Scotland
Summerlee
Glasgow
38
Edinburgh
32
Newcastle
132
Beamish
Northern Ireland
Isle of Man
Douglas
Blackpool
16
Liverpool
46
Manchester
118
Sheffield
144
Dublin
Baile Átha Cliath
22
Llandudno
Birkenhead
Crich
Nottingham
138
Ireland
Éire
Birmingham
8
Lowestoft
Wales
Cymru
England
London
52
Brighton
Seaton
Moderne Straßenbahn / U-Bahn
Modern Tramway / Metro
Straßenbahnmuseum / Museumstram
Tram Museum / Heritage Tram

Edinburgh

TRAM ATLAS Großbritannien & Irland Britain & Ireland

Robert Schwandl Verlag
Hektorstraße 3
D-10711 Berlin

Tel. 030 - 3759 1284 (0049 - 30 - 3759 1284)
Fax 030 - 3759 1285 (0049 - 30 - 3759 1285)

www.robert-schwandl.de
books@robert-schwandl.de

1. Auflage 2015

English Translation by Robert Schwandl & Mark Davies

Druck: Ruksaldruck, Berlin
ISBN 978-3-936573-45-9

Thanks to Bernhard Kußmagk, Brendan Fox, Brian Hardy, Craig Moore, Felix Thoma, Hildegard Schweitzer-Thoma, Jörg Häseler, Urs Mattmann

Wir möchten Sie einladen, uns etwaige Fehler bzw. Veränderungen mitzuteilen, denn hoffentlich wird es in einigen Jahren eine neue, aktualisierte Ausgabe dieses Atlas geben.

We'd like to encourage you to report any errors or updates, because hopefully in a few years, there will be a new, updated edition of this atlas.

Alle Angaben zu Fahrpreisen ohne Gewähr!
All fares listed are for your information only and subject to change!

Newcastle

Blackpool

• VORWORT

In gewisser Weise handelt es sich bei diesem Buch um eine überarbeitete und aktualisierte Ausgabe des Bandes „Metros in Britain“ von 2006. Die Änderung des Titels weist schon darauf hin, dass nun der Schwerpunkt etwas mehr bei den Straßenbahnen und Stadtbahnen liegt, zumal es in dieser europäischen Region außer in London und Glasgow ohnehin keine Metro bzw. U-Bahn im klassischen Sinn gibt.

In einigen Fällen war die Aktualisierung einfach, denn wie etwa in Sheffield oder Croydon hat sich in den letzten zehn Jahren wenig getan, lediglich ein neuer Anstrich für die Fahrzeuge, während Manchester und Nottingham ihre Netze erheblich ausgebaut haben. Mit dabei ist nun natürlich Edinburgh, auf absehbare Zeit allerdings auch die letzte neue Stadt der Britischen Inseln mit einer Tram. Trotz anfänglicher Ängste ist es mir dann doch gelungen, selbst in dieser vom Regen häufig heimgesuchten Gegend genügend Sonnentage zu erwischen, um Ihnen auch in diesem Atlas vorwiegend Bilder mit blauem Himmel anbieten zu können.

Trotz gründlichster Recherche, persönlicher Besichtigung aller Netze und Unterstützung vieler Straßenbahnfreunde kann der eine oder andere Fehler natürlich nicht ausgeschlossen werden. Im Hinblick auf eine zweite Ausgabe bin ich für jeden Hinweis dankbar und wünsche eine gute Fahrt mit diesem Reisebegleiter!

Berlin, im Oktober 2015

Robert Schwandl

• *FOREWORD*

In some way, this book is a revised and updated edition of my 2006 book "Metros in Britain". The change in the title should have given you a hint that the focus is now a little more on trams and light rail systems, particularly as, except for those in London and Glasgow, there are no classic metros in this part of Europe anyway.

In some cases, the update was easy because like in Sheffield or Croydon, little has happened in the last ten years, just a new coat of paint for the tramcars, while Manchester and Nottingham have considerably expanded their networks. For the foreseeable future, Edinburgh, a new city in this edition, will remain the last city in the British Isles to have introduced a completely new tramway. Despite initial fears, in the end I was lucky enough to get lots of photographs on sunny days for this atlas, even in this region so frequently covered by rain and clouds.

Despite the most thorough research, personal visits to every system, and the dedicated support of many tramway enthusiasts, this atlas is unlikely to be free of errors. So in view of a future second edition, any feedback is very much appreciated. We wish you a nice journey with your new travel companion!

Berlin, October 2015

Robert Schwandl

Sheffield

Birmingham

Einleitung

Wie etwa Frankreich und Spanien schaffte es auch Großbritannien, die Straßenbahnen der ersten Generation bald wieder verschwinden zu lassen. Die letzten städtischen Betriebe wurden bereits Ende der 1950er bzw. Anfang der 1960er Jahre geschlossen, nämlich 1957 in Liverpool, 1958 in Aberdeen, 1959 in Leeds, 1960 in Sheffield und schließlich 1962 in Glasgow. Irland war bereits 1949 weitgehend straßenbahnfrei, lediglich die „Hill of Howth Tramway" nordöstlich von Dublin überlebte bis 1959 – außerhalb des Großraums Dublin gab es in der Republik Irland allerdings ohnehin nur in Cork von 1898 bis 1931 eine elektrische Tram. Etwas länger hielten sich einige der einst zahlreichen britischen Obus-Betriebe, z.B. in Cardiff und Walsall bis 1970, in Middlesbrough (Teeside) bis 1971 und in Bradford bis 1972. Während im nordirischen Belfast zwar auch bis 1968 Obusse fuhren, konnte sich dieses Verkehrsmittel in der Republik Irland hingegen nie etablieren. Der einzige überlebende Straßenbahnbetrieb auf den Britischen Inseln war, abgesehen von einzelnen Nostalgiebahnen, der im Seebad Blackpool, da die Strecke weitgehend vom Straßenverkehr unabhängig war und man rechtzeitig dessen touristisches Potenzial erkannte.

Nachdem in Frankreich Mitte der 1980er Jahre die ersten modernen Straßenbahnen (Nantes, Grenoble) eröffnet worden waren, entdeckte auch Großbritannien die Tram wieder für sich. Als erstes entstand 1992 unter Einbeziehung von ehemaligen Eisenbahnstrecken das Hochflurstadtbahnnetz in Manchester, doch da mittlerweile Niederflurtechnologie zur Verfügung stand, wurden alle

Introduction

Like France and Spain, Britain also abandoned virtually all of its first-generation tram systems rather early. The last urban networks had been closed by the late 1950s or early 1960s, namely in Liverpool in 1957, Aberdeen in 1958, Leeds in 1959, Sheffield in 1960, and finally in Glasgow in 1962. Ireland was already almost completely tram-free by 1949, with just the 'Hill of Howth Tramway' northeast of Dublin surviving until 1959 – in fact, outside Greater Dublin, Cork was the only city in the Republic of Ireland that had an electric tramway, which operated from 1898 until 1931. Some of the once numerous British trolleybus companies survived a little longer, e.g. in Cardiff and Walsall until 1970, in Middlesbrough (Teeside) until 1971, and in Bradford until 1972. While trolleybuses also operated in Belfast, Northern Ireland, until 1968, this form of transport was never able to establish itself in the Republic of Ireland. Other than some heritage lines, the only surviving tram operation in the British Isles was the one in the seaside resort of Blackpool, as its route was largely separated from road traffic and its potential as part of the city's tourist attractions was realised in time.

By the mid-1980s, France had opened the first modern tramways (in Nantes and Grenoble), which led to Britain also rediscovering this form of urban transport. The first system to open was the high-floor light rail network in Manchester in 1992, which incorporated some old railway lines, but as low-floor technology had in the meantime become available, all the subsequent systems were brought into service using low-floor cars: in 1994 in

Manchester - Piccadilly > New Islington (Kehranlage | *turnback facility*)

London Underground - Metropolitan Line @ Kilburn

Benutzerhinweise | *User Instructions*

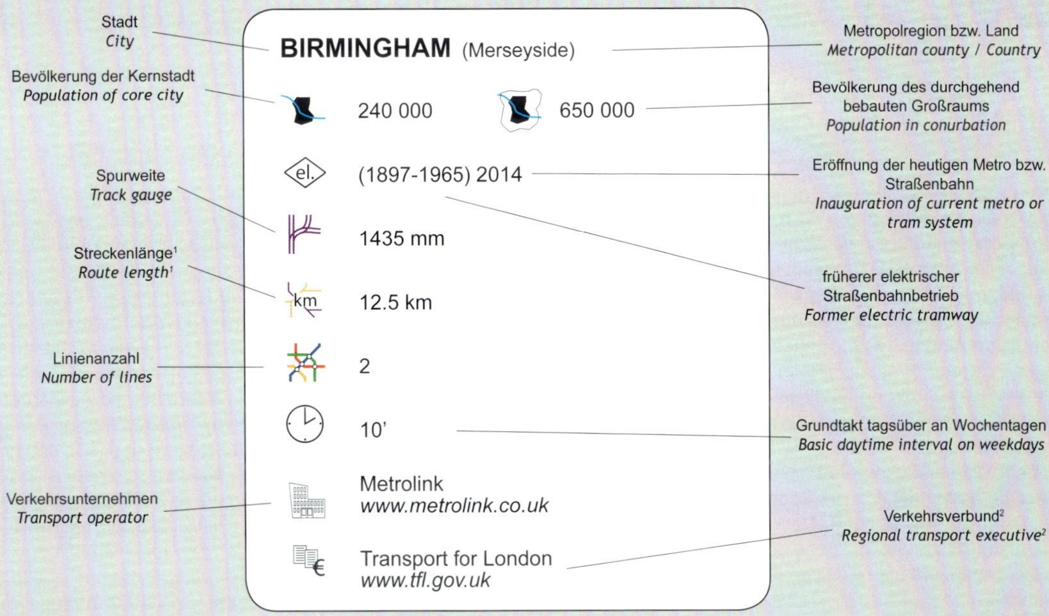

1) Berücksichtigt sind alle im Linienverkehr befahrenen Abschnitte, jedoch keine Betriebsstrecken und nachgeschaltete Kehranlagen. Diese Zahl kann daher erheblich von offiziellen Angaben abweichen. Richtungsweise unterschiedlich geführte Abschnitte werden nur einfach gezählt.

2) Ein Tarifverbund im Sinne deutscher Verkehrsverbünde ist auf den Britischen Inseln nirgends vorhanden, einige Großräume wie London, Manchester oder Birmingham bieten allerdings zumindest Tageskarten an, die in allen verfügbaren Verkehrsmitteln gültig sind.

1) The route length includes all sections served in regular passenger service, but excludes sidings, depot access tracks or other non-revenue tracks. This figure may therefore differ significantly from official numbers. Sections with single-track parallel routes going in opposite directions are only counted once.

2) Full fare integration is not available in any city included in this atlas, although many metropolitan regions, e.g. London, Manchester and Birmingham, offer day passes which cover all the transport modes available within a certain area.

! In Bildtexten bedeutet das Zeichen **>** (z.B. Gyle Centre > Gogarburn) die **Blickrichtung** und nicht die Fahrtrichtung des abgebildeten Fahrzeugs!
In captions, the sign **>** *(e.g.* Gyle Centre > Gogarburn*) indicates the* ***viewing direction*** *and not the travelling direction of the depicted vehicle!*

Nottingham - NET - Wilford Lane > Wilford Village

späteren Netze für Niederflurwagen errichtet: 1994 in Sheffield, 1999 von Birmingham nach Wolverhampton, 2000 im Londoner Stadtbezirk Croydon und 2004 in Nottingham sowie in der irischen Hauptstadt Dublin. Aus einer flächendeckenden Wiedereinführung wie in Frankreich wurde allerdings nichts, was größtenteils am mangelnden Willen der Zentralregierung in London scheiterte. Vor allem die weit fortgeschrittenen Projekte in Leeds und Liverpool konnten nicht umgesetzt werden. Lediglich die Tram in Edinburgh im mittlerweile weitgehend autonom regierten Schottland konnte, wenn auch mit einiger Verspätung, 2014 noch das Licht der Welt erblicken. Von möglichen neuen Trambetrieben ist heute kaum noch die Rede (aktuelle Vorschläge gibt es z. B. in Oxford), selbst Netzerweiterungen erscheinen oft mühsam durchzusetzen. Umso bewundernswerter sind die Erfolge der letzten Jahre diesbezüglich in Manchester und Nottingham.

In Leeds, mit rund 770.000 Einwohnern immerhin eine der größten Stadtgemeinden Englands, wird derzeit als „New Generation Transport" (NGT) eine rund 15 km lange Obus-Linie von Nordwest (Holt Park) nach Südost (Stourton) durch das Stadtzentrum und weitgehend auf Eigentrassen geplant [Info unter *www.ngtmetro.com*].

Neben dem Obus in Leeds könnte die nächste Ausgabe dieses Atlasses bereits den „Tram-Train" von Sheffield nach Rotherham enthalten, der derzeit mit Unterstützung des Transportministeriums als Versuchsbetrieb umgesetzt wird. Sollte man mit den Ergebnissen zufrieden sein, könnte dieses Modell auf andere Großstadtregionen übertragen werden. Im Großraum Cardiff soll mittelfristig eine Regionalstadtbahn nach dem Modell von Manchester entstehen [Info unter *metroconsortium.co.uk*].

Sheffield, in 1999 from Birmingham to Wolverhampton, in 2000 in the London Borough of Croydon, and finally in 2004 in Nottingham and the Irish capital Dublin. A nationwide reintroduction of tramways like in France, however, was not achieved, mostly due to a lack of will on the part of the national government in London. In particular, the well-advanced projects in Leeds and Liverpool were unable to be implemented. With Scotland now largely governed autonomously, Edinburgh opened its new tramway in 2014, albeit with some delay. Today, there is hardly any talk of entirely new systems (e.g. a new tramway has been proposed for Oxford), and even extensions to the existing networks seem difficult to push through, which makes the achievements in this regard in Manchester and Nottingham in recent years all the more admirable.

Leeds, with some 770,000 inhabitants one of the largest cities in England, is currently planning a trolleybus route branded 'New Generation Transport' (NGT), a 15 km long line from the northwest (Holt Park) to the southeast (Stourton), passing through the city centre and running mostly on a dedicated road.
[More information at www.ngtmetro.com]

Besides the trolleybus in Leeds, the next edition of this atlas may already contain the 'tram-train' from Sheffield to Rotherham, which is currently being implemented with the support of the Department of Transport as a pilot project. Should the results be satisfactory, this form of transport might also be chosen for other metropolitan areas. In the medium term, a regional light rail system similar to that in Greater Manchester is planned for the Cardiff area.
[More information at metroconsortium.co.uk]

Dublin - Luas - Red Line @ Suir Road

Bei den bestehenden Trambetrieben sind kleinere Erweiterungen in Birmingham, Manchester, Blackpool und hoffentlich auch in Edinburgh zu erwarten. Ambitionierte Projekte gibt es hingegen in Dublin, deren Umsetzung wird jedoch weiterhin durch die abebbende Finanzkrise ausgebremst.

Im Bereich U-Bahn/Metros hat sich in den letzten Jahrzehnten ebenfalls wenig getan. Das Londoner *Tube*-Netz wurde seit der wesentlichen Verlängerung der Jubilee Line im Jahr 2000 lediglich durch einen 2 km langen Abzweig der Piccadilly Line zum Terminal 5 des Flughafens Heathrow im Jahr 2008 erweitert. In naher Zukunft soll ein 3 km langer Ast der Northern Line bis Battersea Park gebaut werden, außerdem im Außenbereich eine rund 3 km lange Spange für die Metropolitan Line zum Anschluss an den Knoten Watford Junction. Das inzwischen weit verzweigte Netz der Docklands Light Railway wurde zuletzt 2011 im Vorfeld der Olympischen Spiele um 4,5 km vergrößert. Die wichtigsten Meilensteine im Londoner Nahverkehr waren in den letzten Jahren der Aufbau des *London Overground*-Netzes, das durchaus den Charakter einer S-Bahn aufweist, sowie die Umsetzung des lange geplanten *Crossrail*-Projekts, wodurch es in einigen Jahren möglich sein wird, Vorortzüge in Ost-West-Richtung gleich dem Pariser RER durch das Zentrum von London durchzubinden.

Die zweite U-Bahn der Britischen Inseln, die *Glasgow Subway*, sowie die beiden metro-ähnlichen S-Bahnen in Newcastle (*Tyne-and-Wear Metro*) und Liverpool (*Merseyrail*) wurden zwar in den vergangenen Jahren modernisiert, jedoch nicht erweitert.

As far as the existing tram networks go, minor extensions can be expected in Birmingham, Manchester, Blackpool and hopefully also in Edinburgh. There are some ambitious projects, however, in Dublin, but their implementation is still foiled by the slowly ebbing financial crisis.

In the field of metros/Underground, little has happened in recent decades. Since the important extension of the Jubilee Line in the year 2000, the London Tube network has only been expanded once, when a 2 km Piccadilly Line branch to Heathrow Airport's Terminal 5 was opened in 2008. In the near future, a 3 km Northern Line branch to Battersea Park is to be built, as well as a roughly 3 km link for the Metropolitan Line in the outskirts to connect it to the hub at Watford Junction. The large network of the Docklands Light Railway was last extended in 2011 in preparation for the Olympic Games, adding 4.5 km. Among the most important milestones for urban rail in London in recent years was the creation of the London Overground network, which certainly has many features of an S-Bahn or RER system, as well as the start of the long-planned Crossrail project, which in a few years will enable suburban trains to pass under central London in an east-west direction, similar to the Paris RER.

The second underground metro in the British Isles, the Glasgow Subway, as well as the two metro-like suburban railways in Newcastle (Tyne-and-Wear Metro) and Liverpool (Merseyrail), have been modernised in recent years, but not expanded.

Urbos #26 @ Soho - Benson Road

BIRMINGHAM

Birmingham ist das Zentrum des Großraums West Midlands, zu dem außerdem die Bezirke Wolverhampton, Walsall, Dudley, Sandwell, Solihull und das etwas abseits gelegene Coventry gehören. Neben der bislang einzigen Stadtbahnlinie, der *Midland Metro*, wird die Region durch mehrere Bahnlinien mit dichtem Verkehr erschlossen. Auch wenn für Einzelfahrten keine Kombitickets erhältlich sind, gibt es für das gesamte *Network West Midlands* eine Reihe von Tageskarten, die verschiedene Verkehrsmittel kombinieren: Metro+Bus+Bahn ab 9:30 Uhr 6,40 £, sonst 8,10 £ (*Daytripper*); Metro+Bus 6,20 £; Einzelfahrten mit der Metro kosten 2,20-3,70 £, ein Metro *Daytripper* 5,40 £ (gültig ab 9:30 Uhr).

Die **Metro**, wie sie heute meist bezeichnet wird, ist eine moderne Stadtbahn. Sie wird von *West Midlands Travel Ltd*, die als *Midland Metro* auftritt und zur *National Express Group* gehört, betrieben. Die Planung des Verkehrsangebots und der Infrastruktur in West Midlands obliegt *Centro*, der *West Midlands Passenger Transport Executive.*

Die ursprüngliche, 1999 eröffnete Strecke verläuft zwar zu ca. 90% auf eigenem Gleiskörper mit nur einem einzigen Bahnübergang südlich der Haltestelle Black Lake, die Fahrgäste müssen allerdings an den meisten Haltestellen die Gleise überqueren,

BIRMINGHAM (West Midlands)

1 100 000 — 2 500 000

(1904-1953) 1999

1435 mm

21.2 km

1 — 8'

West Midlands Travel Ltd
(National Express)
www.nxbus.co.uk/the-metro

Network West Midlands
www.networkwestmidlands.com

Centro
www.centro.org.uk

Birmingham is the centre of the metropolitan area known as the West Midlands, which also contains Wolverhampton, Walsall, Dudley, Sandwell, Solihull and Coventry, the latter located some distance from Birmingham. Besides the single light rail line, the so-called 'Midland Metro', the area is also served by several suburban rail lines with dense headways. Although no combined tickets are available for single rides, there is a wide range of day tickets for the entire 'Network West Midlands', combining different modes of transport: Daytripper for Metro+Bus+Rail after 09:30 - £6.40, full day - £8.10; Metro+Bus £6.20; single fares for the Metro range from £2.20 to £3.70, while a Metro Daytripper valid after 09:30 is £5.40.

*The **Metro**, as it is commonly referred to, is a modern light rail system. It is operated by 'West Midlands Travel Ltd', which trades as 'Midland Metro' and is part of the National Express Group. The planning authority is 'Centro', the West Midlands Passenger Transport Executive.*

Although the original line runs segregated from other traffic along 90% of its length and has only one level crossing, which lies south of Black Lake, passengers have to cross the tracks at most stops to get to

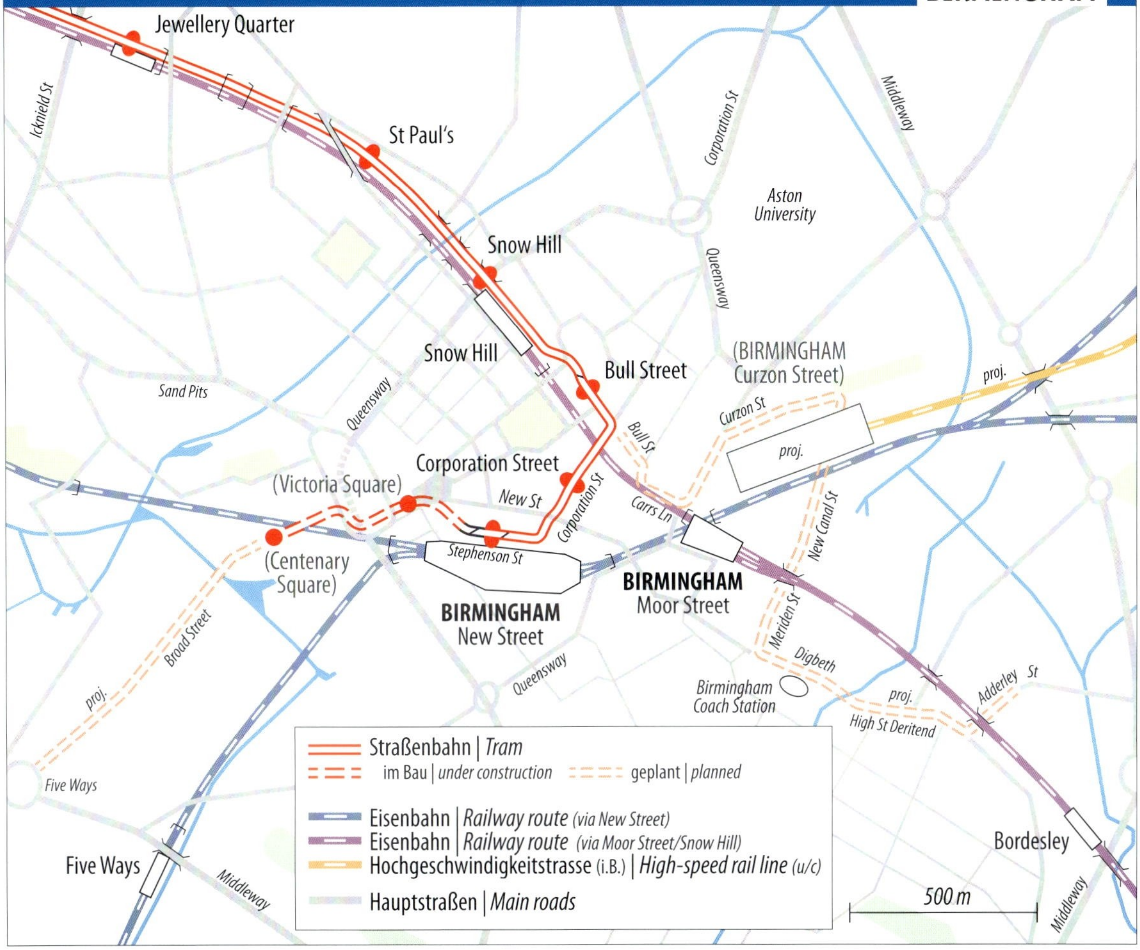

um auf den gegenüberliegenden Bahnsteig oder zum Ausgang zu gelangen. Lediglich am westlichen Ende in Wolverhampton, von kurz hinter Priestfield bis St. George's, fährt die Tram auf der Straße.

1984 wurde ein umfangreiches Netz mit mehreren vom Stadtzentrum ausgehenden Linien geplant. Die erste Strecke sollte in die östlichen Vororte Hodge Hill und Chelmsley Wood gebaut werden, wozu einige Häuser abgerissen werden sollten. Das führte zu heftigen Protesten, so dass schließlich die am einfachsten zu bauende Strecke vorgezogen wurde. Diese führt von Birmingham über das „Black Country" nach Wolverhampton meist auf der Trasse einer stillgelegten Eisenbahn, so dass keine Häuser betroffen waren.

Die ursprüngliche Eisenbahnstrecke von Snow Hill nach Wolverhampton (Low Level) war 1854 von der *Great Western Railway* eröffnet worden und auf ihr verkehrten in ihren besten Tagen Fernzüge von London Paddington nach Birkenhead. Der Fahrgastverkehr wurde 1972 eingestellt, da die Strecke weitgehend parallel zur Hauptbahn vom Bahnhof New Street in Birmingham nach Wolverhampton verlief. Erst 1995 wurde die Strecke im südlichen Abschnitt bis zur neuen Station The Hawthorns (*Jewellery Line*) und von dort Richtung Kidderminster als Teil einer Durchmesserlinie wieder in Betrieb genommen.

Anders als etwa in Manchester oder Newcastle findet man bei der Midland Metro, abgesehen vom

the opposite platform or the exit. The tracks are only embedded in the roadway on the westernmost section, from right after Priestfield to the St. George's terminus in Wolverhampton,

The first of a number of routes proposed in 1984, most of which radiated from the Birmingham city centre, was to have been built to the eastern suburbs of Hodge Hill and Chelmsley Wood, which would have required the demolition of many homes. Due to strong opposition in those areas, the least controversial route was chosen instead. The line from Birmingham to Wolverhampton via the Black Country would run mostly along a former railway alignment, so no private property would be affected.

Urbos #32 @ St Paul's

BIRMINGHAM

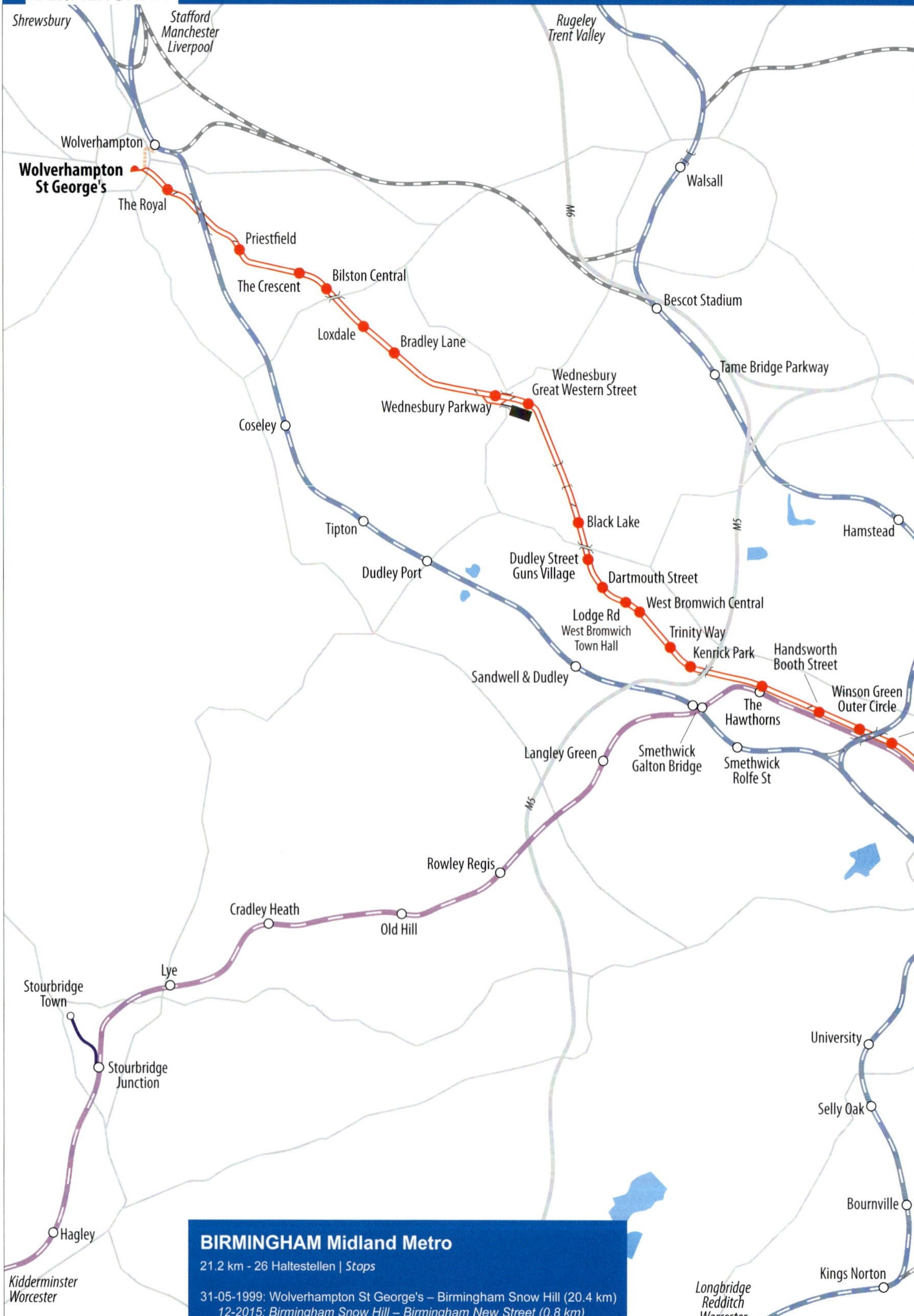

BIRMINGHAM Midland Metro

21.2 km - 26 Haltestellen | *Stops*

31-05-1999: Wolverhampton St George's – Birmingham Snow Hill (20.4 km)
12-2015: Birmingham Snow Hill – Birmingham New Street (0.8 km)

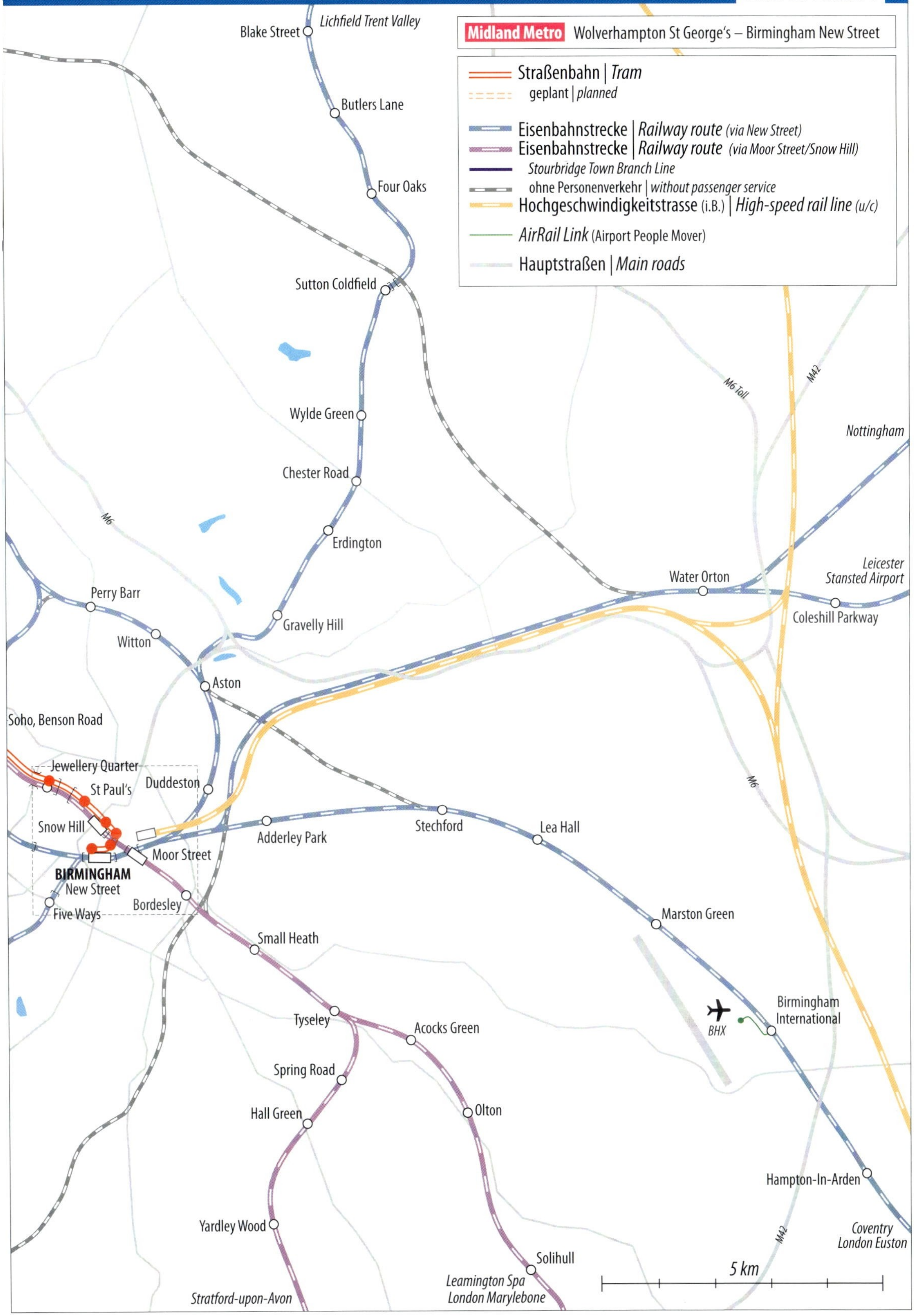
Midland Metro Wolverhampton St George's – Birmingham New Street
Straßenbahn | Tram
geplant | planned
Eisenbahnstrecke | Railway route (via New Street)
Eisenbahnstrecke | Railway route (via Moor Street/Snow Hill)
Stourbridge Town Branch Line
ohne Personenverkehr | without passenger service
Hochgeschwindigkeitstrasse (i.B.) | High-speed rail line (u/c)
AirRail Link (Airport People Mover)
Hauptstraßen | Main roads
Blake Street
Lichfield Trent Valley
Butlers Lane
Four Oaks
Sutton Coldfield
Wylde Green
Chester Road
Erdington
Gravelly Hill
Perry Barr
Witton
Aston
Soho, Benson Road
Jewellery Quarter
St Paul's
Duddeston
Snow Hill
Moor Street
BIRMINGHAM
New Street
Five Ways
Bordesley
Adderley Park
Stechford
Lea Hall
Marston Green
Birmingham International
BHX
Hampton-In-Arden
Coventry
London Euston
Water Orton
Leicester
Stansted Airport
Coleshill Parkway
Nottingham
M6 Toll
M42
M6
Small Heath
Tyseley
Acocks Green
Spring Road
Hall Green
Olton
Yardley Wood
Solihull
Leamington Spa
London Marylebone
Stratford-upon-Avon
5 km

Urbos #18 @ Priestfield > The Royal
(straßenbündiger Abschnitt | *on-street section*)

Hill Top Tunnel, kaum Reste der ehemaligen Eisenbahn. Auf der ganzen Strecke wurden neue Gleise verlegt und einfache Haltestellen mit 35 cm hohen Bahnsteigen eingerichtet.

Nach Inbetriebnahme der ersten Strecke gab es immer wieder Bemühungen für ergänzende Linien. Vorrangig schien lange Zeit eine 11,7 km lange Strecke von Wednesbury über Dudley nach Brierley Hill größtenteils auf der Trasse der ehemaligen *South Staffordshire Line*, nur im Zentrum von Dudley waren straßenbündige Abschnitte vorgesehen. Doch die einzige bislang in Angriff genommene Erweiterung ist eine etwa 800 m lange Innenstadtstrecke von Snow Hill zum Hauptbahnhof New Street, die Ende 2015 in Betrieb gehen soll. Dafür wird die ursprüngliche, unter Geländeniveau liegende Endstelle aufgegeben, denn die Tram erreicht nun parallel dazu über eine Rampe die Straßenebene. Sie fährt auf der Corporation Street hinunter und endet vorerst in der Stephenson Street, direkt vor dem neuen Nordzugang zum Hauptbahnhof Birmingham New Street. Die Finanzierung für den Weiterbau über Victoria Square (Town Hall) bis zum Centenary Square (700 m) scheint gesichert. Später soll diese Strecke entlang der Broad Street bis Five Ways weiterführen.

In Wolverhampton war lange ein Ring um die Innenstadt vorgesehen, derzeit scheint eine kurze Verlängerung zum Bahnhof (550 m) wahrscheinlich.

Im Zusammenhang mit der Ankunft der Hochgeschwindigkeitszüge im neuen Bahnhof Curzon Street Mitte der 2020er Jahre wird ein Abzweig für die Tram geplant. Die sog. „Eastside Extension“ soll weiter über die New Canal Street zur Digbeth Coach Station führen und vorerst in der Adderley Street enden.

Die *Midland Metro* startete 1999 mit 16 Fahrzeugen vom italienischen Hersteller Ansaldo. Die T69 waren 60% niederflurig, die Endabschnitte hatten eine Fußbodenhöhe von 85 cm. Da man mit diesen Fahrzeugen nie wirklich zufrieden war, wurden sie bis August 2015 durch die 21 neuen, 100% niederflurigen Urbos vom spanischen Hersteller CAF ersetzt. Einige der T69 bekamen vor ihrer Ausmusterung noch einen neuen Anstrich in Pink und Silber.

The original railway line from Snow Hill to Wolverhampton (Low Level) was opened in 1854 by the Great Western Railway, and during its heyday it was used by long-distance trains from London Paddington to Birkenhead. Passenger service was eventually withdrawn in 1972 as the line paralleled the route from New Street Station. In 1995, a rail service was reintroduced between Snow Hill and a new station at The Hawthorns (Jewellery Line project), and from there on to Kidderminster, creating a new cross-city service.

Unlike in Manchester or Newcastle, the Midland Metro does not preserve anything of the former railway line, except for the Hill Top Tunnel. New track was laid along the entire route, and simple uniform stops with 35 cm high platforms were established.

With the first line in service, several attempts have been made to add more routes. For a long time, the 11.7 km extension from Wednesbury to Dudley and Brierley Hill seemed to be a priority. This line would mostly have been built along the abandoned South Staffordshire Line, with some street-running sections in the Dudley town centre. The only new section, however, is a mere 800 m city centre extension from Snow Hill to Birmingham's main railway station, New Street, scheduled to open by the end of 2015. This extension requires the original terminus to be abandoned as the trams will use a ramp on the eastern side of the railway station to reach street level before running down on Corporation Street to terminate on Stephenson Street, right in front of the new northern entrance to Birmingham New Street railway station. Funding for a further 700 m stretch to Centenary Square via Victoria Square (Town Hall) has been secured. In a later stage, the trams may continue along Broad Street to reach Five Ways.

In Wolverhampton, a loop around the city centre was once on the drawing board, but currently, a short 550 m extension to the railway station is more likely.

In conjunction with the future arrival of high-speed trains at the planned Curzon Street station in the mid-2020s, a branch for the tram is being designed. The so-called 'Eastside Extension' will allow trams to continue from the new railway station along New Canal Street to Digbeth Coach Station, and on to an initial terminus on Adderley Street.

The Midland Metro service was launched in 1999 with a fleet of 16 trams, all built by Ansaldo of Italy. These T69 vehicles were 60% low-floor, while the end sections were 85 cm above the rails. As their performance was never very satisfactory, by August 2015 they had all been withdrawn from service and replaced with new rolling stock, a total of 21 100% low-floor Urbos trams from Spanish manufacturer CAF. Some of the T69s still received a new livery in pink and silver before being retired from service.

Fahrzeuge | *Rolling Stock* (750 V DC)

Nummer *Number*	Anzahl *Quantity*	Hersteller *Manufacturer*	Typ *Class*	Länge *Length*	Breite *Width*	Ausgeliefert *Delivered*
01-16* 17-37	16* 21	Ansaldo CAF	T69 Urbos 3	24.4 m 33.0 m	2.60 m 2.65 m	1998-1999 2013-2015

* alle seit August 2015 außer Betrieb | *all withdrawn from service since August 2015*

Urbos #23 @ Lodge Road (West Bromwich Town Hall)

Urbos #33 @ Snow Hill (ursprüngliche Endstelle | *original terminus*)

Ansaldo T69 #02 @ Wednesbury Parkway (2005)

Ansaldo T69 #10 @ Wednesbury Parkway (2014)

Foto B. Kußmagk

Cross City Line – elektrische S-Bahn | *electric suburban rail service* @ Selly Oak

Vorortverkehr

In den West Midlands findet auf den Gleisen von Network Rail ein reger Vorortverkehr statt. Besonders erwähnenswert ist die *Cross City Line*, die ähnlich einer S-Bahn zwischen Four Oaks im Norden und Longbridge im Süden im 10-Minuten-Takt mit modernen Elektrotriebzügen verkehrt, allerdings werden die Gleise auf dem südlichen Abschnitt auch von Fernzügen benutzt. Weiter bis Lichfield Trent Valley im Norden bzw. Redditch im Süden fahren die Züge von *London Midland* im Halbstundentakt. Mehrmals stündlich erreicht man Walsall mit der Regionalbahn, während zwischen Birmingham und Wolverhampton genauso wie zwischen Birmingham und dem Flughafen bzw. Coventry neben Regionalzügen auch zahlreiche Fernzüge zur Verfügung stehen. Sechs Mal pro Stunde fahren Vorortzüge auch auf der nicht elektrifizierten Strecke zwischen Stourbridge und Birmingham Moor Street. Sie durchqueren das Stadtzentrum in einem bereits 1852 eröffneten Tunnel.

Teil des von *London Midland* betriebenen Regionalbahnnetzes ist auch die 1,3 km lange *Stourbridge Town Branch Line*. Die Shuttle-Linie wird nicht mit herkömmlichen Dieseltriebwagen betrieben, sondern seit 2009 von einer Art Schienenbus, dem 9,6 m langen Parry People Mover (BR-Baureihe 139). Für den Pendelbetrieb im 10-Minuten-Takt bei einer Fahrzeit von drei Minuten stehen zwei Fahrzeuge zur Verfügung.

Suburban Rail

A dense suburban rail service is provided on Network Rail tracks through the West Midlands. The 'Cross City Line' deserves a special mention, as, like an S-Bahn, it offers a train every 10 minutes between Four Oaks in the north and Longbridge in the south with modern electric multiple units, though it shares tracks with other services along the southern leg. On the northern extension to Lichfield and the southern to Redditch, London Midland operates a half-hourly service like on most other routes. Walsall can be reached several times an hour, whereas Wolverhampton and Coventry (via the airport) are also connected to Birmingham New Street by numerous long-distance trains. The non-electrified route between Stourbridge and Moor Street via Snow Hill is likewise served by six trains an hour. They cross the city centre in a tunnel which opened in as early as 1852.

Forming part of the regional rail network operated by London Midland, the 1.3 km 'Stourbridge Town Branch Line' is a shuttle service that does not work with conventional diesel units, but since 2009, with a kind of railbus, the 9.6 m long Parry People Mover (BR class 139). Two vehicles are available to provide a 10-minute headway with a journey time of three minutes.

Stourbridge Town Branch Line

Jewellery Line @ Smethwick Galton Bridge
Vorortverkehr mit Dieseltriebwagen | *diesel-powered suburban rail service*

Der Peoplemover **AirRail Link** verbindet seit 2003 den Bahnhof Birmingham International mit dem Terminalgebäude des Flughafens. Die 585 m lange vollautomatische Hochbahn besitzt einen Kabelantrieb. Die Cable Liner-Technologie stammt von Doppelmayr. Anders als bei den meisten Standseilbahnen verkehren die beiden Kabinen unabhängig voneinander. Sie können gratis genutzt werden.

Die aufgeständerte Trasse wurde bereits 1984 errichtet, und zwar für die erste Magnetschwebebahn weltweit. Diese wurde jedoch 1995 aufgrund fehlender Ersatzteile und teurer Instandhaltungskosten stillgelegt.

AirRail Link

*Since 2003, a people mover called **AirRail Link** has connected Birmingham International railway station with the airport terminal building. The 585 m cable-hauled system is operated automatically using Cable Liner technology from Doppelmayr. Unlike most funiculars, the two cars work independently. They can be used free of charge.*

The elevated structure had already been built in 1984 for the first maglev line in the world, but this system was closed down in 1995 due to a lack of spare parts and high maintenance costs.

In Großbritannien gibt es zahlreiche Standseilbahnen, die meisten davon findet man in verschiedenen Küstenorten, zum Beispiel in Torquay, Hastings und Folkestone im Süden oder auch in Scarborough und Saltburn-by-the-Sea im Nordosten, wo sie eine Verbindung von den höher gelegenen Orten zu deren Stränden herstellen, weshalb sie meist als *Cliff Railway* oder *Cliff Tramway* bezeichnet werden.

Die einzige Standseilbahn der Britischen Inseln mit einer städtischen Nahverkehrsfunktion findet man hingegen im Landesinneren, nämlich in **Bridgnorth** rund 35 km westlich von Birmingham in der Grafschaft Shropshire. Die als „Castle Hill Railway" bezeichnete Bahn verbindet die Unter- mit der Oberstadt und wurde 1892 mit Wasserballastantrieb in Betrieb genommen. 1944 wurde die zweigleisige Bahn mit 1067 mm Spurweite auf elektrischen Antrieb (415 V) umgestellt. Die beiden Wagen, die aus dem Jahr 1955 stammen, überwinden auf einer Länge von 61 m einen Höhenunterschied von 33,8 m. Eine Berg- und Talfahrt kostet 1,20 £.

Bridgnorth Castle Hill Railway

In the UK, there are numerous funiculars, most of which are found in coastal towns, for example Torquay, Hastings and Folkestone in the south, or Scarborough and Saltburn-by-the-Sea in the northeast. They connect the higher towns to their respective beaches, which is why they are often referred to as 'Cliff Railways' or 'Cliff Tramways'.

*The only funicular in the British Isles with an urban transport function, however, can be found in the interior, namely in **Bridgnorth**, some 35 km west of Birmingham in Shropshire. Known as the 'Castle Hill Railway', it links the Low Town with the High Town. Opened in 1892, it was built using the water ballast system. In 1944, the double-track railway, which has 1067 mm gauge, was converted to electric traction (415 V). On the 61 m long line, the two cars from 1955 negotiate a difference in altitude of 33.8 m. A return trip costs £1.20.*

Bombardier Flexity #004 @ North Pier

BLACKPOOL

Der Badeort Blackpool in der Grafschaft Lancashire ist die einzige Stadt Großbritanniens, in der die Straßenbahn der ersten Generation bis heute überlebt hat. Die 2012 grundlegend modernisierte Strecke wird wie das städtische Busnetz von *Blackpool Transport Services Ltd* betrieben, die Bahninfrastruktur sowie die Fahrzeuge sind Eigentum der Stadt Blackpool. Für die moderne Tram gilt bei Einzelfahrten ein Entfernungstarif, von 1,00 £ zur nächsten Haltestelle bis 2,50 £ ab 16 Haltestellen. Mit einem Blackpool1 Ticket kann man unbegrenzt die moderne Tram sowie alle Stadtbusse nutzen: 1 Tag - 5,00 £, 3 Tage - 11,00 £ oder 7 Tage - 14,00 £. Für die Oldtimer-Fahrzeuge gelten jedoch eigene Fahrpreise (5,00 £ hin und zurück auf einer Teilstrecke, 10,00 £ für eine Tageskarte)!

Die erste elektrische Tramway des Landes wurde hier am 29. September 1885 entlang der Promenade zwischen North und South Pier in Betrieb genommen, anfangs erfolgte die Stromversorgung über eine Stromschiene, die in einer Rille im Boden angebracht war. 1899 wurde die Stromzufuhr auf konventionelle Oberleitung umgestellt. 1898 hatte die *Blackpool and Fleetwood Tramroad Company* eine eigenständige Linie von Gynn Square bis Fleetwood Ferry

The seaside resort of Blackpool in Lancashire is the only city in Britain where a first-generation tram system has survived. Like the city buses, the tram line, which was completely upgraded in 2012, is operated by Blackpool Transport Services Ltd, while the tram infrastructure and vehicles are owned by Blackpool Council. Single tickets for the modern tramway cost between £1.00 for 1 stop and £2.50 for 16 stops or more. "Blackpool1 Tickets" allow unlimited travel on the modern tram and buses for £5.00 a day, and £11.00 or £14.00 for three and seven days, respectively. The heritage trams require a special ticket (£5 for one round trip on a section of the route; £10 for a day pass)!

The country's first electric tramway system opened along the Promenade between North and South Piers on 29 September 1885. Initially powered via a current rail fitted into an underground conduit between the rails, the power supply system was changed to conventional overhead wire in 1899. In 1898, the Blackpool and Fleetwood Tramroad Company had opened a separate line between Gynn Square and Fleetwood Ferry. The two lines were only connected and operated jointly after the Blackpool Corporation had taken

BLACKPOOL (Lancashire)

142 000 | 240 000

(1885-2011) 2012

1435 mm

17.8 km

1

Mo-Do | *Mon-Thu*: 12'
Fr-So | *Fri-Sun*: 10'

Blackpool Transport
www.blackpooltransport.com

Flexity #014 @ Central Pier > Tower

Flexity #016 @ Little Bispham > Anchorsholme Lane

Flexity #010 @ North Pier

Flexity #008 @ Little Bispham > Anchorsholme Lane

eröffnet, beide Strecke wurden erst 1920, als die Fleetwood-Linie von der Blackpool Corporation übernommen wurde, betrieblich verknüpft. Daneben gab es in Blackpool zu dieser Zeit noch weitere Linien, etwa nach Layton und Marton oder entlang des Central Drive.

Nachdem die verbliebene, rund 18 km lange Nord-Süd-Linie jahrzehntelang als Museumsstraßenbahn betrieben worden war, gab das *Department for Transport* 2008 grünes Licht für eine grundlegende Instandsetzung und den Kauf neuer Niederflurfahrzeuge. Während für diese knapp 30 m lange Niedrigbahnsteige errichtet wurden, wurde die Anzahl der Haltestellen um fast die Hälfte verringert, der mittlere Stationsabstand beträgt nun ca. 500 m. Gleichzeitig wurde die Strecke saniert und die Stromspannung von zuvor 550 V auf 600 V Gleichstrom erhöht. Der reguläre Betrieb mit den neuen Flexity-Fahrzeugen begann am 4. April 2012.

Die Strecke verläuft größtenteils auf eigenem Gleiskörper, zwischen Starr Gate im Süden und Cabin (ca. 7 km) auf einer asphaltierten Eigentrasse entlang der Strandpromenade, danach ca. 7,5 km auf einem Schottergleisbett kleinbahnartig bis zur Haltestelle Fisherman's Walk, mit Überlandabschnitten zwischen Rossall Beach und Broadwater. Lediglich die knapp 1,2 km durch das Ortszentrum von Fleetwood bis zur Blockumfahrung am Fährhafen sind straßenbündig. Der zuvor straßenbündige Abschnitt im Zentrum von Blackpool zwischen North Pier und Pleasant Street wurde im Zuge der Streckenmodernisierung durch Bordsteine von der Fahrbahn abgetrennt. Ein rund 600 m langer Abzweig zum Hauptbahnhof Blackpool North ist

over the Fleetwood line in 1920. Besides this north-south line, Blackpool had several other routes in those days, like those to Layton and Marton or the one along Central Drive.

The surviving, approximately 18 km north-south line was operated with heritage tram vehicles for many decades until eventually the Department for Transport granted funds in 2008 to upgrade the line to modern light rail standard, including the purchase of new vehicles. While low-level platforms approximately 30 m long were built for the future trams, almost half the stops were eliminated, resulting in an average station distance of some 500 m. The tracks were replaced and the tension of the overhead power supply was increased from 550 to 600 V DC. Regular service with the new Flexity fleet was launched on 4 April 2012.

The trams run mostly on a dedicated right-of-way, first on a paved reservation along the Promenade between Starr Gate in the south and Cabin (approximately 7 km), before moving to a railway-style ballast trackbed and heading north to Fisherman's Walk, with some interurban stretches between Rossall Beach and Broadwater. A mere 1.2 km through the Fleetwood town centre has the tracks embedded in the roadway, including the loop at the ferry terminal. The former on-street section between North Pier and Pleasant Street in the centre of Blackpool was separated from road traffic by curb stones during the route upgrade. A branch approximately 600 m long to Blackpool's main railway station is planned, with the necessary points already in place.

Flexity #013 @ Manchester Square

Bombardier Flexity

Flexity #015 @ Lord Street (London St > Victoria St)

geplant, die notwendigen Weichen dafür wurden bereits eingebaut.

Neben den modernen Trams fahren von April bis Oktober an Wochenenden und im Hochsommer an fast allen Tagen auf einzelnen Abschnitten, vor allem zwischen North Pier und Pleasure Beach, auch weiterhin Oldtimer-Fahrzeuge. Dafür stehen zahlreiche Wagen zur Verfügung, die meisten aus den 1930er Jahren, z.B. neun für den Betrieb an den neuen Bahnsteigen angepasste, doppelstöckige „Widened Balloon Cars“ (Tw. 700...724). Außerdem gibt es viele offene Wagen, sowohl doppelstöckig als auch einstöckig („boat cars“). Eine aktuelle Fahrzeugliste ist unter der Internetadresse unten zu finden.

Besides the modern trams, the route is busy from April until October with a number of heritage tram vehicles. They run every weekend, but also during the week in high season, when they serve certain sections of the route. The heritage fleet includes a large number of different cars, most of which date back to the 1930s, like the nine "widened balloon cars" which were adapted to serve the new low-level platforms (nos. 700...724). The fleet also comprises many open cars, both single-deck ("boat cars") and double-deck. An updated fleet list can be found at the web address below.

Flexity #004 @ Fleetwood Schleife | *loop*

Fahrzeuge | *Rolling Stock* (600 V DC)

Nummer *Number*	Anzahl *Quantity*	Hersteller *Manufacturer*	Typ *Class*	Länge *Length*	Breite *Width*	Ausgeliefert *Delivered*
001-016	16	Bombardier	Flexity 2	32.2 m	2.65 m	2011-2012

Oldtimer-Fahrzeugliste unter | *Heritage tram fleet list at* www.britishtramsonline.co.uk/blackpoolfleet.html

Flexity #010 + 009 @ Cliff's Hotel

Stockport #5 + Blackpool #726 @ Central Pier (2005)

Flexity #007 @ Waterloo Road > St. Chad's Road

Blackpool #761 @ London Street (2005)

Blackpool 'Balloon' #726 (1925) @ Tower (2005)

Bolton Standard Tram #66 (1901) @ Manchester Square > Central Pier

Blackpool 'Boat' #602 (1933) @ St. Chad's Road

Alstom Citadis #3019 @ Abbey Street

DUBLIN

Die irische Hauptstadt Dublin (gälisch *Baile Átha Cliath*) liegt beiderseits des Flusses Liffey kurz vor dessen Mündung in die Irische See. Seit 2004 verkehrt in der Stadt wieder eine Straßenbahn (Luas), nachdem bereits 1984 eine elektrische S-Bahn-Linie (DART) eingerichtet worden war.

Einen Verkehrsverbund im deutschen Sinn gibt es im Großraum Dublin nicht, jeder Betreiber hat sein eigenes Zonensystem und auch unterschiedliche Tarife. Das Tramnetz ist in 9 Zonen unterteilt, Einzelfahrten kosten demnach von 1,80 bis 3,00 €, uneingeschränkt kann man das zweigeteilte Netz mit einem *1-Day Flexi Ticket* für 6,80 € erkunden. Günstiger sind Einzelfahrten mit der *Leap Card*, einer aufladbaren kontaktlosen Wertkarte. Mit dieser werden in der Tram max. 6,40 € pro Tag abgezogen, oder max. 10,00 €, wenn man mit derselben Karte neben der Straßenbahn auch die städtischen Busse und DART bzw. andere Vorortzüge nutzen möchte. Allerdings ist für die *Leap Card* ein Pfand von 5,00 € zu entrichten.

DUBLIN (Ireland | Éire)

530 000 | 1 300 000

el. (1896-1959) 2004

1435 mm

km 37 km

2

6-15'

Luas
www.luas.ie

Transport for Ireland
www.transportforireland.ie
www.leapcard.ie

Transport Infrastructure Ireland
www.tii.ie

The Irish capital Dublin (Baile Átha Cliath in Gaelic) lies on both sides of the River Liffey shortly before it flows into the Irish Sea. Since 2004, the city has once again had a tram system (Luas), while an electric S-Bahn-style suburban railway (DART) was already established in 1984.

The Greater Dublin area does not have a unified fare system, and instead, each operator has its own zonal system and different fares. The tram network is divided into 9 zones, with single tickets costing from €1.80 to €3.00; the two parts of the split network can be explored using a 1-Day Flexi Ticket for €6.80. Single fares are cheaper when paid with the Leap Card, a rechargeable contactless smartcard. As long as you just ride on the tram, the daily fare is capped at €6.40, and if urban buses, DART and other suburban trains are used, too, a maximum of €10.00 will be charged. For the Leap Card itself, however, a deposit of €5.00 is payable.

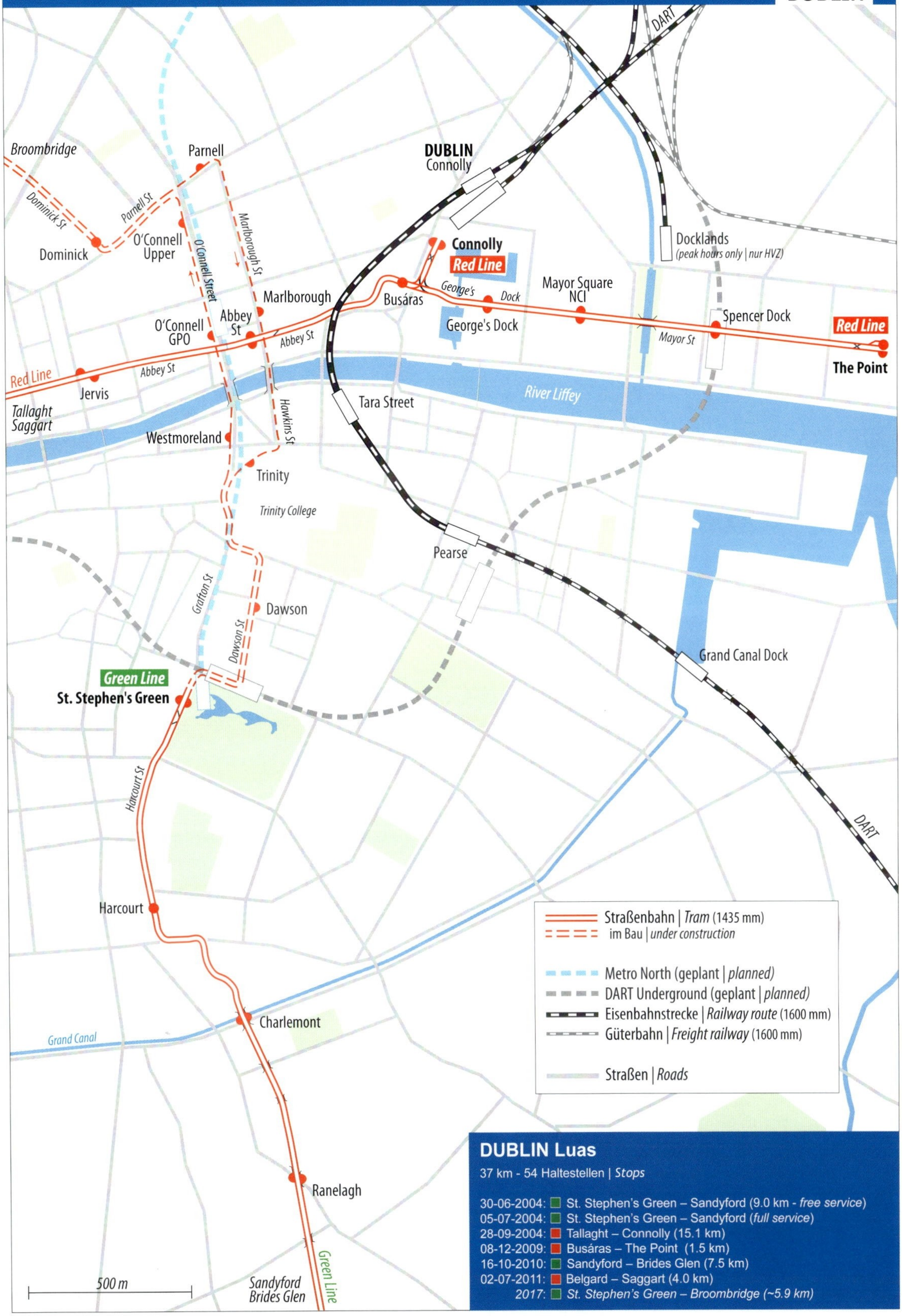

DUBLIN Luas

37 km - 54 Haltestellen | *Stops*

30-06-2004: St. Stephen's Green – Sandyford (9.0 km - *free service*)
05-07-2004: St. Stephen's Green – Sandyford (*full service*)
28-09-2004: Tallaght – Connolly (15.1 km)
08-12-2009: Busáras – The Point (1.5 km)
16-10-2010: Sandyford – Brides Glen (7.5 km)
02-07-2011: Belgard – Saggart (4.0 km)
2017: St. Stephen's Green – Broombridge (~5.9 km)

DUBLIN

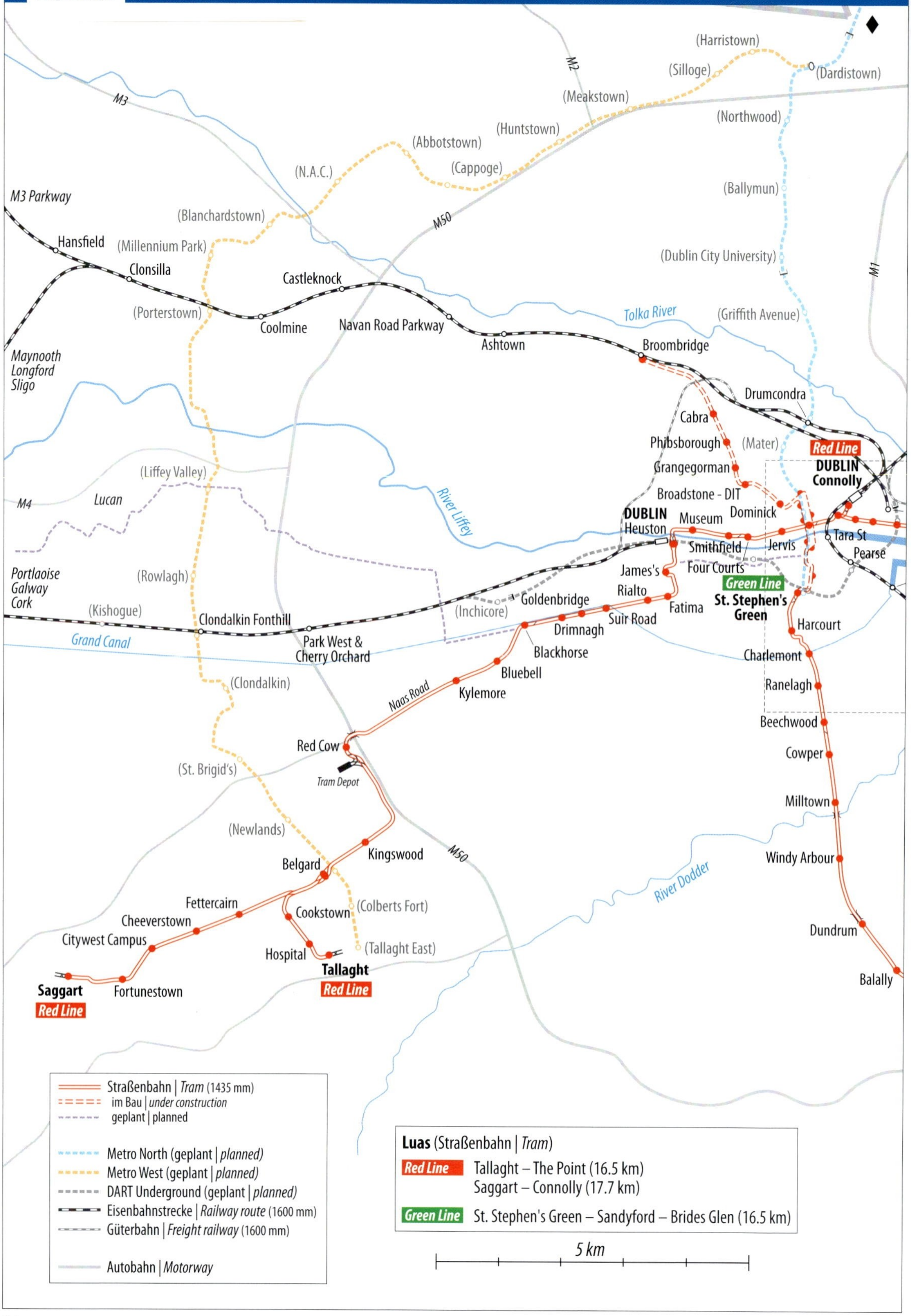

(Harristown)
(Silloge)
(Dardistown)
(Meakstown)
(Northwood)
(Huntstown)
(Abbotstown)
(Cappoge)
(N.A.C.)
(Ballymun)
M3 Parkway
(Blanchardstown)
Hansfield
(Millennium Park)
Clonsilla
Castleknock
(Dublin City University)
(Porterstown)
Coolmine
Navan Road Parkway
Ashtown
Tolka River
(Griffith Avenue)
Broombridge
Maynooth
Longford
Sligo
Drumcondra
Cabra
Phibsborough
(Mater)
Red Line
DUBLIN
Connolly
Grangegorman
(Liffey Valley)
Broadstone - DIT
M4
Lucan
River Liffey
DUBLIN
Heuston
Museum
Dominick
Tara St
Smithfield
Jervis
Pearse
Four Courts
James's
Portlaoise
Galway
Cork
(Rowlagh)
Green Line
Rialto
St. Stephen's
Green
Goldenbridge
Fatima
(Kishogue)
(Inchicore)
Suir Road
Harcourt
Clondalkin Fonthill
Drimnagh
Grand Canal
Park West &
Cherry Orchard
Blackhorse
Charlemont
Bluebell
(Clondalkin)
Ranelagh
Naas Road
Kylemore
Beechwood
Red Cow
Cowper
(St. Brigid's)
Tram Depot
Milltown
(Newlands)
Kingswood
M50
Windy Arbour
Belgard
River Dodder
Fettercairn
(Colberts Fort)
Cheeverstown
Cookstown
Dundrum
Citywest Campus
Hospital
(Tallaght East)
Tallaght
Red Line
Balally
Saggart
Red Line
Fortunestown
M3
M2
M1
Straßenbahn | Tram (1435 mm)
im Bau | under construction
geplant | planned
Metro North (geplant | planned)
Metro West (geplant | planned)
DART Underground (geplant | planned)
Eisenbahnstrecke | Railway route (1600 mm)
Güterbahn | Freight railway (1600 mm)
Autobahn | Motorway
Luas (Straßenbahn | Tram)
Red Line Tallaght – The Point (16.5 km)
Saggart – Connolly (17.7 km)
Green Line St. Stephen's Green – Sandyford – Brides Glen (16.5 km)
5 km

Portmarnock
Malahide
Drogheda
Dundalk
Belfast
DART
Clongriffin
Howth Junction & Donaghmede
Bayside
Sutton
DART
Howth
National Transport Museum
Kilbarrack
Harmonstown
Raheny
Killester
Clontarf Road
Docklands
The Point
Red Line
Grand Canal Dock
Lansdowne Road
Sandymount
Sydney Parade
Booterstown
Blackrock
Seapoint
Dun Laoghaire Mallin
Salthill & Monkstown
Sandycove & Glasthule
Glenageary
Dalkey
Killiney
DART
Bray
Greystones
Rosslare
Kilmacud
Green Line
Sandyford
Stillorgan
Tram Depot
Central Park
Glencairn
M50
The Gallops
Leopardstown Valley
Ballyogan Wood
Carrickmines
Laughanstown
Cherrywood
Green Line
Brides Glen
Irish Sea
Muir Éireann
(Estuary)
(Seatown)
(Swords Central)
(Fosterstown)
DUB
(Airport)
(Dardistown)

Alstom Citadis #5005 @ Dundrum

LUAS

Die moderne Straßenbahn von Dublin wurde nach dem gälischen Wort für „Geschwindigkeit“ benannt. Die irische Sprache ist auch an Haltestellenschildern an erster Stelle zu sehen, auch wenn sonst die meiste Information nur auf Englisch vermittelt wird. Luas wird bis mindestens 2019 von *Transdev* betrieben, für den Ausbau ist nun die *Transport Infrastructure Ireland* (TII) zuständig.

Bislang besteht das Dubliner Tramnetz aus zwei voneinander isolierten Strecken, zwischen denen auch keine Gleisverbindung besteht. Umsteiger müssen einen 15-minütigen Fußmarsch einlegen oder einen Bus nutzen. Diese Situation wird sich glücklicherweise voraussichtlich 2017 durch den Bau von *Luas Cross City* ändern.

Die **Red Line**, die die südwestlichen Außenbezirke mit dem Stadtzentrum verbindet, besteht eigentlich aus zwei Linien, Tallaght – The Point und Saggart – Connolly, wobei allerdings zu Schwachlastzeiten der Abschnitt Saggart – Belgard als Shuttle betrieben und der Bahnhof Connolly, der nur 130 m vom Busbahnhof Busáras liegt, nicht direkt bedient wird. Zwischen Belgard und Busáras verkehrt tagsüber meist alle 4-5 Minuten eine Tram.

Diese Ost-West-Linie fährt durch die Innenstadt wie eine klassische Straßenbahn auf teils abmarkierter Trasse. Erst an der Haltestelle James's beginnt ein eigener Gleiskörper. Die Trasse liegt ab Fatima erst auf einem zugeschütteten Seitenkanal und verläuft dann bis Blackhorse parallel zum Grand Canal. Anschließend folgt die Trasse dem Mittelstreifen der Naas Road. Der Kreuzungsbereich am Kreisel über der Ringautobahn M50 kurz vor dem Betriebshof Red Cow wurde 2008 kreuzungsfrei umgebaut. Die Haltestelle Belgard, etwa 500 m von der eigentlichen Verzweigung entfernt, wurde 2011 dreigleisig ausgebaut, um zeitweise

Dublin's modern tramway was named after the Gaelic word for 'speed'. The Irish language is also visible on station signs, occupying the first place, even though most other information is only given in English. Until at least 2019, Luas will be run by Transdev, while the expansion of the network is now the responsibility of 'Transport Infrastructure Ireland' (TII).

For now, the Dublin tram network consists of just two separate lines, with no physical connection between them. Transferring passengers need to take a 15-minute walk or hop on a bus. Fortunately, this situation will change in 2017, when the construction of 'Luas Cross City' is set to be completed.

*The **Red Line**, which connects the southwestern districts to the city centre, actually consists of two overlapping lines, Tallaght – The Point and Saggart – Connolly; however, during off-peak hours, the Saggart – Belgard section is operated as a shuttle, and Connolly Station, which is located just 130 m from the Busáras Bus Station, is not served. Between Belgard and Busáras, trams run every 4-5 minutes during daytime hours.*

Through the city centre, this east-west line resembles a classic tramway, with partly marked-off tracks. A dedicated right-of-way is only available from James's stop; from Fatima, the route first follows a filled-in side canal before continuing parallel to the Grand Canal to Blackhorse. Subsequently, the route runs in the median strip of Naas Road. The intersection with the roundabout above the M50 motorway, shortly before the Red Cow depot, was rebuilt in 2008, and is now completely grade-separated. The stop at Belgard, some 500 m from the actual junction where the two western branches split,

Alstom Citadis #3023 @ Rialto > Suir Road

einen bequemen Umstieg zum Shuttle-Betrieb auf dem neuen Saggart-Ast anbieten zu können. Auf der Red Line fahren ausschließlich die älteren Citadis-Fahrzeuge, von denen die 14 in der Langversion ausgelieferten Wagen von der Green Line übernommen wurden, während die ursprünglich nur 30 m langen wenige Jahre nach Inbetriebnahme um zwei Module verlängert wurden.

Die Trassierung der **Green Line** unterscheidet sich wesentlich von der der Red Line, da sie auf langen Abschnitten die alte Eisenbahntrasse der 1958 stillgelegten Harcourt Street Line nutzt. Im Vergleich zur alten Bahn dringt die Tram jedoch ca. 650 m weiter ins Stadtzentrum vor und endet am Stadtpark St. Stephen's Green. Die alte Bahntrasse beginnt nördlich der Haltestelle Charlemont und reicht bis zum ursprünglichen Endpunkt in Sandyford, wo sich auch der Betriebshof für die Green Line befindet. Allerdings mussten auch auf diesem Abschnitt einige Brücken neu errichtet

was expanded to three tracks in 2011 to enable a convenient shuttle service on the new Saggart branch at certain times. On the Red Line, only the older Citadis vehicles are in service; 14 of the long type, which had originally been delivered for the Green Line, were transferred to the Red Line, while the initially just 30 m long vehicles on that line were extended with two additional sections only a few years after the opening of the system.

*The alignment of the **Green Line** is rather different from that of the Red Line, as on long sections it uses the railway formation of the Harcourt Street Line, which had been abandoned since 1958. However, unlike the old railway, the tramway runs some 650 m further into the city centre before terminating at St. Stephen's Green. The old railway route starts north of Charlemont station and extends all the way to the original terminus in Sandyford, where the depot for the Green Line is located. Nonethe-*

Alstom Citadis #5006 @ Ranelagh

Alstom Citadis #3003 @ Belgard

Alstom Citadis #4006 @ Fortunestown

werden, die spektakulärste ist eine Spannseilbrücke nördlich der Station Dundrum. Außerdem bestehen mehrere Bahnübergänge, meist direkt an Haltestellen. Für die 2010 fertiggestellte Verlängerung nach Brides Glen wählte man jedoch eine neue Trasse, um die Bürostadt Central Park sowie die Stadtteile Glencairn und Leopardstown anzuschließen. Dafür überquert die Green Line zweimal die Ringautobahn M50. Durch sehr spärlich bebautes Gebiet erreicht sie schließlich die Endstation Brides Glen in Cherrywood, wo große Flächen seit Jahren zur Bebauung vorbereitet sind. Ab Carrickmines liegt die Tramstrecke wieder teilweise auf der alten Trasse der Harcourt Road Line. Zwischen Carrickmines und Laughanstown ist eine weitere Haltestelle baulich vorbereitet, unmittelbar südlich davon wurde sogar ein 150 m langer Tunnel in die Landschaft gesetzt. Aufgrund der geringeren Nachfrage verkehrt auf dem südlichen Abschnitt tagsüber nur alle 10-13 Minuten eine Bahn, bis Sandyford hingegen alle 5-7 Minuten.

less, this section also required some bridges to be rebuilt, the most spectacular being a cable-stayed bridge north of Dundrum station. There are also several level crossings, mostly located directly at tram stops. For the extension to Brides Glen, which was completed in 2010, the tram route diverges from the old railway corridor to serve the Central Park business area as well as the districts of Glencairn and Leopardstown. To do so, the Green Line crosses the M50 motorway twice. After passing through a sparsely built-up area, the trams finally reach the terminus at Brides Glen in Cherrywood, where large areas have been awaiting development for years. South of Carrickmines, the tram route again runs partly on the old route of the Harcourt Road Line. Between Carrickmines and Laughanstown, provisions were made for another station, and immediately to its south, a 150 m tunnel was even dug into the open countryside. On the southern section, trams run every 10-13 minutes during daytime off-peak hours, but every 5-7 minutes as far as Sandyford.

Citadis #3023 @ Tallaght

Citadis #5003 @ Central Park

Alstom Citadis #5005 @ Dundrum (William Dargan Bridge)

Nach dem Erfolg der ersten Linien entwickelte Dublin ein weitreichendes Ausbauprogramm: Als **Metro North** wird eine großteils unterirdische Stadtbahn vom Stadtzentrum über den Flughafen bis Swords bezeichnet. Wie die Tangentiallinie **Metro West** soll sie durchgehend kreuzungsfrei werden, jedoch mit ähnlichen (jedoch längeren) Fahrzeugen wie Luas betrieben werden. Langfristig könnte die gut ausgebaute Green Line mit Metro North direkt verknüpft werden. Im Stil der Red Line soll hingegen die Strecke nach Lucan gebaut werden. Trotz fortgeschrittener Planungen wurden diese Projekte infolge der Finanzkrise 2011 auf Eis gelegt, nach einer Entscheidung im September 2015 soll Metro North in einer abgespeckten Version ab 2021 gebaut werden (16,5 km, davon 8,5 km unterirdisch).

Als einziges Projekt wurde 2013 das wesentliche Bindeglied zwischen den beiden Luas-Linien in Angriff genommen. Unter dem Projektnamen **Luas Cross City** entsteht bis Ende 2017 eine knapp 6 km lange Nordverlängerung der Green Line. Durch die Innenstadt handelt es sich um eine klassische Straßenbahnstrecke, teils durch parallele Straßen. Richtung Norden wird die Tram den Liffey auf der traditionellen O'Connell Bridge überqueren, Richtung Süden hingegen auf der erst 2014 eröffneten und für den ÖPNV reservierten Rosie Hackett Bridge. Ab Broadstone-DIT bis zur Endstelle Broombridge steht wiederum eine seit 1961 ungenutzte, im Einschnitt liegende Eisenbahntrasse zur Verfügung.

*Following the success of the first lines, Dublin developed an ambitious expansion program: **Metro North** has been designed as a mostly underground light rail line from the city centre via the airport to Swords. Like the tangential **Metro West**, it should run on a grade-separated route throughout, but it should be operated with vehicles similar to those in service on Luas, just longer. In the long term, the well-aligned Green Line could be directly linked to Metro North. The route to Lucan, however, is planned to be built in the style of the Red Line. Despite having reached an advanced stage of planning, these projects were all postponed indefinitely in 2011 as a result of the financial crisis. After a decision taken in September 2015, Metro North will be realised in a reduced version, with construction now set to start in 2021 (16.5 km, with 8.5 km underground).*

*The only project under construction since 2013 is the essential link between the two Luas lines. Labelled '**Luas Cross City**', this nearly 6 km northern extension of the Green Line will be completed by the end of 2017. Through the city centre this will be a classic tramway, running partly through parallel streets – northbound trams will cross the Liffey River on the traditional O'Connell Bridge, while southbound they will use the Rosie Hackett Bridge, which was only opened in 2014 for the exclusive use of public transport. From Broadstone-DIT to the terminus at Broombridge, an old railway corridor in a cutting out of use since 1961 is available.*

Luas > Fahrzeuge | *Rolling Stock* (750 V DC)

Nummer *Number*	Anzahl *Quantity*	Hersteller *Manufacturer*	Typ *Class*	Länge *Length*	Breite *Width*	Ausgeliefert *Delivered*
3001-3026*	26	Alstom	Citadis 401 (Red Line)	40 m*	2.40 m	2003-2004
4001-4014	14	Alstom	Citadis 401 (Red Line)	40 m	2.40 m	2003-2004
5001-5026	26	Alstom	Citadis 402 (Green Line)	43 m	2.40 m	2010

* 2007-08 verlängert | *extended*

DART @ Connolly

DART

Seit dem 23. Juli 1984 verfügt Dublin über eine moderne S-Bahn auf der bislang einzigen elektrifizierten Eisenbahnstrecke Irlands. Die sicherlich Schnelligkeit und Zielgenauigkeit suggerierende Bezeichnung DART steht für *Dublin Area Rapid Transit*, etwa zeitgleich entstand im texanischen Dallas dieselbe Marke. DART ist Teil des Netzes der Staatsbahn Iarnród Éireann/Irish Rail. Während Luas mit internationaler Standardspurweite (1435 mm) errichtet wurde, hat DART wie das übrige irische Bahnnetz Breitspur (1600 mm).

DART fuhr anfangs zwischen Howth im Nordosten und Bray im Süden (38 km) mit 24 Bahnhöfen innerhalb des Stadtgebiets von Dublin. Durch die Innenstadt nutzt DART die aufgeständerte Verbindungsbahn mit der Loop Line Bridge über den Liffey aus dem Jahre 1891. Der südliche Abschnitt zwischen Pearse und Salthill & Monkstown war im Jahr 1834 die erste Eisenbahnstrecke Irlands.

Für den DART-Betrieb wurde die Nord-Süd-Strecke mit 1500 V Gleichstrom unter Oberleitung elektrifiziert und mit einem neuen Signalsystem ausgerüstet. Die ersten 2,8 m breiten Elektrotriebwagen kamen von Linke-Hoffmann-Busch (BR 8100). Zwischen 2000 und 2004 wurde die Flotte durch drei Serien aus japanischer Produktion (Tokyu Car Corporation) aufgestockt (BR 8500/8510/8520). Die wenigen Fahrzeuge der BR 8200 von GEC/Alsthom waren nur von 2000 bis 2008 im Einsatz.

Nachdem am 1. September 1997 der Halt Clontarf Road eröffnet worden war, wurde der elektrische Betrieb am 10. April 2000 im Süden von Bray bis Greystones (7,9 km) und am 9. Oktober 2000 im Norden von Howth Junction bis Malahide (7 km) erweitert. Am 22. Januar 2001 kam

Since 23 July 1984, Dublin has had a modern S-Bahn-style system on what is so far the only electrified railway route in Ireland. DART, which clearly suggests speed and accuracy, stands for 'Dublin Area Rapid Transit'; coincidentally, the same brand name was created in Dallas, Texas, at about the same time. DART is part of the state railway company Iarnród Éireann/Irish Rail. While the Luas system was built with international standard gauge (1435 mm), DART features broad gauge (1600 mm) like the rest of the Irish railway network.

DART initially ran between Howth in the northeast and Bray in the south (38 km), serving 24 stations within the Dublin city boundaries. Through the city centre, DART takes advantage of the elevated railway link, including the Loop Line Bridge over the Liffey River, which dates back to 1891. The southern section between Pearse and Salthill & Monkstown became the first railway in Ireland when it opened in 1834.

Before DART was launched, the north-south route was electrified at 1500 V DC using an overhead catenary and equipped with a new signalling system. The first 2.8 m wide EMUs (electric multiple units) came from Linke-Hoffmann-Busch (class 8100). Between 2000 and 2004, the fleet was enlarged with three series of trains (class 8500/8510/8520) manufactured in Japan by Tokyu Car Corporation. The few vehicles of class 8200 from GEC/Alsthom only remained in service between 2000 and 2008.

After Clontarf Road station had opened on 1 September 1997, electric service was extended south from Bray to Greystones (7.9 km) on 10 April 2000, and north from Howth Junction to Malahide (7 km) on 9 October 2000.

DART @ Dun Laoghaire

die innenstadtnahe Station Grand Canal Dock hinzu. Von Howth fahren 2-3 Züge pro Stunde bis Bray, manche weiter bis Greystones. Auf dem Nordast nach Malahide verkehren nur 1-2 DART-Züge pro Stunde, allerdings wird dieser Abschnitt auch von zahlreichen Regionalzügen von und nach Drogheda oder Dundalk bedient, die ab Howth Junction ohne Halt bis Connolly durchfahren und meist in Pearse enden. Auf der Südstrecke verkehren hingegen nur vereinzelt Regionalzüge nach Rosslare.

Neben DART betreibt Iarnród Éireann im Großraum von Dublin einen regen Vorortverkehr mit Dieseltriebwagen, die als *Commuter* bezeichnet werden. Um den etwas abseits vom Zentrum gelegenen Westbahnhof Heuston besser an das Nord-Süd-Netz anzuschließen, ist eine unterirdische Verbindungsbahn, **DART Underground** (7,6 km), durch das Stadtzentrum mit vier tief liegenden Stationen geplant: Christchurch, St. Stephen's Green, Pearse und Spencer Dock. Gleichzeitig sollen die sowohl von Heuston als auch von Connolly nach Westen führenden Strecken elektrifiziert und in das DART-Netz integriert werden, so dass zwei Hauptachsen entstehen:

1) (Drogheda –) Malahide / Howth – Docklands – Pearse – Heuston – Hazelhatch & Celbridge
2) Maynooth / M3 Parkway – Connolly – Pearse – Greystones.

Wie die ambitionierten Luas- und Metro-Projekte verzögert sich auch der Ausbau des DART-Netzes aus finanziellen Gründen.

DART @ Malahide

On 22 January 2001, Grand Canal Dock station was added not far from the city centre. From Howth, 2-3 trains an hour run to Bray, with some continuing to Greystones. The northern branch to Malahide only has 1-2 DART trains an hour, as this section is also served by numerous regional trains to and from Drogheda or Dundalk. These run nonstop between Howth Junction and Connolly, and usually terminate at Pearse. The southern section, however, is only shared with a few regional trains to Rosslare.

In addition to DART, Iarnród Éireann operates a busy suburban service in Greater Dublin called 'Commuter', which uses diesel multiple units (DMUs). Dublin's western railway station, Heuston, is located some distance from the city centre, and to better connect it to the north-south network, a tunnel link called ***DART Underground*** *(7.6 km) has been planned through the city centre with four deep-level stations: Christchurch, St Stephen's Green, Pearse and Spencer Dock. At the same time, the routes leading west from Heuston and Connolly will be electrified and integrated into the DART network, resulting in two main axes:*

1) (Drogheda –) Malahide / Howth – Docklands – Pearse – Heuston – Hazelhatch & Celbridge
2) Maynooth / M3 Parkway – Connolly – Pearse – Greystones.

Like the ambitious Luas and metro projects, the expansion of the DART network is also on hold due to the financial crisis.

CAF Urbos #259 @ St. Andrew Square

EDINBURGH

Die schottische Hauptstadt ist seit 2014 das neueste und auf absehbare Zeit auch das letzte neue Mitglied im Club der britischen Straßenbahnstädte.

Zusammen mit der Eröffnung der Tram-Linie wurde *Transport for Edinburgh* gegründet und somit eine Tarifgemeinschaft mit *Lothian Buses* geschaffen, einer Verkehrsgesellschaft in öffentlicher Hand, die neben der Stadt Edinburgh auch die umliegenden Gebiete in Midlothian und East Lothian bedient. Eigentümer der Straßenbahngesellschaft *Edinburgh Trams* ist die City of Edinburgh.

Alle Tram-Haltestellen sind mit Fahrkartenautomaten ausgestattet. Einzelfahrscheine gelten nur in der Tram und kosten für fast die gesamte Strecke (City Zone) 1,50 £, zum Flughafen (Airport Zone) allerdings 5,00 £ (hin und retour 8,00 £). Tageskarten schließen das Netz von *Lothian Buses* mit ein und sind für 4,00 £ (bzw. 9,00 £ inkl. Flughafen) erhältlich. Wochen- und Monatskarten werden in der Form einer kontaktlosen Smartcard (*Ridacard*) ausgegeben. Die Nahverkehrszüge von *ScotRail* (Abellio) sind nicht in dieses Tarifsystem integriert.

Die bislang einzige Straßenbahnlinie von Edinburgh verbindet auf einer 14 km langen Strecke das Stadtzentrum mit dem Flughafen im Westen der Stadt. Die stadtseitige Endstelle York Place ist provisorisch und daher nur eingleisig, sie würde im Fall einer Verlängerung etwas nach Osten verlegt. Am St. Andrew Square besteht ein Übergang zum Busbahnhof und zum etwas weiter entfernten Hauptbahnhof Waverley. Die Tram fährt dann entlang der Princes

In 2014, the Scottish capital became the latest, and for the foreseeable future, also the last new member of the club of British tramway cities.

Along with the opening of the city's first tram line, Transport for Edinburgh was founded, thus creating a joint fare system with Lothian Buses, a publicly owned transport company which operates buses both within the City of Edinburgh as well as in the surrounding areas in Midlothian and East Lothian. The tramway company Edinburgh Trams is owned by the City of Edinburgh.

All tram stops are equipped with automatic ticket vending machines. Single tickets are only valid on the tram and cost £1.50 for most of the route (City Zone), but £5.00 all the way to the airport (Airport Zone; round trip £8.00). Day tickets include the Lothian Buses network and are available for £4.00 (or £9.00 incl. the airport). Weekly and monthly tickets are issued in the form of a contactless smartcard (Ridacard). The local trains operated by ScotRail (Abellio) are not integrated into this fare system.

Edinburgh has only one tram line so far, which is 14 km long and connects the city centre to the airport in the west of the city. The city-side terminus at York Place is temporary and therefore has just a single track; in the case of an extension, this stop would be moved further east. At St. Andrew Square, interchange is provided to the city's major bus station and, though requiring a longer walk, Edinburgh's main railway station, Waverley. The trams then travel west along Princes Street, the city's

CAF Urbos #266 @ Haymarket

Street, der Haupteinkaufsstraße der Stadt, nach Westen und bietet linker Hand über die Princes Street Gardens hinweg eine schöne Aussicht auf das Edinburgh Castle. Der städtische, knapp 2,6 km lange Abschnitt, auf dem die Trasse zwar meist abmarkiert ist, jedoch teils von Linienbussen mitgenutzt wird, endet an der Haltestelle Haymarket neben dem zweitwichtigsten Bahnhof der Stadt.

Die Trassierung der restlichen 12,4 km entspricht eher der einer typischen amerikanischen *Light Rail* mit eigenem Gleiskörper unter teilweiser Nutzung von Eisenbahnkorridoren. Dafür überquert die Tram zweimal die Bahnstrecke Richtung Glasgow, wobei westlich der Station Edinburgh Park zu diesem Zweck ein rund 300 m langer Viadukt errichtet wurde. Das aufwendigste Stationsbauwerk ist am Murrayfield Stadium zu finden. Zwischen Saughton und Bankhead (1,5 km) wurde der *West Edinburgh Busway,* eine im Dezember 2004 errichtete Bustrasse mit Spurführung ähnlich wie in Essen, für die Tram umgebaut. Zwei Querstraßen werden auf diesem Abschnitt somit kreuzungfrei überquert.

Der Betriebshof liegt unmittelbar nördlich der Unterquerung der Nationalstraße A8, hier entsteht derzeit ein Umsteigepunkt von und zu den Zügen Richtung Perth, Dundee oder Aber-

EDINBURGH (Scotland)

490 000 — 700 000

el. (1905-1956) 2014

1435 mm

14 km

1

8-10'

Edinburgh Trams
www.edinburghtrams.com

Transport for Edinburgh
www.transportforedinburgh.com

Transport Scotland
www.transportscotland.gov.uk

main shopping street, providing great views of Edinburgh Castle on the left looking over Princes Street Gardens. The urban, almost 2.6 km long section runs mostly on marked-off lanes, which are, however, also partly used by buses. This section ends at the Haymarket stop, which lies next to the city's second most important railway station.

The alignment of the remaining 12.4 km resembles a typical American light rail line, with its own dedicated right-of-way making partial use of railway corridors. The trams therefore cross the railway line to Glasgow twice, and for that purpose a 300 m long viaduct was built to the west of Edinburgh Park station. The most substantial station can be found at Murrayfield Stadium. Between Saughton and Bankhead (1.5 km), the former West Edinburgh Busway was reused to form the trackbed. Established in December 2004 and featuring a bus guidance system similar to that in Essen (Germany), its integration into the new line enabled two road intersections to be avoided.

The tram depot is located just north of the crossing under national road A8; at this point, an interchange is currently under construction to allow transfer to and from trains towards Perth, Dundee and Aberdeen.

deen. Durch weitgehend unbebautes Gebiet, jedoch mit teils trotzdem sehr engen Kurvenradien geht es weiter über die Park-and-Ride Anlage Ingliston zum Flughafen. Eine Fahrt von St. Andrew Square zum Flughafen dauert 40 Minuten.

Die am 31. Mai 2014 eröffnete Strecke entspricht nur etwa der Hälfte des 2006 vom schottischen Parlament beschlossenen und bereits abgespeckten Netzes. Neben der logischen Verlängerung ins Hafengebiet von Leith (4,5 km) sollte in einer nächsten Phase noch ein Ast von Haymarket Richtung Norden nach Granton gebaut werden, ursprünglich sollten beide Nordäste eine Ringlinienführung ergeben. Nachdem der Bau im Sommer 2008 begonnen hatte, kam es wiederholt zu Verzögerungen, Kostensteigerungen und vertraglichen Problemen mit den Baufirmen, so dass das gesamte Projekt zeitweise auf der Kippe stand und nur durch Kürzung der Anfangsstrecke gerettet werden

Travelling through largely undeveloped areas, though still with some rather tight curves, the trams then pass the park-and-ride facility at Ingliston before reaching the airport. A trip from St. Andrew Square to the airport takes 40 minutes.

The tram route which opened on 31 May 2014 represents just about a half of what the Scottish Parliament approved in 2006, and that had already been trimmed down from the original proposal. In addition to the logical extension towards the port area of Leith (4.5 km), a northern branch from Haymarket towards Granton was to be built in the following phase, with the two northern branches originally meant to become a circular route of sorts. After construction had begun in the summer of 2008, there were repeated delays, cost overruns and problems with the contractors. At times, the entire project was in danger of being scrapped, and it was only rescued by truncating the initial

CAF Urbos #263 @ York Place

CAF Urbos

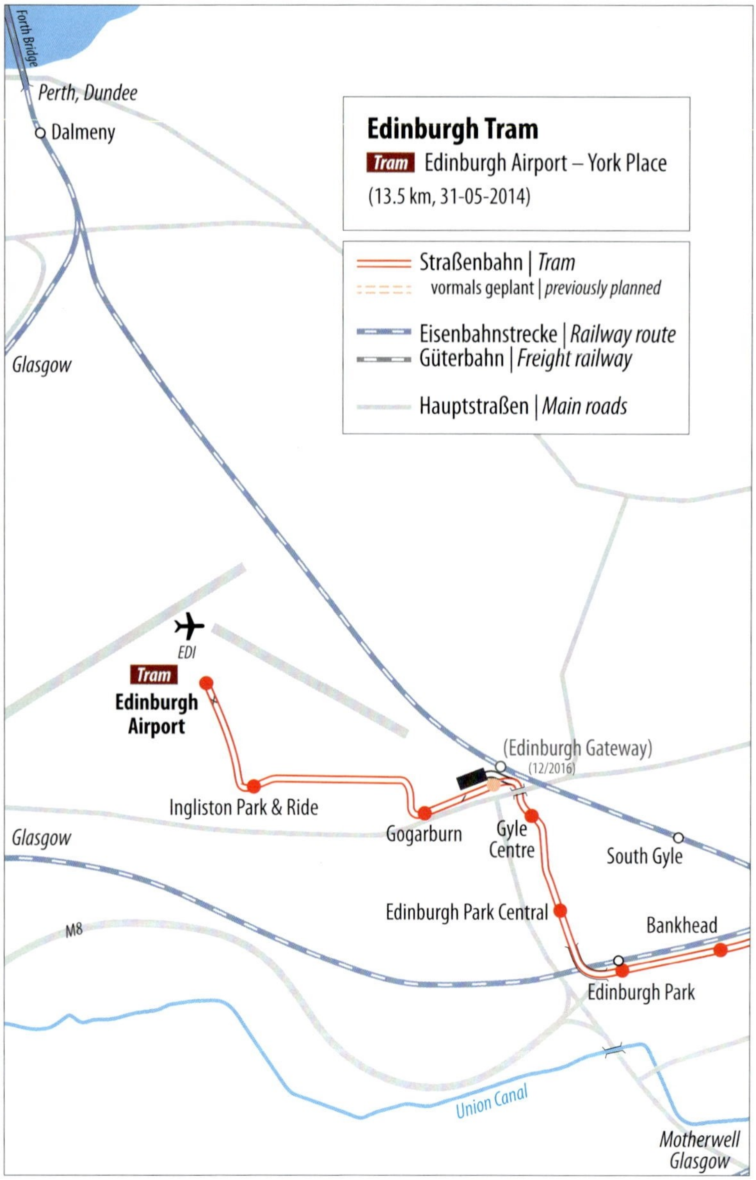

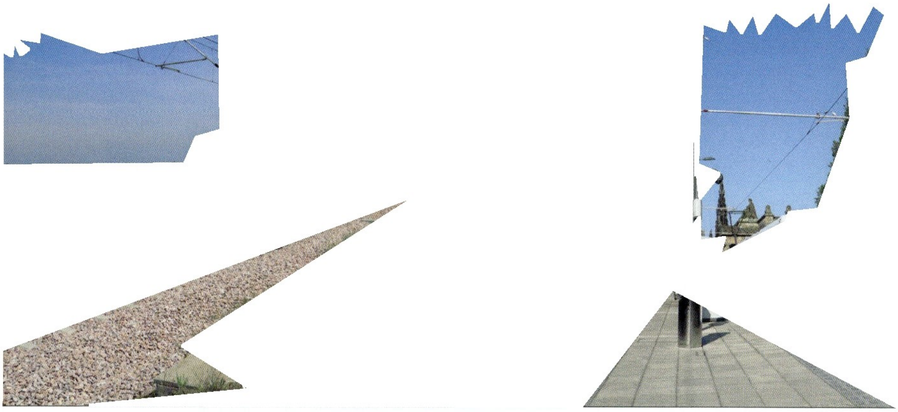

Firth of Forth
Granton
(Ocean Terminal)
(Newhaven)
(Port of Leith)
Leith
(Bernard Street)
(Foot of the Walk)
Water of Leith
Leith Walk
(Balfour Street)
(McDonald Road)
Tram
York Place
(Picardy Place)
Newcastle
London
St Andrew Square
Princes Street
Princes St
Palace of Holyroodhouse
Scottish Parliament
West End - Princes Street
EDINBURGH
Waverley
Haymarket
Edinburgh Castle
EDINBURGH
Haymarket
Murrayfield Stadium
Balgreen
Saughton
Slateford
Kingsknowe
Wester Hailes
1 km

CAF Urbos #274 @ Gogarburn > Gyle Centre

konnte. Anlässlich der Eröffnung der heutigen Strecke erklärte die schottische Regierung, nicht weiter in die Tram investieren zu wollen. Der Stadtrat hingegen spricht sich für eine Verlängerung bis Leith aus. Die Zukunft wird zeigen, ob es in der schottischen Hauptstadt mit der Tram weitergeht.

Angesichts der optimistischen Planungen bestellte man bereits im November 2007 beim spanischen Hersteller CAF insgesamt 27 durchgehend niederflurige Urbos-Fahrzeuge, von denen heute im Normalbetrieb jedoch nur 17 benötigt werden. Die ersten Testfahrten begannen 2011, drei Jahre vor Inbetriebnahme. Die Fahrzeuge sind großzügig mit Gepäckablagen ausgerüstet. Der weinrot-weiße Anstrich sowie die Nummerierung der Fahrzeuge setzt die Tradition der 1956 eingestellten Straßenbahn der ersten Generation fort.

stretch. At the opening of the present route, the Scottish government declared their unwillingness to continue their investment in the tramway. The City Council, however, is in favour of an extension to Leith. Time will tell whether the Scottish capital's tram network is one day expanded or not.

With such optimistic plans, Edinburgh placed an order in November 2007 for a total of 27 100% low-floor Urbos trams from the Spanish manufacturer CAF, of which just 17 are now required for normal operation. The first test runs began in 2011, three years before commissioning. The vehicles are generously equipped with luggage racks. The burgundy-and-white livery as well as the vehicle numbering system are a continuation of the tradition of Edinburgh's first-generation tramway, which was abandoned in 1956.

Gyle Centre > Gogarburn

Tram > Fahrzeuge | *Rolling Stock* (750 V DC)

Nummer *Number*	Anzahl *Quantity*	Hersteller *Manufacturer*	Typ *Class*	Länge *Length*	Breite *Width*	Ausgeliefert *Delivered*
251-277	27	CAF	Urbos 3	42.8 m	2.65 m	2010-2012

CAF Urbos #261 @ Gyle Centre

CAF Urbos #259 + 267 @ Airport

Ibrox

GLASGOW

In der größten Stadt Schottlands fährt seit nunmehr 120 Jahren eine U-Bahn, die allerdings seit ihrer Inbetriebnahme 1896 nie erweitert wurde. Die als *Subway* bezeichnete Untergrundbahn wird in der Region Greater Glasgow durch ein weitverzweigtes elektrisches Vorortbahnnetz mit S-Bahn-Charakter ergänzt.

Die Subway wird direkt von SPT (*Strathclyde Partnership for Transport*, bis 2006 *Strathclyde Passenger Transport Executive*) betrieben. SPT ist als regionale Nahverkehrsplanungsbehörde auch für die Koordination von Bussen und Bahnen zuständig, trotzdem ist der Tarifverbund im Vergleich zu anderen britischen Großräumen sehr unzureichend.

Eine Einzelfahrt nur mit der Subway kostet 1,60 £, zwei Fahrten 3,00 £, eine Tageskarte exklusiv für die Subway ist für 4,00 £ erhältlich. Günstiger fährt man mit der *Subway Smartcard*, die jedoch nur für registrierte Nutzer verfügbar ist. Möchte man auch andere Verkehrsmittel nutzen, bietet sich ein *Roundabout Ticket* für die Subway und Vorortbahnen in Greater Glasgow für 6,50 £ (ab 9 Uhr) an, das *Daytripper Ticket* für £20,30 gilt in der gesamten Region Strathclyde ab 9 Uhr, auch in den meisten Bussen und auf manchen Fähren.

Die Subway verkehrt wochentags von 6:30 bis 23:30, sonntags allerdings erst ab 10:00 und nur bis 18:00 Uhr! Eine volle Runde auf der Ringlinie dauert 24 Minuten. Die Subway ist nicht behindertengerecht zugänglich.

The largest city in Scotland has boasted a metro line for the past 120 years, but since its opening in 1896, it has never been expanded. The system known as the 'Subway' is complemented by an extensive electric S-Bahn-style suburban rail network which covers the whole of Greater Glasgow.

The Subway is operated directly by SPT ('Strathclyde Partnership for Transport', until 2006 'Strathclyde Passenger Transport Executive'). As a regional transport authority, SPT is responsible for the coordination of buses and trains, but in comparison with other British metropolitan areas, fare integration is still rather inadequate.

A single ticket just for the Subway costs £1.60, two trips are £3.00, while a day pass also exclusively for the Subway is priced at £4.00. The fares are cheaper when using a Subway smartcard, but this is available just for registered users. For those who also want to use other means of transport, a Roundabout Ticket for the Subway and suburban trains in Greater Glasgow is on offer for £6.50 (after 09:00), while a Daytripper Ticket worth £20.30 is valid throughout the Strathclyde region after 09:00, and can also be used on most buses and some ferries.

While the Subway operates from 06:30 to 23:30 on weekdays, on Sundays it only opens at 10:00 and already closes at 18:00! A full round trip on the circular line takes 24 minutes. The Subway is not accessible for disabled people.

Cessnock

Die **Glasgow Subway** war bei ihrer Eröffnung 1896 nach London (1863, elektrisch seit 1890) und Budapest (ebenfalls 1896) die dritte Untergrundbahn der Welt.

Die ersten Pläne für eine U-Bahn vom Stadtzentrum zum West End entstanden 1887. Ein Jahr später wurde das Projekt durch eine Strecke auf der Südseite des Flusses Clyde und zwei Unterwasserverbindungen erweitert, so dass daraus eine Ringlinie mit 15 Stationen wurde. Durch unterschiedliche Gesteinsschichten, von Ton und Sandstein bis hin zu hartem Felsgestein, wurden zwei eingleisige Röhren gegraben. Der Tunneldurchmesser beträgt nur 3,35 m und ist somit noch kleiner als bei der Londoner *Tube*. Etwa ein Drittel der Tunnelstrecken wurde mit Eisentübbings gesichert, der Rest mit Ziegelsteinen. Auf der Südseite des Flusses wurden zwei kurze Abschnitte in offener Bauweise errichtet. Alle Stationen hatten 3 m breite Bahnsteige mit nur einem Ausgang. Der U-Bahnhof Buchanan Street liegt in 12 m Tiefe und ist somit die tiefste Station der Ringlinie. Die Subway wurde ursprünglich von einem zwischen den Schienen laufenden Kabel gezogen. Die Züge mussten sich außer beim Halt in den Stationen an das Kabel anklemmen, ähnlich wie die *Cable Cars* in San Francisco. Die Spurweite beträgt bis heute

GLASGOW (Scotland)

600 000 — 1 200 000

1896

1219 mm

10.4 km

1

4-8'

SPT (Strathclyde Partnership for Transport)

www.spt.co.uk

When it opened in as early as 1896, the ***Glasgow Subway*** *became the third urban underground railway in the world, after London (1863, electric from 1890) and Budapest (also 1896).*

The first proposals for an underground line to link the city centre to the West End were made in 1887. A year later, the project became more ambitious with two river crossings and a route on the south bank of the River Clyde to form a full circle line with 15 stations. Two single-track tunnels were excavated through numerous different strata, ranging from various types of clay and sandstone to solid rock. The tunnels have a diameter of only 3.35 m, and are thus slightly narrower than the London tube tunnels. About a third of all the tunnels was lined with cast-iron rings, the rest being secured with brickwork. Two short sections on the south bank were built by the cut-and-cover method. Every station had a 3 m wide island platform, with exits at only one end. At 12 m below street level, Buchanan Street is the deepest station. The original subway trains were hauled by a cable running between the rails, and the trains had to grip onto it except when stopping at stations, much like the Cable Cars in San Francisco still do today. The

1219 mm (4 Fuß). Bis 1980 gab es zwischen den beiden Streckentunneln keine Gleisverbindung, außerdem fehlten Abstellgleise.

1923 wurde die Subway an die städtische *Municipal Corporation* übergeben, die auch ein weitreichendes Straßenbahnnetz betrieb. Dass die Subway modernisiert werden musste, war zu diesem Zeitpunkt bereits klar. 1935 konnte schließlich die Elektrifizierung mit 600 V Gleichstrom über seitliche Stromschiene vollendet werden. Gleichzeitig wurde die Subway offiziell in „Underground" umbenannt, was ein moderneres Erscheinungsbild vermitteln sollte, auch wenn für den elektrischen Betrieb keine neuen Fahrzeuge angeschafft worden waren. Stattdessen wurden die bestehenden Fahrzeuge mit Stromabnehmern ausgerüstet und Fahrmotoren an den Drehgestellen montiert. Die Fahrzeit auf dem Gesamtring konnte immerhin von 39 auf 28 Minuten reduziert werden.

Nach Gründung der *Greater Glasgow Passenger Transport Executive* im Jahr 1973 wurde das nächste Modernisierungsprogramm verabschiedet. 1975 ging die Subway in die Verantwortung des *Strathclyde Regional Council* über. Für die Modernisierungsarbeiten wurde der gesamte Ring ab 1977 für fast drei Jahre geschlossen. Auf der gesamten Strecke wurden neue Gleise auf einem Betonunterbau verlegt, alle Stationen wurden umgebaut, allerdings wurden nur die wichtigsten erweitert. Metro-Cammell in Birmingham lieferte neue Fahrzeuge, die elektrische Ausrüstung kam von GEC Traction (heute Alstom). Im Bereich Govan fanden

track gauge was (and still is) 1219 mm (4 ft); there was no link between the two circular tracks, and neither were there any sidings.

In 1923, the Subway was handed over to the Municipal Corporation, which also ran an extensive tramway network. The need to modernise the Subway had become obvious, and eventually in 1935, an electrification scheme (600 V dc, third rail) was completed. At the same time, the Subway was officially renamed the 'Underground' to give it a more modern image, although no new rolling stock had been acquired; instead, the existing cars were retrofitted with current collector shoes and the bogies were motorised. Journey times were thus reduced from 39 to 28 minutes for a full circuit.

Once the Greater Glasgow Passenger Transport Executive had been founded in 1973, a wide-ranging modernisation plan was approved. In 1975, the Subway was transferred to the new Strathclyde Regional Council. Modernisation began in earnest in 1977, when the entire system was closed for almost three years. New tracks were laid on a concrete bed and all the stations were upgraded, although only the busiest were enlarged. New rolling stock was ordered from Metro-Cammell in Birmingham, with electrical equipment being supplied by GEC Traction (now Alstom). Major construction work was carried out at Govan, where a direct track link to the depot was built, the cars having been lifted from the tunnels by a crane for the previous 80 years.

St. George's Cross

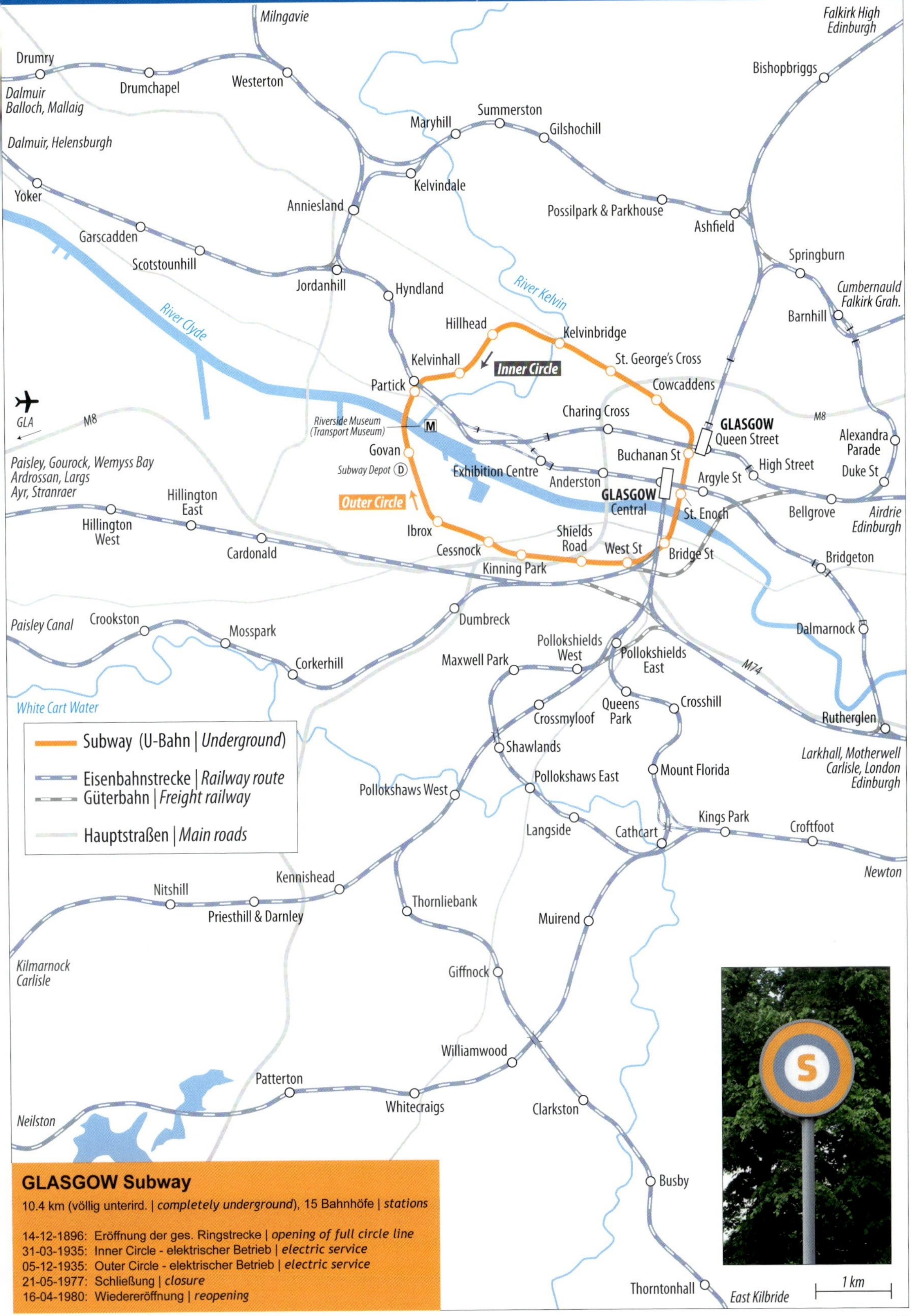

GLASGOW Subway

10.4 km (völlig unterird. | *completely underground*), 15 Bahnhöfe | *stations*

14-12-1896: Eröffnung der ges. Ringstrecke | *opening of full circle line*
31-03-1935: Inner Circle - elektrischer Betrieb | *electric service*
05-12-1935: Outer Circle - elektrischer Betrieb | *electric service*
21-05-1977: Schließung | *closure*
16-04-1980: Wiedereröffnung | *reopening*

St. Enoch

umfangreiche Bauarbeiten statt, denn hier wurde eine Rampe von den beiden Tunneln zum Betriebshof errichtet. Die ersten 80 Jahre lang waren die Züge nämlich mit Hilfe eines Krans aus den Tunneln gehoben worden.

Ein 3-Wagen-Zug ist 38 m lang und nur 2,65 m hoch. Die Fußbodenhöhe beträgt 695 mm und ermöglicht stufenloses Einsteigen. Die Züge fahren automatisch im ATO-Modus, wobei sich die Aufgaben des Fahrers darauf beschränken, die Türen zu schließen und den Zug in Bewegung zu setzen. Die Stromzufuhr erfolgt über eine seitliche Stromschiene.

2003 bekam die Underground ihren alten Namen „Subway“ zurück, nachdem die lokale Bevölkerung nie aufgehört hatte, die kleine U-Bahn so zu nennen. In jüngster Vergangenheit wurden zahlreiche Stationen modernisiert und dabei eine neue Beschilderung eingeführt. Die mittlerweile 35 Jahre alten Fahrzeuge bekamen einen neuen Anstrich, wobei Orange die dominante Farbe blieb. Die Fahrtrichtungen sind mit ‚Outer Circle‘ (Äußerer Ring - im Uhrzeigersinn, orangefarbene Beschilderung) und ‚Inner Circle‘ (Innerer Ring - gegen den Uhrzeigersinn, graue Beschilderung) angegeben.

A 3-car train is 38 m long and just 2.65 m high; the floor height is 695 mm above the top of the rail, allowing level access. The trains are operated automatically in ATO mode, with the drivers merely required to close the doors and put the trains in motion. The trains are fed via a third-rail power supply system.

In 2003, the 'Underground' returned to its original name 'Subway', a designation it had never lost among the local population. In recent years, many stations have been refurbished and new signage has been implemented. The trains, now 35 years old, have received a new livery, with orange remaining the dominant colour. The Subway route is signposted as an 'Outer Circle' (clockwise – orange signage) and an 'Inner Circle' (anti-clockwise – grey signage).

Subway > Fahrzeuge | *Rolling Stock* (600 V DC)

Nummer *Number*	Anzahl *Quantity*	Hersteller *Manufacturer*	Typ *Class*	Länge *Length*	Breite *Width*	Ausgeliefert *Delivered*
101-133	33	Metro-Cammell	Triebwagen | *Power cars*	12.7 m	2.34 m	1978-1979
201-208	8	Metro-Cammell	Beiwagen | *Trailers*	12.7 m	2.34 m	1992

Kelvinhall (2006)

Hillhead

Subway

Partick

Kelvinhall

Glasgow Central (Low level)

Suburban Rail

Die Region Greater Glasgow verfügt neben der bescheidenen Subway über ein großes, als S-Bahn einzustufendes Vorortbahnnetz, welches jedoch unter keiner besonderen Marke, sondern als Teil des *ScotRail*-Netzes seit 2015 von Abellio betrieben wird. Die *ScotRail*-Franchise umfasst fast alle Strecken in Schottland, lediglich Fernzüge nach England werden von anderen Anbietern betrieben.

Auf allen Strecken in Greater Glasgow verkehren die S-Bahn-Züge im 30-Minuten-Takt, auch wenn deren Linienführung aufgrund fehlender Liniennummern oder entsprechender Darstellung auf neueren Netzplänen etwas unübersichtlich ist. Vom Kopfbahnhof Glasgow Central geht neben mehreren Radiallinien die tropfenförmige Cathcart Circle-Linie aus, die jeweils halbseitig auch von den Zügen nach Neilston bzw. Newton befahren wird. In Ost-West-Richtung wird das Stadtzentrum von zwei Tunnelstrecken mit insgesamt fünf unterirdischen Bahnhöfen durchquert, zwei liegen rechtwinkelig unter den jeweiligen Kopfbahnhöfen Glasgow Central und Glasgow Queen Street. Der nördliche, zur North Clyde Line gehörende Tunnel stammt bereits aus dem Jahr 1886 und hat bis heute einige Öffnungen zur Entlüftung. Der Tunnel der Argyle Line geht ebenfalls bereits auf das Jahr 1896 zurück, er ging jedoch 1964 außer Betrieb und wurde schließlich 1979 in seiner heutigen Form als S-Bahn-Tunnel wiedereröffnet.

Der größte Teil der Network Rail-Infrastruktur rund um Glasgow ist bereits elektrifiziert (25 kV 50 Hz AC), seit 2012 auch die gesamte Strecke bis Paisley Canal, die Nordstrecke nach Edinburgh soll bis 2016 folgen. Dann sollen im Vorortverkehr nur noch die Strecken von Glasgow Central nach Kilmarnock und East Kilbride sowie die Nordspange

Besides the rather modest Subway, the Greater Glasgow region also boasts a large suburban rail network. However, this is not operated under any particular brand, but is part of the ScotRail network, since 2015 run by Abellio. The ScotRail franchise includes almost every route in Scotland, and only the long-distance trains to England are operated by other companies.

Trains run every 30 minutes on all the suburban lines in Greater Glasgow, even though their routes are somewhat confusing due to the absence of line numbers or distinctive colours for each line on the newer network maps. Besides several radial lines, the teardrop-shaped Cathcart Circle line starts from the terminal station Glasgow Central, with one side of the loop being shared with trains to Neilston and Newton, respectively. In an east-west direction, the city centre is traversed in two tunnels featuring a total of five underground stations, two of which are located perpendicularly below their respective terminal stations, Glasgow Central and Glasgow Queen Street. The northern tunnel, which is part of the North Clyde Line, dates back to as early as 1886 and still has some openings for ventilation. The tunnel on the Argyle Line was already opened in 1896, but went out of service in 1964, before finally being reopened in 1979 in its present form as a suburban rail tunnel.

The majority of Network Rail infrastructure around Glasgow has already been electrified (25 kV 50 Hz AC). Since 2012, the electrification has continued all the way to Paisley Canal, with the northern route to Edinburgh due to follow by 2016. Only the routes from Glasgow Central to Kilmarnock and East Kilbride as well as the northern link line from Queen Street to Anniesland

Glasgow Queen Street (Low level)

von Queen Street nach Anniesland (Maryhill Line) mit Dieseltriebwagen befahren werden.

Die Planungen für einen 2 km langen Abzweig von Paisley zum internationalen Flughafen von Glasgow (Glasgow Airport Rail Link) waren bereits weit fortgeschritten, als diese im Jahr 2009 aus Budgetgründen auf Eis gelegt wurden. Derzeit ist die Option eines Tram-Train im Gespräch.

(Maryhill Line) will then still be operated with diesel railcars (DMUs).

Plans for a 2 km branch from Paisley to Glasgow International Airport ('Glasgow Airport Rail Link') were well advanced when they were shelved in 2009 for financial reasons. Currently, the option of a tram-train is under discussion.

Argyle Street

Wirral Line – Liverpool Central (modernisierter U-Bahnhof | *refurbished underground station*)

LIVERPOOL

Die Hafenstadt Liverpool ist das Zentrum des Großraums Merseyside, der sich im Nordwesten Englands auf beiden Seiten des Flusses Mersey erstreckt. Zu Merseyside gehören die Kommunen Liverpool, Wirral (Birkenhead), Sefton, St. Helens und Knowsley, die Region grenzt im Osten jedoch direkt an den Ballungsraum Greater Manchester. Liverpool liegt ca. 55 km westlich von Manchester, beide Städte sind durch drei Eisenbahnstrecken verbunden.

Liverpool hat zwar abgesehen von der Museumstram in Birkenhead (siehe S. 153) weder eine Straßenbahn (ein fortgeschrittenes Projekt *Merseytram* mit drei Linien scheiterte 2005 an der finanziellen Unterstützung der Zentralregierung und wurde 2013 endgültig aus dem Nahverkehrsplan gestrichen) noch eine klassische U-Bahn, trotzdem verdient es wegen seiner besonderen S-Bahn *Merseyrail* in diesem Atlas enthalten zu sein.

Merseyrail ist Teil des *Merseytravel*-Netzes. *Merseytravel* ist die Verkehrsbehörde für die 2014 geschaffene ‚Liverpool City Region Combined Authority'. Mit einem *Day Saver* kann man für 4,90 £ das gesamte *Merseyrail*-Netz (Northern und Wirral Line) erkunden, mit einem *Saveaway Dayticket* für 5,10 £ neben den Bahnen auch Busse und Fähren benutzen. Für Einzelfahrten gilt ein Zonentarif (1,75-4,90 £).

The port city of Liverpool is the centre of the (former) metropolitan county of Merseyside, which extends on both sides of the River Mersey in the northwest of England. Merseyside includes the boroughs of Liverpool, Wirral (Birkenhead), Sefton, St. Helens and Knowsley, and on its eastern side adjoins the metropolitan area of Greater Manchester. Liverpool lies some 55 km west of Manchester, the two cities being linked by three railway routes.

Other than the heritage tramway in Birkenhead (see p. 153), Liverpool has neither a tram system nor a classical metro – the 3-line 'Merseytram' project was well-advanced when it was refused financial support from the British government in 2005, before eventually being completely shelved in 2013 – but nonetheless the city deserves to be included in this atlas for its special suburban railway called 'Merseyrail'.

Merseyrail is part of the Merseytravel transport system. Merseytravel is the regional transport authority, which is under the control of the Liverpool City Region Combined Authority, created in 2014. A Day Saver ticket allows unlimited rides on the Merseyrail system (Northern and Wirral Lines) for £4.90, while a Saveaway Dayticket for £5.10 includes buses and ferries, too. Single fares are charged according to the zones travelled through (£1.75-4.90).

LIVERPOOL (Merseyside)

470 000 | 1 500 000

1903

1435 mm

118.5 km

2 (6)

15'; außer | *except*: Hooton – Ellesmere Port / Chester

Merseyrail
www.merseyrail.org

Merseytravel
www.merseytravel.gov.uk

Wirral Line – West Kirby

Merseyrail ist mit der Berliner oder Hamburger S-Bahn vergleichbar, da sie als Vollbahn auf einem fast völlig unabhängigen Bahnnetz mit seitlicher Stromschiene (750 V Gleichstrom) betrieben wird und einen ganztägigen, dichten Verkehr anbietet. Eine ähnliche Stromversorgung findet man sonst nur im Network Rail-Netz südlich von London. Im Stadtzentrum gibt es außerdem einige nur von Merseyrail genutzte unterirdische Stationen. Wegen dieser besonderen Eigenschaften wurde das einst zu *British Rail* gehörende Netz nicht wie anderswo Anfang des Jahrtausends im Zuge der Privatisierung von der damaligen nationalen *Strategic Rail Authority*, sondern von der regionalen *Merseyside Passenger Transport Executive* (heute *Merseytravel*) vergeben. Seit 2003 wird Merseyrail von *Merseyrail Electrics*, einem Konsortium aus Serco und Abellio (je 50%), betrieben.

Merseyrail besteht aus zwei Liniengruppen, der Wirral Line und der Northern Line. Andere vom Hauptbahnhof Lime Street abfahrende, größtenteils mit Dieseltriebwagen betriebene Strecken werden als City Line bezeichnet. Lange Zeit war, abgesehen vom Merseyrail-Netz, im Großraum von Liverpool lediglich die Hauptstrecke Richtung London über Runcorn als Abzweig der West Coast Main Line elektrifiziert (25 kV 50 Hz AC-Oberleitung). Seit Frühjahr 2015 fährt nun „Northern Electrics" von Liverpool nach Wigan und Manchester.

Neben dem heutigen Merseyrail-Netz hatte Liverpool einst eine wirkliche ‚Metro', nämlich die ***Liverpool Overhead Railway*** (LOR). Diese elektrifizierte Hochbahn fuhr ab 1893 auf einer 11,5 km langen Strecke am Hafen entlang. Der südliche Endpunkt Dingle, 1896 eröffnet, lag unterirdisch etwas landeinwärts. Am nördlichen Ende war die LOR mit den Bahnen nach Southport und Aintree verbunden,

Merseyrail *is not a conventional underground or light rail network, but is similar to the S-Bahn systems in Berlin and Hamburg. Almost entirely segregated from other rail traffic, it has a third-rail power supply (750 V DC), offers a frequent service throughout the day, and there are even several exclusive underground stations in the city centre. These special characteristics also explain why Merseyrail was the only former British Rail franchise to be awarded by the Merseyside Passenger Transport Executive (now Merseytravel) rather than the now abolished Strategic Rail Authority. Since 2003, Merseyrail has been operated by Merseyrail Electrics, a 50/50 joint venture between Serco and Abellio.*

Merseyrail comprises two line groups, the Wirral Line and the Northern Line. Other local rail services, most of which are diesel-operated, depart from Lime Street station and are referred to as the City Line. For a long time, the only electrified railway route in the Liverpool region besides Merseyrail was the main line to London via Runcorn, which is a branch off the West Coast Main Line (25 kV 50 Hz AC overhead line). Starting in spring 2015, 'Northern Electrics' now links Liverpool to Wigan and Manchester.

Apart from the present Merseyrail system, Liverpool once had a proper 'metro', the ***'Liverpool Overhead Railway'*** *(LOR). This electrified elevated line opened in 1893 and ran along the riverside for 11.5 km, linking many of the once important docks. The southern terminus Dingle, opened in 1896, lay underground and was located further inland. At its northern end, the LOR was linked to the rail lines to Southport and Aintree, which were electrified from the early 20th century. Due to a lack of*

LIVERPOOL

Merseyrail
Northern Line
Wirral Line
Eisenbahnstrecke | Railway route
Autobahn | Motorway
Southport
Meols Cop
Birkdale
Hillside
Ainsdale
Bescar Lane
New Lane
Preston
Burscough Bridge
Burscough Junction
Hoscar
Parbold
LANCASHIRE
Appley Bridge
Gathurst
Wigan
Sefton
Freshfield
Formby
Ormskirk
Aughton Park
Town Green
Upholland
Pemberton
Orrell
M58
High Town
Rainford
M6
Wigan
Blackpool
Maghull
Hall Road
Blundellsands & Crosby
Old Roan
Kirkby
Garswood
St. Helens
Irish Sea
Waterloo
Aintree
Seaforth & Litherland
Orrell Park
Fazakerley
Walton
Rice Lane
Bootle - New Strand
Bootle
Oriel Road
Knowsley
St. Helens Central
Manchester
New Brighton
Bank Hall
Kirkdale
Thatto Heath
Eccleston Park
M57
Wallasey Grove Road
Sandhills
Liverpool
Prescot
St. Helens
Junction
Wallasey Village
Lea Green
LIVERPOOL
Lime Street
Broad
Green
Roby
Leasowe
Bidston
Birkenhead
North
Moorfields
Edge Hill
Huyton
Whiston
Rainhill
Meols
Moreton
James St
Wavertree
Technology Park
M62
Warrington
Manchester
Manor Road
Hoylake
Birkenhead Park
Liverpool
Central
Conway Park
Hamilton
Square
Upton
Birkenhead Central
Brunswick
MERSEYSIDE
Green Lane
St. Michaels
Mossley Hill
West Kirby
Rock Ferry
West Allerton
Hough Green
Widnes
Hunts Cross
Aigburth
Cressington
Halewood
Wirral
Bebington
Liverpool
South Parkway
Port Sunlight
LPL
Runcorn
Warrington
Manchester
Spital
Heswall
Bromborough Rake
Runcorn
East
River Dee
River Mersey
Bromborough
Eastham Rake
Llandudno
Holyhead
Crewe
Birmingham
London
Hooton
Neston
Frodsham
Little Sutton
Ellesmere Port
Overpool
MERSEYSIDE
Ince & Elton
Stanlow & Thornton
Helsby
M53
Capenhurst
M56
Flint
Mouldsworth
Stockport
Manchester
WALES
Delamere
Hawarden Bridge
Shotton
Bache
Chester
CHESHIRE
5 km
Wrexham
Chester
Wrexham
Holyhead
Crewe

welche bereits Anfang des 20. Jahrhunderts elektrifiziert wurden. Da Geld für eine Modernisierung fehlte, wurde die LOR schließlich 1956 stillgelegt und bald danach abgetragen.

Die **Wirral Line** gehört zu den ältesten unterirdischen Bahnen der Welt. Ähnlich wie die PATH-Linien, die New York und New Jersey unter dem Hudson River verbinden, entstand die Wirral Line als Verbindung zwischen dem Liverpooler Stadtzentrum und Birkenhead auf der Halbinsel Wirral jenseits des Flusses Mersey. Die 2,7 km lange Tunnelstrecke, davon etwa 1,6 km unter dem Fluss, wurde 1886 zwischen James Street und Green Lane eröffnet. 1888 kam ein Abzweig bis Birkenhead Park hinzu. Zwei kurze Verlängerungen bis Rock Ferry (1891) und Liverpool Central (1892) vervollständigten das ursprüngliche Netz der *Mersey Railway*. Ähnlich wie bei den ersten U-Bahn-Strecken in London war der anfängliche Betrieb mit Dampflokomotiven im Tunnel nicht sehr zufriedenstellend, so dass die *Mersey Railway* 1903 elektrifiziert wurde. Bis dahin waren die Züge von Liverpool kommend auf der *Wirral Railway* nach West Kirby und New Brighton durchgefahren. Für die folgenden 35 Jahre wurde die elektrische *Mersey Railway* getrennt betrieben und die Fahrgäste mussten an den Bahnhöfen Birkenhead Park und Rock Ferry umsteigen. Während die Äste nach West Kirby und New Brighton bereits 1938 elektrifiziert waren, wurde der elektrische Betrieb auf dem südlichen Ast erst während

funds for modernisation, the LOR was closed down in 1956 and demolished a year later.

The ***Wirral Line*** *is one of the oldest electric underground lines in the world. Similar to the PATH routes that link New York to New Jersey under the Hudson River, it was initially built to link the Liverpool city centre to Birkenhead on the Wirral peninsula on the other side of the River Mersey. The 2.7 km tunnel, of which approx. 1.6 km runs under the river, was opened in 1886 to connect Green Lane to James Street. In 1888, a branch to Birkenhead Park was added, and in 1891 and 1892, two short extensions to Rock Ferry and Liverpool Central completed the original 'Mersey Railway'. As with the first underground routes in London, steam operation through the tunnels was rather dissatisfactory, so in 1903 the 'Mersey Railway' was electrified. Up to then, cross-river trains had continued their journey on the 'Wirral Railway' to West Kirby and New Brighton. For the following 35 years, however, the electrified 'Mersey Railway' remained an isolated network, and passengers had to change trains at Birkenhead Park and Rock Ferry. Whereas the West Kirby and New Brighton lines were electrified in 1938, the southern leg of the present Wirral Line was only equipped with a power rail in various stages during the 1980s and 1990s. During daytime hours on weekdays, the Wirral Line offers a train every 15 minutes to West Kirby and New Brighton, and four trains per hour to Chester and two*

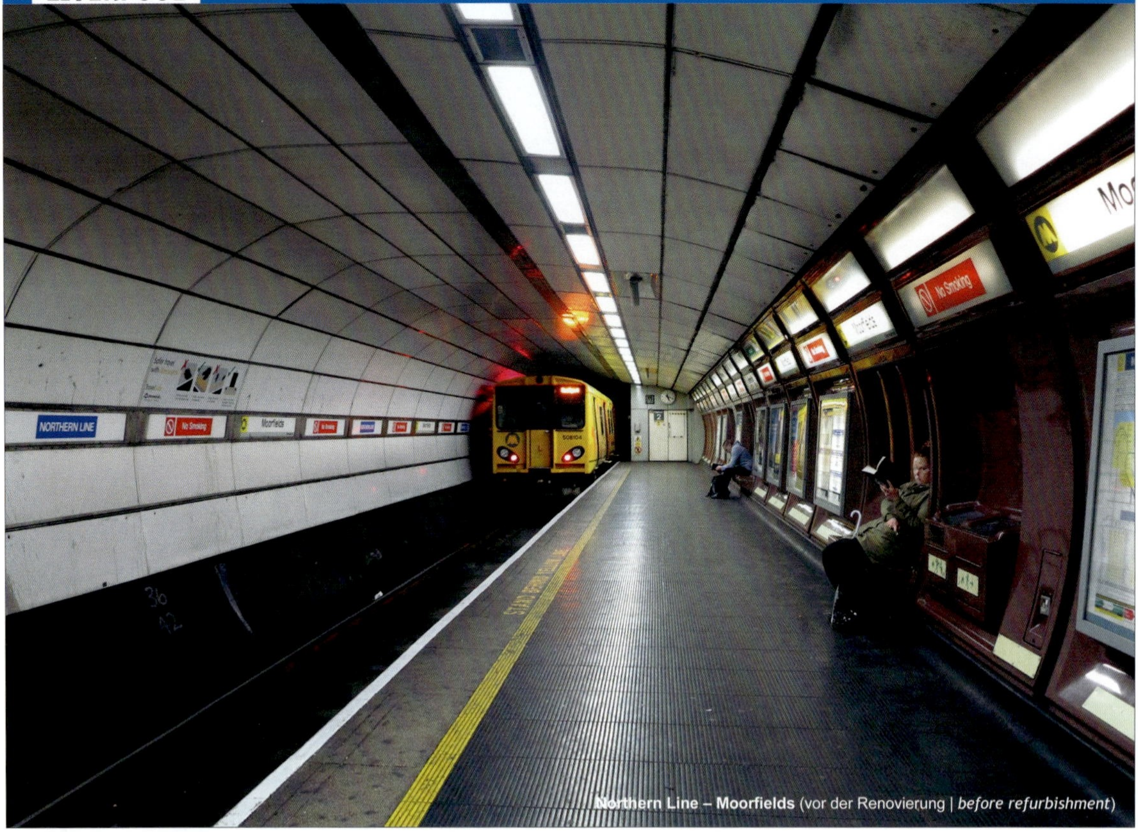

Northern Line – Moorfields (vor der Renovierung | *before refurbishment*)

der 1980er/1990er Jahre in mehreren Stufen Richtung Chester und Ellesmere Port ausgedehnt. An Wochentagen verkehren tagsüber acht Züge pro Stunde abwechselnd nach West Kirby und New Brighton sowie vier Züge pro Stunde nach Chester und zwei nach Ellesmere Port. Die Wirral Line hat eine Gesamtlänge von 52,8 km, davon sind ca. 8 km in Liverpool und Birkenhead unterirdisch.

Die **Northern Line** entstand 1977, als die drei nördlichen Strecken, die früher an der *Exchange Station* (unweit der heutigen Station Moorfields) endeten, durch einen Tunnel mit einer einzigen Strecke im Süden, die bis zu ihrer Stilllegung 1972 am oberirdischen Bahnhof Liverpool Central begann, verbunden wurden. Eine ursprünglich geplante Einbindung der östlichen Strecken nach St. Helens, bis Edge Hill im Tunnel, kam nicht zustande. Während die Strecken nach Southport und Ormskirk bereits Anfang des 20. Jahrhunderts elektrifiziert worden waren, fuhren auf dem Kirkby-Ast bis zur Inbetriebnahme des Innenstadttunnels 1977 Dieseltriebwagen. Die Züge der Northern Line verkehren auf allen Ästen wochentags tagsüber alle 15 Minuten. Der südliche Ast ist dabei direkt mit dem Southport-Ast verbunden, während die Züge der beiden anderen Nordäste am Bahnhof Liverpool Central wenden. Die Northern Line hat eine Gesamtlänge von 65,6 km, davon liegen etwa 5 km im Tunnel.

Das Herzstück der Merseyrail sind die in den 1970er Jahren gebauten unterirdischen Innenstadtstrecken: die 3,2 km lange und in 17-38 m Tiefe verlaufende eingleisige ***Loop*** (Schleife) für die Wirral Line, und der 2,6 km lange zweigleisige ***Link*** (Verbindung) für die Nord-Süd-Strecken. Der Großteil der Tunnelstrecken wurde mit sogenannten Roadheadern (mit Fräsköpfen) statt im Schildvortrieb

to Ellesmere Port. The Wirral Line has a total length of 52.8 km, of which approximately 8 km runs underground in Liverpool and Birkenhead.

Today's ***Northern Line*** *was created in 1977, when the northern branches, which up to then had terminated at Exchange Station, were connected underground to a single line in the south. Until its closure in 1972, this line used to have its terminus at Liverpool Central surface station. The initially planned integration of the eastern lines to St. Helens via a tunnel curve up to Edge Hill did not materialise. While the Southport and Ormskirk branches had been electrified in the early 20th century, the present Kirkby line remained diesel-operated until the central tunnel was completed in 1977. The Northern Line provides trains every 15 minutes on all branches during daytime hours on weekdays. The southern leg is linked to the Southport branch, with the Ormskirk and Kirkby services terminating at Liverpool Central. The Northern Line has a total length of 65.6 km, with approximately 5 km in tunnel.*

The centrepiece of the present Merseyrail network is the so-called ***'Loop and Link'****, built in the 1970s. This scheme included a 3.2 km single-track loop at a depth of 17-38 m for the Wirral Line, and a 2.6 km double-track link for the north-south lines. Most parts of the central underground sections were excavated with roadheaders instead of tunnel-boring machines. The tube-shaped tunnels were lined with precast concrete elements. An underground track link exists between the two tunnel routes.*

Merseyrail service is provided by a fleet of 59 three-car trains of class 507 (001...033) and 508 (101...143), built by British Rail Engineering Ltd. in York in 1978-80.

Northern Line – Maghull

Northern Line – Kirkdale

Wirral Line – Birkenhead North

Wirral Line – James Street (Ausgang | *Exit* Water Street)

gebaut. Die Röhrentunnel wurden mit Betontübbings ausgekleidet. Zwischen beiden Tunnelstrecken besteht eine Gleisverbindung.

Die Merseyrail wird mit 59 3-Wagen-Zügen der Baureihen 507 (001...033) und 508 (101...143), die 1978-80 von British Rail Engineering Ltd. in York gebaut wurden, betrieben. Alle Fahrzeuge wurden Anfang der 2000er Jahre modernisiert. Eine neuerliche Auffrischung des Innenraums ist ab 2015 vorgesehen, nachdem den Fahrzeugen erst kürzlich äußerlich ein *New Look* in sechs Varianten verpasst wurde. In den Hauptverkehrszeiten sind auch Doppeltraktionen zu sehen.

Thoroughly refurbished during the early 2000s, the units are currently undergoing a further interior facelift, their exteriors having recently received a 'new look' featuring six different designs. During busy hours, double units can also be seen in service.

LIVERPOOL Merseyrail

118.5 km (~ 13 km unterirdisch | *underground*), 69 Bahnhöfe | *stations*

Elektrischer Betrieb | *Electric service:*

03-05-1903: Liverpool Central – Birkenhead Park / Rock Ferry
22-03-1904: *Exchange Station* – Southport
07-12-1906: Sandhills – Aintree
01-10-1909: Aintree – Maghull
03-07-1911: Maghull – Town Green
12-07-1913: Town Green – Ormskirk
14-03-1938: Birkenhead Park – West Kirby / New Brighton
02-05-1977: *Link*: Liverpool Central – Sandhills – Kirkby
09-05-1977: *Loop*: James Street – Central – James Street
31-10-1977: + Lime Street
03-01-1978: Liverpool Central – Garston
08-05-1978: + Moorfields (Loop station)
16-05-1983: Garston – Hunts Cross
30-09-1985: Rock Ferry – Hooton (+ Bromborough Rake)
04-10-1993: Hooton – Chester
29-05-1994: Hooton – Ellesmere Port
03-04-1995: + Eastham Rake
09-03-1998: + Brunswick
22-06-1998: + Conway Park

Modernisierter Merseyrail-Zug | *Refurbished Merseyrail train*

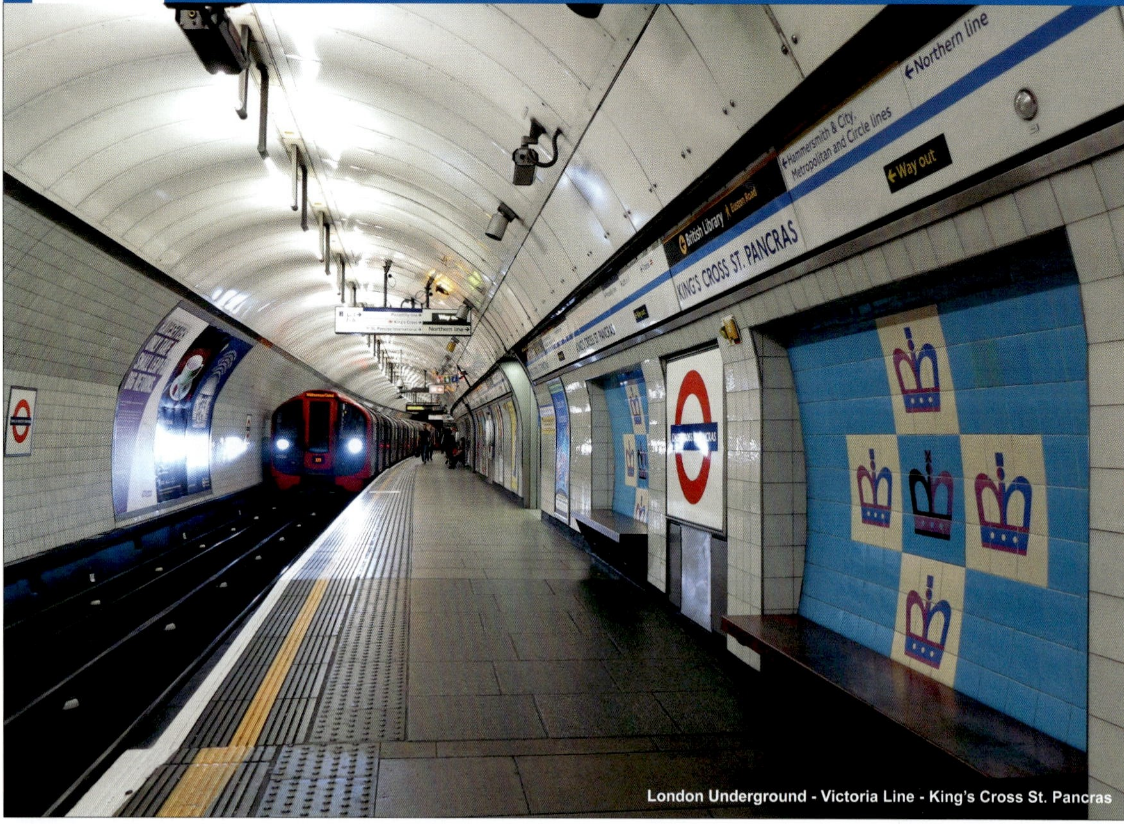

London Underground - Victoria Line - King's Cross St. Pancras

LONDON

Die britische Hauptstadt, mit einer Fläche von 1579 km^2 (*Greater London*) etwa doppelt so groß wie Berlin, ist bekannt für die älteste U-Bahn der Welt, und auch wenn das Netz in den letzten Jahren wenig gewachsen ist, gehört es weiterhin zu den größten der Welt. Neben der *London Underground* gibt es aber noch weitere städtische Schienenverkehrsmittel wie das wachsende S-Bahn-Netz *London Overground*, zahlreiche Vorortbahnen, die als „National Rail" von verschiedenen Privatfirmen betrieben werden, die fahrerlose *Docklands Light Railway* und nicht zuletzt das bescheidene Straßenbahnnetz *Tramlink* in Croydon im Süden der Stadt.

Das Londoner Nahverkehrsnetz ist im Wesentlichen in sechs ringförmige Zonen eingeteilt. Im Norden (Cheshunt), Nordwesten (Richtung Watford und Chesham) und Nordosten (TfL Rail Richtung Shenfield) gibt es noch zusätzliche Zonen. Fahrscheine werden für alle möglichen Zonenkombinationen angeboten, allgemein günstiger ohne die Innenzonen 1+2. Für Einzelfahrscheine in Papierformat werden stolze 4,80 £ für 1-3 Zonen oder 6,00 £ für 6 Zonen verlangt (mit der aufladbaren Wertkarte *Oyster Card* nur 2,30 £ bzw. 3,10 £ – die Karte selbst einmalig 5,00 £). Eine *Visitor Oyster Card* kann für 3,00 £ + den gewünschten Geldwert online bestellt werden. Der entsprechende Fahrpreis wird je nach durchfahrenen Zonen abgebucht. Die Tarife gehen von 1,50 £ für eine Busfahrt über 2,30 £ für eine U-Bahn-Fahrt außerhalb der Stoßzeiten (off-peak) in den inneren Zonen 1+2 bis max 6,90 £ für eine Fahrt bis in die Außenzone 9. Bleibt man in den Zonen 1-2, zahlt man max. 6,40 £

With an area of 1579 km^2 (Greater London), the British capital is about twice the size of Berlin. London is famous for having the oldest underground railway in the world, and even though the London Underground network has hardly grown in recent years, it is still one of the world's largest metro systems. In addition to the Underground, there are several other urban rail systems, such as the growing S-Bahn-style network called the 'London Overground'; numerous suburban railways, which are operated by various private companies under the joint label 'National Rail'; the driverless Docklands Light Railway; and last but not least, the modest Tramlink network in Croydon in the south of the city.

The London transport network is basically divided into six concentric zones. Additional zones can be found in the north (Cheshunt), the northwest (to Watford and Chesham) and the northeast (TfL Rail towards Shenfield). Tickets are available for every possible combination of zones, generally being cheaper without the inner zones 1+2. For single paper tickets, no less than £4.80 is payable for 1-3 zones and £6.00 for 6 zones (with the rechargeable prepaid Oyster Card just £2.30 or £3.10, respectively – the card itself is available for £5.00). A Visitor Oyster card can be ordered online for £3.00 + the desired credit. The corresponding fare will be deducted according to the zones travelled through. Single fares range from £1.50 for a bus ride and £2.30 for a metro ride off-peak in the inner zones 1+2 to a maximum of £6.90 for a ride all the way to the outer zone 9. If you stay within zones 1-2, you

London Tramlink - Croydon

pro Tag, für 1-6 Zonen max. 11,70 £ (sog. ‚Daily Capping'). Für Bahnfreunde, die das Netz intensiv erkunden wollen, ist allerdings weiterhin die traditionelle *Travelcard* für die Zonen 1-6 für 12,00 £ pro Tag (Mo-Fr gültig ab 9:30 Uhr) oder eine entsprechende Wochenkarte empfehlenswert, da die ‚Pay-as-you-go'-Oyster Card bei ungewöhnlichem Reiseverhalten häufig Fehlbuchungen vornimmt! Auf die Oyster Card können jedoch auch verschiedene *Travelcards* geladen werden, die ein uneingeschränktes Durchschreiten der Zugangssperren ermöglichen sollten. Alle *Travelcards* sind auch in sämtlichen in London verkehrenden Bussen, in denen übrigens kein Fahrscheinverkauf mehr stattfindet, gültig. Zum Flughafen Heathrow gelten Verbundtarife (Zone 6) nur in der Piccadilly Line, nicht jedoch im Heathrow Express ab Paddington.

will pay a maximum of £6.40 a day, or £11.70 for zones 1-6 (so-called 'daily capping'). For railway enthusiasts who want to explore the network intensively, however, the traditional Travelcard for zones 1-6 for £12.00 per day (Mon-Fri valid after 09:30) or a corresponding weekly pass is still recommended, as the 'Pay-as-you-go' Oyster Card easily gets confused and charges excessive fares for unusual travel patterns! Various types of passes can, however, be loaded onto the Oyster Card, which should allow unrestricted passage through the access barriers. All Travelcards are valid on all of London's bus services, where cash fares are no longer accepted. Going to Heathrow Airport, standard fares apply on the Piccadilly Line (zone 6), but not on the Heathrow Express from Paddington.

London Overground - Finchley Road & Frognal

Docklands Light Railway - Limehouse

London Underground - Circle/District Line - Gloucester Road

LONDON (Greater London)

8 550 000

el. Ⓣ (1901-1952) 2000
Ⓤ 1890
Ⓓ 1987

1435 mm

km Ⓣ 28 km
Ⓤ 403 km
Ⓓ 35.5 km

Ⓣ 4
Ⓤ 11
Ⓓ 6

TfL - Transport for London
www.tfl.gov.uk

Ⓣ Tramlink Ⓤ Underground Ⓓ Docklands Light Railway

London Underground - District & Piccadilly Lines - Earl's Court

London Tramlink - Mitcham

Docklands Light Railway - Canning Town

HEATHROW POD

Ein besonders kurioses und innovatives Verkehrsmittel findet man seit Mai 2011 im Bereich des Terminal 5 am Londoner Flughafen Heathrow: Der vollautomatisierte „Pod" von Ultra Global bringt bis zu vier Fahrgäste gleichzeitig direkt von der Terminal-Station (einige Etagen über dem Bahnhof des Heathrow Express) kostenlos zu einem der beiden Langzeitparkplätze (ca. 1,4 km). Die computergesteuerten, gummibereiften Kabinen sind 3,7 m lang und 1,5 m breit, mit einer Gesamthöhe von 1,8 m jedoch relativ niedrig. Sie erreichen eine Höchstgeschwindigkeit von 40 km/h. Das gewünschte Fahrtziel wählt man vor dem Einsteigen am Bildschirm aus.

A rather curious and innovative means of transport has been available in the Terminal 5 area at London's Heathrow Airport since May 2011: the fully automated 'pod' designed by Ultra Global carries up to four passengers directly from the T5 station (several floors above the Heathrow Express station) to one of the two long-term car parks (about 1.4 km) for free. The computer-controlled, rubber-tyred cabins are 3.7 m long and 1.5 m wide, though relatively low with a total height of 1.8 m. They can reach a top speed of 40 km/h. The desired destination has to be chosen on the screen before boarding.

LONDON

Luton Airport Parkway
Bedford
Northern Line
Edgware
Northern Line
High Barnet
Mill Hill East
Barking
Jubilee Line
Metropolitan Line
Stanmore
Watford, Amersham, Uxbridge
Cricklewood
Hampstead
Hampstead Heath
Gospel Oak
Tufnell Park
Neasden
Dollis Hill
Finchley Road & Frognal
Kentish Town
Hemel Hempstead
Birmingham
Manchester
Liverpool
Glasgow
Willesden Green
West Hampstead
Belsize Park
Kilburn
Finchley Road
Kentish Town West
Brondesbury
Swiss Cottage
Chalk Farm
Camden Road
South Hampstead
Brondesbury Park
Camden Town
Bakerloo Line
Harrow & Wealdstone
Kilburn High Road
Mornington Crescent
Willesden Junction
Kensal Rise
Kilburn Park
St. John's Wood
King's Cross St. Pancras
Queen's Park
Kensal Green
Maida Vale
Central Line
West Ruislip
Ealing Broadway
Euston
Metropolitan Line
Baker Street
Great Portland Street
Euston Sq
Russell Square
Warren St
Warwick Avenue
Marylebone
Greenford
Slough
Heathrow
Edgware Road
Regent's Park
Goodge Street
Royal Oak
Richmond
Westbourne Park
Paddington
Circle Line
District Line
Tottenham Court Road
East Acton
Paddington
Bond Street
Covent Garden
Ladbroke Grove
Oxford Circus
Latimer Road
Bayswater
Marble Arch
Leicester Square
White City
Lancaster Gate
Piccadilly Circus
Wood Lane
Queensway
Notting Hill
Charing Cross
Green Park
Embankment
Shepherd's Bush Market
Holland Park
Hyde Park Corner
West-minster
Shepherd's Bush
Goldhawk Road
High Street Kensington
District Line
Kensington (Olympia)
Knightsbridge
St. James's Park
District Line
Piccadilly Line
Ealing Broadway, Richmond
Heathrow Airport, Uxbridge
Circle Line
Hammersmith & City Line
South Kensington
Victoria
Turnham Green
Stamford Brook
Ravenscourt Park
Hammersmith
Gloucester Road
Sloane Square
Barons Court
Earl's Court
Pimlico
West Kensington
West Brompton
Docklands Light Railway
London Overground
TfL Rail
Crossrail (im Bau | u/c)
National Rail
Channel Tunnel Rail Link
London Underground Depot
London Transport Museum
Vauxhall
River Thames
Fulham Broadway
(Battersea) 2020
(Nine Elms)
Battersea Park
Hounslow, Woking
Parsons Green
Queenstown Road (Battersea)
Stockwell
Barnes Bridge
Imperial Wharf
Wandsworth Rd
Clapham North
Barnes
Putney Bridge
Kingston
Windsor & Eton Riverside
Clapham High Street
Clapham Junction
London Underground
Metropolitan Line
District Line
Circle Line
Hammersmith & City Line
Northern Line
Central Line
Bakerloo Line
Piccadilly Line
Victoria Line
Jubilee Line
Waterloo & City Line
Putney
Wandsworth Town
Clapham Common
East Putney
Clapham South
Wandsworth Common
Southfields
Hampton Court
Chessington South
Epsom
Guildford
Earlsfield
Balham
Wimbledon
District Line
Northern Line
Morden
Croydon

Victoria Line
Walthamstow Central
Piccadilly Line
Cockfosters
Finsbury Park
Arsenal
Holloway Road
Caledonian Road
Drayton Park
Canonbury
Highbury & Islington
Caledonian Rd & Barnsbury
Essex Road
Enfield Town
Rectory Road
Clapton
Chingford
Stansted Airport
Cambridge
Dalston Kingsland
Dalston Junction
Hackney Downs
Hackney Central
Homerton
London Fields
Haggerston
Hoxton
Cambridge Heath
Cambridge
Central Line
Epping
Hainault
Leyton
Shenfield
Chelmsford
Stratford International
Maryland
Hackney Wick
Stratford
Jubilee Line
Stratford High Street
District Line
Hammersmith & City Line
Pudding Mill Lane
Abbey Rd
Plaistow
Angel
Bethnal Green
Bow Church
Bromley by-Bow
West Ham
Barking
Upminster
Southend
Old Street
Shoreditch High St
Bethnal Green
Mile End
Bow Road
Devons Road
Stepney Green
Whitechapel
Star Lane
Farringdon
Barbican
Chancery Lane
Moorgate
Liverpool Street
Holborn
City Thameslink
W&C
Bank
Met
Aldgate
Aldgate East
Langdon Park
Blackfriars
St. Paul's
Fenchurch St
Tower Gateway
Temple
Mansion House
Cannon St
Monument
Tower Hill
Shadwell
Limehouse
Docklands Light Railway
All Saints
Canning Town
Westferry
Poplar
East India
West India Quay
Blackwall
London Bridge
River Thames
Wapping
Waterloo East
Southwark
Waterloo
W&C
Lambeth North
Borough
Canary Wharf
Rotherhithe
Heron Quays
Bermondsey
Canada Water
South Quay
North Greenwich
Emirates Air Line
Bakerloo Line
Elephant & Castle
Crossharbour
Surrey Quays
Kennington
Mudchute
South Bermondsey
Island Gardens
(New Bermondsey)
Dartford
Oval
Cutty Sark
Maze Hill
Deptford
Greenwich
New Cross
Queens Road Peckham
New Cross Gate
Deptford Bridge
Peckham Rye
Denmark Hill
Elverson Road
Gillingham
St. Johns
Lewisham
Blackheath
Loughborough Junction
Nunhead
Brockley
Dartford
Brixton
Victoria Line
East Dulwich
Crofton Park
Ladywell
Herne Hill
North Dulwich
Hither Green
Lee
Honor Oak Park
Dartford
Catford
Catford Bridge
Sutton
Orpington
1 km
Crystal Palace
Croydon
Hayes
Sevenoaks
Orpington
Sevenoaks

LONDON

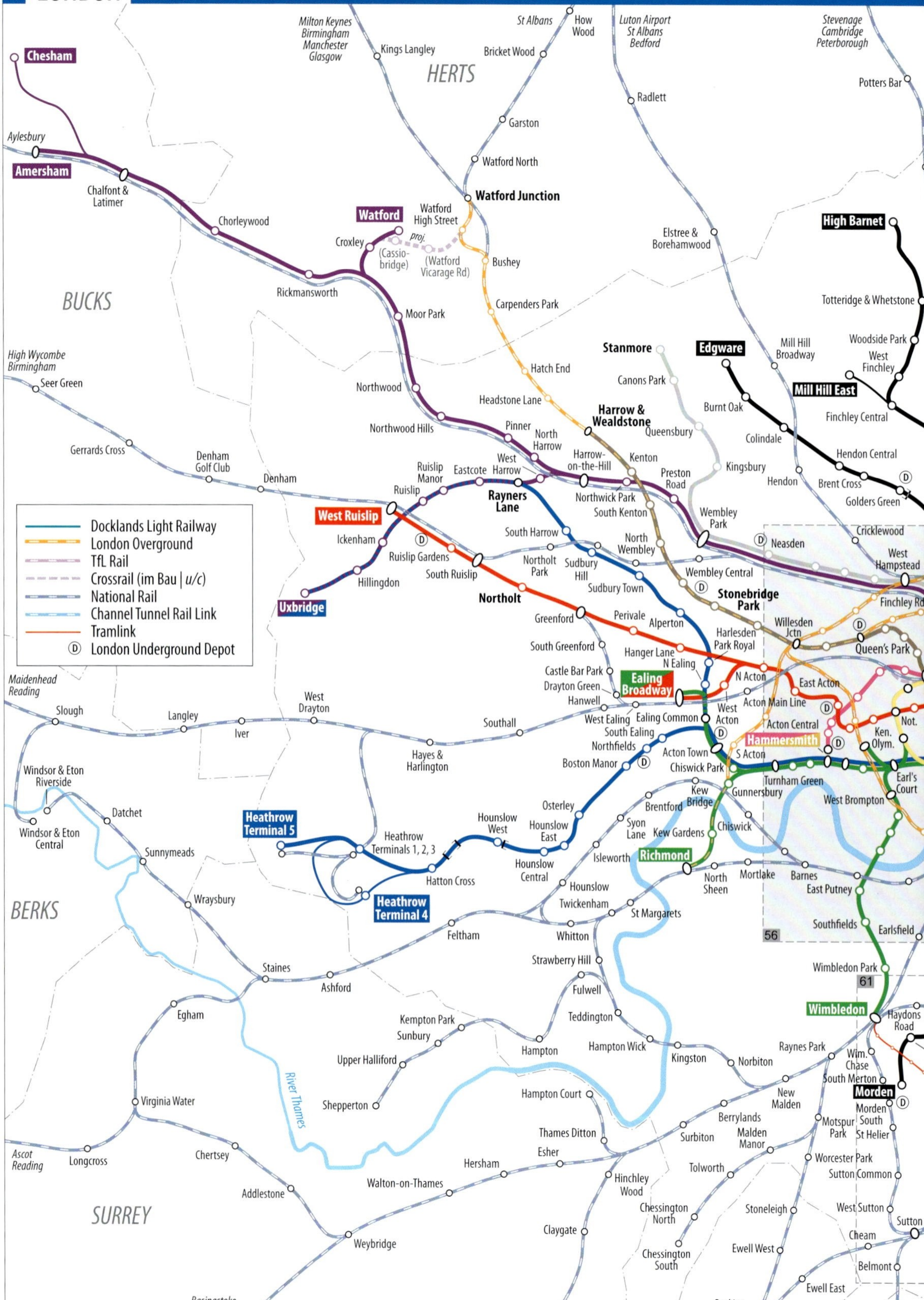

Chesham
Milton Keynes
Birmingham
Manchester
Glasgow
Kings Langley
HERTS
St Albans
How Wood
Bricket Wood
Luton Airport
St Albans
Bedford
Stevenage
Cambridge
Peterborough
Potters Bar
Radlett
Garston
Aylesbury
Amersham
Chalfont & Latimer
Watford North
Watford Junction
Watford
Watford High Street
Chorleywood
Croxley
proj.
(Cassio-bridge)
(Watford Vicarage Rd)
Bushey
Elstree & Borehamwood
High Barnet
Rickmansworth
BUCKS
Moor Park
Carpenders Park
Totteridge & Whetstone
Woodside Park
Stanmore
Edgware
Mill Hill Broadway
West Finchley
High Wycombe
Birmingham
Seer Green
Hatch End
Canons Park
Northwood
Mill Hill East
Headstone Lane
Burnt Oak
Harrow & Wealdstone
Finchley Central
Northwood Hills
Pinner
North Harrow
Queensbury
Colindale
Gerrards Cross
Hendon Central
Denham Golf Club
Ruislip Manor
Eastcote
West Harrow
Harrow-on-the-Hill
Kenton
Preston Road
Kingsbury
Hendon
Brent Cross
Denham
Ruislip
Rayners Lane
Northwick Park
Golders Green
West Ruislip
South Kenton
Wembley Park
Docklands Light Railway
London Overground
TfL Rail
Crossrail (im Bau | u/c)
National Rail
Channel Tunnel Rail Link
Tramlink
London Underground Depot
Cricklewood
Ickenham
South Harrow
North Wembley
Neasden
West Hampstead
Ruislip Gardens
Northolt Park
Sudbury Hill
Wembley Central
South Ruislip
Hillingdon
Sudbury Town
Uxbridge
Northolt
Stonebridge Park
Finchley Rd
Greenford
Perivale
Alperton
Willesden Jctn
Harlesden
Park Royal
Queen's Park
South Greenford
Hanger Lane
N Ealing
Castle Bar Park
N Acton
Drayton Green
Ealing Broadway
East Acton
Maidenhead
Reading
Hanwell
West Acton
Acton Main Line
West Drayton
Slough
Langley
Southall
West Ealing
Ealing Common
Not.
Iver
South Ealing
Acton Central
Ken. Olym.
Hayes & Harlington
Northfields
Hammersmith
Acton Town
S Acton
Boston Manor
Chiswick Park
Windsor & Eton Riverside
Turnham Green
Earl's Court
Kew Bridge
Gunnersbury
Osterley
Brentford
West Brompton
Datchet
Heathrow Terminal 5
Hounslow West
Hounslow East
Syon Lane
Kew Gardens
Chiswick
Windsor & Eton Central
Heathrow Terminals 1, 2, 3
Sunnymeads
Isleworth
Richmond
Hounslow Central
Mortlake
Barnes
North Sheen
Hatton Cross
East Putney
Hounslow
Heathrow Terminal 4
Wraysbury
Twickenham
St Margarets
BERKS
Southfields
Earlsfield
Feltham
Whitton
56
Strawberry Hill
Wimbledon Park
Staines
61
Fulwell
Ashford
Wimbledon
Haydons Road
Egham
Kempton Park
Teddington
Sunbury
Hampton
Hampton Wick
Raynes Park
Upper Halliford
Kingston
Norbiton
Wim. Chase
South Merton
River Thames
Morden
New Malden
Virginia Water
Hampton Court
Shepperton
Berrylands
Morden South
Motspur Park
St Helier
Thames Ditton
Surbiton
Malden Manor
Ascot
Reading
Longcross
Chertsey
Esher
Worcester Park
Hersham
Tolworth
Sutton Common
Hinchley Wood
Walton-on-Thames
Addlestone
Chessington North
Stoneleigh
West Sutton
SURREY
Sutton
Claygate
Cheam
Weybridge
Ewell West
Chessington South
Belmont
Ewell East
Basingstoke
Guildford
Byfleet & New Haw
Guildford
Oxshott
Dorking
Horsham
Epsom
Epsom Downs

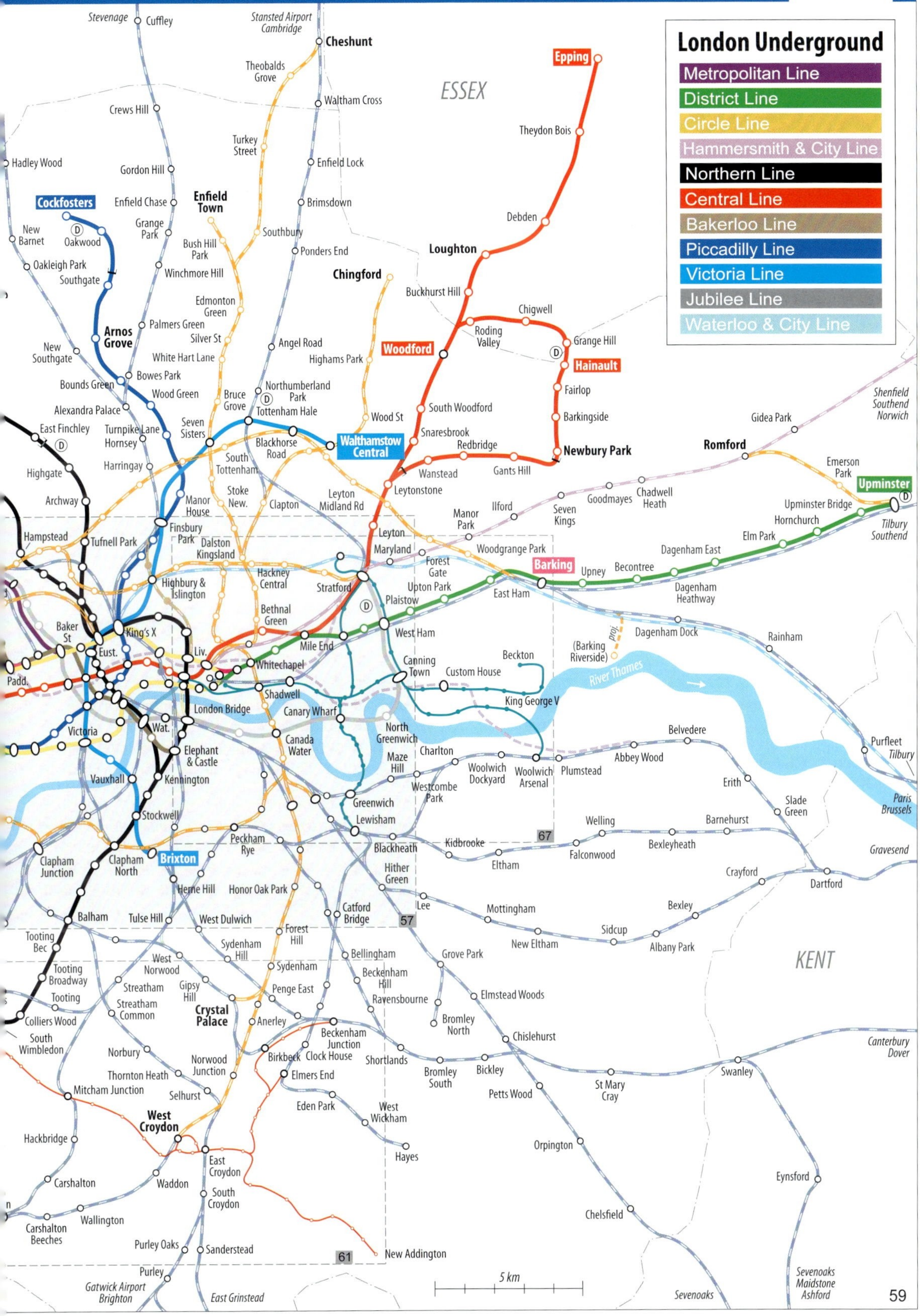
London Underground
Metropolitan Line
District Line
Circle Line
Hammersmith & City Line
Northern Line
Central Line
Bakerloo Line
Piccadilly Line
Victoria Line
Jubilee Line
Waterloo & City Line
ESSEX
KENT
River Thames
Stevenage
Cuffley
Stansted Airport
Cambridge
Cheshunt
Theobalds Grove
Waltham Cross
Epping
Theydon Bois
Crews Hill
Turkey Street
Enfield Lock
Hadley Wood
Gordon Hill
Brimsdown
Cockfosters
Enfield Chase
Enfield Town
Debden
New Barnet
Oakwood
Grange Park
Bush Hill Park
Southbury
Ponders End
Loughton
Oakleigh Park
Southgate
Winchmore Hill
Chingford
Buckhurst Hill
Edmonton Green
Chigwell
Arnos Grove
Palmers Green
Silver St
Angel Road
Roding Valley
Grange Hill
New Southgate
White Hart Lane
Highams Park
Woodford
Hainault
Bowes Park
Bounds Green
Wood Green
Bruce Grove
Northumberland Park
Fairlop
Alexandra Palace
Tottenham Hale
South Woodford
Shenfield
Southend
Norwich
East Finchley
Turnpike Lane
Seven Sisters
Wood St
Barkingside
Gidea Park
Hornsey
Blackhorse Road
Walthamstow Central
Snaresbrook
Redbridge
Newbury Park
Romford
Highgate
Harringay
South Tottenham
Wanstead
Gants Hill
Emerson Park
Upminster
Archway
Stoke New.
Clapton
Leyton Midland Rd
Leytonstone
Manor House
Ilford
Seven Kings
Goodmayes
Chadwell Heath
Upminster Bridge
Hornchurch
Tilbury
Southend
Hampstead
Tufnell Park
Finsbury Park
Dalston Kingsland
Leyton
Manor Park
Elm Park
Maryland
Forest Gate
Woodgrange Park
Dagenham East
Hackney Central
Barking
Upney
Becontree
Highbury & Islington
Stratford
Upton Park
East Ham
Dagenham Heathway
Plaistow
Baker St
King's X
Bethnal Green
Eust.
West Ham
Dagenham Dock
Rainham
Mile End
Liv.
Whitechapel
(Barking Riverside)
proj.
Padd.
Canning Town
Beckton
Custom House
Shadwell
London Bridge
Canary Wharf
King George V
Belvedere
Victoria
Wat.
North Greenwich
Purfleet
Tilbury
Elephant & Castle
Canada Water
Charlton
Abbey Wood
Maze Hill
Woolwich Dockyard
Woolwich Arsenal
Plumstead
Vauxhall
Kennington
Westcombe Park
Erith
Paris
Brussels
Greenwich
Slade Green
Stockwell
Lewisham
Welling
Barnehurst
Peckham Rye
Kidbrooke
Bexleyheath
Gravesend
Clapham Junction
Clapham North
Brixton
Blackheath
Falconwood
Eltham
Hither Green
Crayford
Dartford
Herne Hill
Honor Oak Park
Lee
Mottingham
Balham
Tulse Hill
West Dulwich
Catford Bridge
Bexley
Tooting Bec
Forest Hill
Sidcup
New Eltham
Albany Park
Sydenham Hill
West Norwood
Sydenham
Bellingham
Grove Park
Tooting Broadway
Streatham
Gipsy Hill
Penge East
Beckenham Hill
Ravensbourne
Elmstead Woods
Tooting
Streatham Common
Crystal Palace
Bromley North
Colliers Wood
Anerley
Chislehurst
South Wimbledon
Beckenham Junction
Canterbury
Dover
Norbury
Norwood Junction
Birkbeck
Clock House
Shortlands
Swanley
Thornton Heath
Elmers End
Bromley South
Bickley
St Mary Cray
Mitcham Junction
Selhurst
Petts Wood
West Croydon
Eden Park
West Wickham
Hackbridge
East Croydon
Hayes
Orpington
Eynsford
Carshalton
Waddon
South Croydon
Wallington
Chelsfield
Carshalton Beeches
Purley Oaks
Sanderstead
New Addington
Purley
Sevenoaks
Maidstone
Ashford
Gatwick Airport
Brighton
East Grinstead
Sevenoaks
5 km
67
57
61
D

Stadler #2559 @ King Henry's Drive

LONDON TRAMLINK

Croydon (340.000 Einw.) ist der südlichste Londoner Bezirk, dessen Zentrum etwa 15 km südlich von Charing Cross liegt. Der Bezirk ist über mehrere Bahnstrecken an die Bahnhöfe Charing Cross bzw. London Bridge einerseits und Victoria andererseits angeschlossen, mit Thameslink kann man durch die City of London hindurch die nördlichen Bezirke direkt erreichen. Seit 2010 bietet auch London Overground über die East London Line eine direkte Verbindung zwischen den Bezirken nördlich und südlich der Themse. Die Londoner U-Bahn hingegen wurde nie so weit nach Süden verlängert, auch wenn es in den 1950er Jahren Planungen gab, die neue Victoria Line bis Croydon zu führen.

Im Jahr 1996 gewann *Tramtrack Croydon Limited* (TCL) die Ausschreibung für die Planung, den Bau, den Betrieb und die Wartung der Straßenbahn von Croydon. Am TCL-Konsortium waren FirstGroup und Bombardier beteiligt. Obwohl der Vertrag über einen Zeitraum von 99 Jahren laufen sollte, erwarb *Transport for London* (TfL) 2008 die Konzession. Im Hinblick auf weitere Straßenbahn- und Stadtbahnlinien in ganz Greater London wurde die Bezeichnung von Croydon Tramlink in London Tramlink, geändert. Mit dem Eigentümerwechsel kam auch ein neues Corporate Design, statt des früheren Rot gibt es nun einen hellgrünen Anstrich der Fahrzeuge, wie zuvor schon bei der Beschilderung. Die Straßenbahn wird derzeit im Auftrag von TfL von *Tram Operations Limited*, einer Tochter der FirstGroup, betrieben. Tramlink ist vollständig in das TfL-Tarifsystem integriert, eine Travelcard, die die Zone 3 abdeckt, ist für das gesamte Tramlink-Netz gültig.

Croydon (340,000 inh.) is the southernmost borough of Greater London, lying about 15 km south of Charing Cross. The borough is served by several rail lines from Victoria and Charing Cross/London Bridge, as well as by Thameslink, which allows through journeys via the City of London to the northern boroughs. Since 2010, the London Overground has also provided direct connections between the boroughs north and south of the River Thames via the East London Line. The London Underground, however, has never been extended that far south, although there were plans in the 1950s for the new Victoria Line to serve Croydon town centre.

In 1996, 'Tramtrack Croydon Limited' (TCL) won a contract to design, build, operate and maintain the Croydon tram system. The TCL consortium included FirstGroup and Bombardier. Although the contract was for a 99-year period, Transport for London (TfL) purchased TCL in 2008 and rebranded it from Croydon Tramlink to London Tramlink, in view of more tram and light rail lines to be built across London. The change in ownership was accompanied by a change in corporate design, from the former red to a lime-green livery, a colour already previously used for

London Tramlink

28 km, 39 Haltestellen | *Stops*

10-05-2000:	West Croydon – New Addington
23-05-2000:	Sandilands – Beckenham Junction
30-05-2000:	Wimbledon – West Croydon
	Arena – Elmers End
10-12-2005:	+ Centrale

Die **London Tramlink** ist eine typische ‚Light Rail' bzw. Stadtbahn britischer Bauart, da sie größtenteils auf bestehenden oder stillgelegten Bahntrassen errichtet wurde. Dazu kommen im Zentrum von Croydon straßenbündige Abschnitte sowie eine Neubaustrecke auf eigenem Gleiskörper nach New Addington. Derzeit besteht das Netz aus vier Linien, die alle im Zentrum von Croydon eine eingleisige Schleife im Uhrzeigersinn befahren. Die Linien 1 und 4 verkehren alle 15 Minuten, die Linie 2 alle 10 und die Linie 3 alle 7-8 Minuten. Während die anderen Linien von 5:00 Uhr bis ca. 1:30 Uhr unterwegs sind, fährt die Linie 4 nur bis 19:00 Uhr.

Der westliche Ast, der größtenteils durch angrenzende Bezirke führt, benutzt die Trasse der ehemaligen *Wimbledon to West Croydon Railway* von 1855. Auf dieser Strecke gibt es mehrere eingleisige Abschnitte, auch die Endstation Wimbledon ist eingleisig (Gleis 10). Nachdem bereits 2012 der eingleisige Abschnitt westlich von Mitcham Junction auf ein Minimum (Carshalton Road) reduziert wurde, soll bis 2016 auch der Abschnitt östlich

signage. The trams are currently operated as a concession by Tram Operations Limited, which is part of FirstGroup. Tramlink is fully integrated into the TfL fare system, and a travelcard including zone 3 is good for all tram routes.

*The **London Tramlink** is a typical modern light rail system, making use of former mainline railway routes, combined with some street-running sections in central Croydon and a new alignment to New Addington. The network is currently operated with four routes, all running around a single-track loop in a clockwise direction in the Croydon town centre. Lines 1 and 4 operate every 15 minutes, line 2 every 10, and line 3 every 7-8 minutes. While the other lines are in service from 05:00 until approx. 01:30, line 4 finishes at 19:00.*

The western leg, most of which runs through the neighbouring boroughs, makes use of the former 'Wimbledon to West Croydon Railway' (1855). Along this branch, there are several single-track sections as well as the Wimbledon terminus, where only platform 10 is available. With the single-track section west of Mitcham Junction

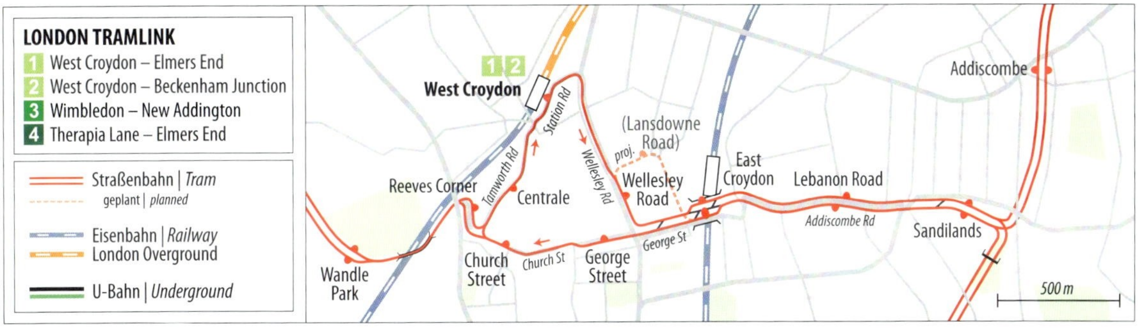

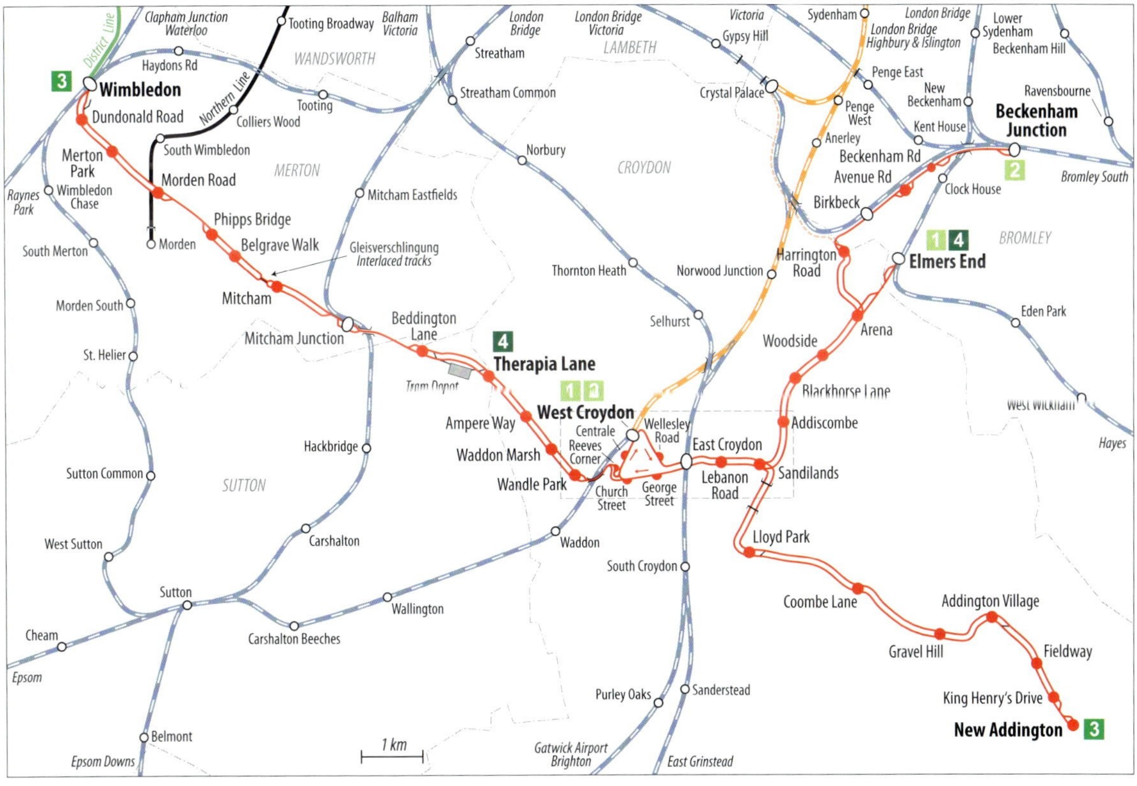

Bombardier #2537 + #2536 @ Therapia Lane

der Brücke über die Thameslink-Strecke bis Beddington Lane zweigleisig werden. Die Endstelle in Wimbledon wird derzeit umgebaut, damit in Zukunft zwei Fahrzeuge gleichzeitig in der Station stehen können. Westlich der Haltestelle Mitcham, wo die Strecke unter der A217 (London Road) hindurchführt, gibt es ein kurzes Stück mit verschlungenen Gleisen. Der Eisenbahnbetrieb wurde erst im Mai 1997 für den Umbau eingestellt. Zu den wichtigsten Bauwerken an diesem Ast zählen die Viadukte über die Vorortbahnstrecken in Mitcham Junction sowie südlich von West Croydon.

Am Bahnhof East Croydon verlässt die Tram das Zentrum und fährt bis kurz vor Sandilands auf der Straße. In Sandilands verzweigen sich die Linien, wobei in beiden Richtungen die Trasse der ehemaligen Bahn von Elmers End Richtung Sanderstead benutzt wird. Auf dem heute von drei Linien befahrenen Abschnitt bis Arena befinden sich mehrere Bahnübergänge. Von Arena fahren die Linien 1 und 4 eingleisig bis Elmers End, die Endhaltestelle liegt an der Nordseite des Bahnhofs an der Strecke von Charing Cross nach Hayes. Die Linie 2 setzt ihre Fahrt auf einer Neubaustrecke am westlichen Rand des South Norwood Country Parks fort und erreicht in Birkbeck die Bahnstrecke von Crystal Palace nach Beckenham. Von dieser Bahnstrecke wurde ein Gleis an die Tramlink abgegeben. An der Haltestelle Avenue Road gibt es ein Ausweichgleis, Birkbeck und Beckenham Road hingegen haben nur eine Bahnsteigkante für beide Richtungen. Die Endhaltestelle der Linie 2 liegt auf der Südseite vor dem Bahnhof Beckenham Junction.

Nach dem Abzweig östlich von Sandilands fährt die Linie 3 erst durch einen 500 m langen Tunnel und verlässt nach etwa 1 km die alte Bahntrasse. Die Strecke von Lloyd Park bis New Addington wurde für die Tramlink neu gebaut. Sie führt durchgehend auf eigenem Gleiskörper meist in Straßenrandlage und hat mehrere Bahnübergänge.

reduced to a minimum (Carshalton Road) in 2012, the section east of the bridge across the Thameslink tracks up to Beddington Lane is to be doubled by 2016. The Wimbledon terminus is currently being rebuilt to accommodate two trams at the same time. Just west of the Mitcham stop, there is a short section of interlaced track that passes under the A217 London Road. The railway was closed for conversion in May 1997. Among the major infrastructure works carried out on this branch are the viaducts across the mainline at both Mitcham Junction and West Croydon.

From East Croydon, the trams leave the town centre on a street alignment up to Sandilands, where the route splits, continuing in either direction along a disused railway which had once linked Elmers End to Sanderstead. The northern route to Arena is now served by three lines and features several level crossings. At Arena, the route splits once again, with the eastern leg becoming single-track and terminating at the north side of Elmers End station on the Hayes – Charing Cross line. Line 2 continues on a new alignment through the western side of the South Norwood Country Park before joining the Crystal Palace – Beckenham railway line at Birkbeck. The Birkbeck – Beckenham Junction section was reduced to single-track, and the former westbound track was converted for the Tramlink. Whereas Birkbeck and Beckenham Road have just a single platform face for both directions, there is a passing loop with two side platforms at Avenue Road. Line 2 terminates at the south side of Beckenham Junction station, with two tracks lying outside the original station compound.

After branching off at Sandilands, line 3 runs 1 km south along the former railway to Sanderstead, including a stretch through a 500 m long tunnel. The route from the stop at Lloyd Park to the terminus at New Addington was purpose-built for the Tramlink, and runs mostly

Bombardier #2551 @ East Croydon

Trotz des Erfolgs des bestehenden Tramlink-Netzes in Croydon und trotz ambitionierter Projekte wurde das Netz seit Inbetriebnahme im Jahr 2000 nicht mehr erweitert. Weiterhin gilt ein Abzweig von Harrington Road bis Crystal Palace als möglich. Dazu würde das zweite Gleis zwischen Beckenham Junction und Birkbeck übernommen und im Bereich Crystal Palace eine neue Strecke gebaut. Weit fortgeschritten waren auch die ‚West London Tram' von Shepherd's Bush über Acton und Ealing bis Uxbridge entlang der Uxbridge Road (A4020) sowie in der Innenstadt die ‚Cross River Tram' von Euston bis Waterloo, mit Ästen an beiden Enden. Die einzige konkrete Planung ist derzeit eine zweite Schleife in Croydon, so dass Bahnen aus dem Osten ab 2019 nicht unbedingt über die Innenstadtschleife fahren müssen.

Bei der Tramlink begann der Betrieb mit 24 Stadtbahnwagen des Typs CR4000 (FLEXITY Swift) von Bombardier im Einsatz. Dieses Fahrzeug ist von der aus Köln bekannten Niederflurstadtbahn K4000 abgeleitet. Das erste gelieferte Fahrzeug bekam die Nummer 2530 und schließt somit an die alte Nummerierung der seit 1952 in London verschwundenen Straßenbahnen an. Um das Angebot zu verbessern, wurden ab 2011 sechs Variobahnen von Stadler geliefert, die ursprünglich zur neuen Stadtbahn im norwegischen Bergen gehen sollten. Vier weitere Variobahnen kamen 2015 hinzu. Beide Fahrzeugtypen können nur als Einzelwagen verkehren.

alongside roads on reserved track with several level crossings.

Despite the success of the Tramlink system in Croydon and several ambitious expansion projects, the network has not been extended since it first opened in 2000. A branch from Harrington Road to Crystal Palace is still an option. It would be achieved by taking over the second track between Beckenham Junction and Birkbeck, and adding a new alignment at the Crystal Palace end. Other tram schemes had reached an advanced stage of planning before being shelved: the 'West London Tram', linking Shepherd's Bush to Uxbridge along Uxbridge Road (A4020) through Acton and Ealing; and in central London, the 'Cross River Tram' linking Euston to Waterloo, with several branches at both ends. The only project currently being pursued is a second loop in Croydon to open in 2019, allowing trams from the eastern branches to turn around without using the Croydon town centre loop.

Tramlink was launched with a fleet of 24 FLEXITY Swift CR4000 trams (2530-2553). Built by Bombardier in Vienna, they are based on the K4000 tram designed for the Cologne low-floor network. The strange number assigned to the first tram delivered (2530) is a continuation of the traditional numbering system, the last trams having disappeared from London's streets in 1952. To improve frequencies, six Variotrams were delivered by Stadler in 2011, vehicles which had initially been intended for the new light rail system in Bergen (Norway). Another four of the same type were added in 2015. Both types of tram are only allowed to operate as single units.

Tramlink > Fahrzeuge | *Rolling Stock* (750 V DC)

Nummer *Number*	Anzahl *Quantity*	Hersteller *Manufacturer*	Typ *Class*	Länge *Length*	Breite *Width*	Ausgeliefert *Delivered*
2530-2553	24	Bombardier	CR4000	30.1 m	2.65 m	1998-1999
2554-2563	10	Stadler	Variobahn	32.3 m	2.65 m	2011-2015

Stadler #2557 @ Church Street (> George Street)

Bombardier #2542 @ Lebanon Road

Bombardier #2539 @ Wimbledon (vor dem Umbau | *before rebuilding*)

Bombardier #2533 @ Gravel Hill
(2005 im Originalanstrich | *in original livery*)

Bombardier #2546 @ Mitcham Junction
(2005 im Originalanstrich | *in original livery*)

Bombardier #2533 @ Blackhorse Lane

Bombardier CR4000

Bombardier #2530 @ George Street

Bombardier #2535 @ Addiscombe Road (Lebanon Rd > Sandilands)

Bombardier #2550 @ Church Street

Canary Wharf

DOCKLANDS LIGHT RAILWAY

Bei der **Docklands Light Railway** (DLR) handelt es sich um eine völlig unabhängige, fahrerlose, automatische Stadtbahn, die auch als „Leicht-Metro" bezeichnet werden könnte. Der Betrieb wird von der Leitzentrale am Bahnhof Poplar überwacht. Das SelTrac-Signalsystem ist eine Entwicklung von Alcatel und arbeitet mit *Moving-Block*-Technologie. Alle Züge sind allerdings mit sog. „Passenger Service Agents" besetzt, deren Aufgabe es ist, die Türen zu schließen, aber auch die Fahrscheine zu kontrollieren, da es an den DLR-Stationen keine Zugangssperren gibt. Die DLR war das erste Bahnsystem Großbritanniens, das barrierefrei zugänglich war. Derzeit wird die DLR von *KeolisAmey Docklands* betrieben und unterhalten.

Auf der DLR gibt es sechs nicht nummerierte oder farblich unterschiedene Grundlinien, die außerhalb der Hauptverkehrszeiten alle 10 Minuten bedient werden (Stratford – Canary Wharf alle 5 Minuten). Daneben kommen in den Spitzenzeiten Zusatzfahrten mit teils verkürzter Streckenführung.

Die Idee für die Docklands Light Railway wurde 1982 geboren. Sie sollte als Stadtbahn die City mit den Entwicklungsgebieten im ehemaligen Hafen, den Docklands, auf der Themse-Halbinsel Isle of Dogs verbinden. Der Bau des Grundnetzes von Tower Gateway bis Island Gardens mit einem Abzweig nach Stratford (12 km) begann 1984 und wurde 1987 vollendet. Längere Abschnitte dieser Strecken konnten auf stillgelegten Bahntrassen errichtet werden. Bald nach Inbetriebnahme des Grundnetzes wurde mit dem

*The **Docklands Light Railway** (DLR) is a fully segregated, driverless automatic system which is better classified as a 'light metro'. It is monitored from the Control Centre at Poplar. The signalling system is based on Alcatel's SelTrac system, which uses the 'moving block' technology. All trains are staffed, however, with Passenger Service Agents, who are responsible for closing doors and inspecting tickets, which is necessary as the system has not been equipped with access barriers. The DLR was the first fully accessible railway in the UK. 'KeolisAmey Docklands' is currently in charge of operation and maintenance.*

The DLR operates six basic off-peak routes (each with trains every 10 minutes, though Stratford – Canary Wharf every 5 minutes), with additional trains during peak hours. The different services are not numbered or distinguished by different colours.

The Docklands Light Railway was conceived in 1982 as a low-capacity rail link from the City to the regeneration area in the former port area on the Isle of Dogs peninsula. Construction started in 1984 on an initial network from Tower Gateway to Island Gardens with a branch to Stratford (12 km), which opened in 1987. Long sections of these routes were built on abandoned railway alignments. Soon after services started, work began on a 1.6 km underground extension to Bank as well as on lengthening the platforms, which used to be just 30 m long as they had been designed for single units. This would allow operation with 2-car trainsets to start from 1991.

Bau einer 1,6 km langen Tunnelstrecke zum Umsteigeknoten Bank direkt in der City begonnen. Außerdem mussten die anfangs nur 30 m langen Bahnsteige sofort verlängert werden, um ab 1991 2-Wagen-Züge einsetzen zu können.

Die ersten Entwürfe für diese Stadtbahn sahen auch die Möglichkeit von straßenbündigen Strecken zum U-Bahnhof Mile End vor. Schließlich entschied man sich aber für ein völlig kreuzungsfreies Netz.

Der Erfolg der DLR führte bald zu weiteren Neubaustrecken, so 1994 von Poplar über Canning Town (damals mit Umsteigemöglichkeit zur North London Line) nach Beckton (8,4 km), unter anderem, um das Kongresszentrum ExCel sowie einen zweiten Betriebshof anzuschließen. Einige Jahre später folgte die erste Unterquerung der Themse, wofür der ursprüngliche Hochbahnhof Island Gardens abgerissen und durch einen unterirdischen Bahnhof ersetzt werden musste. In Greenwich und Lewisham besteht Anschluss an zahlreiche Vorortbahnen, die den Süden Londons erschließen. Ein weiterer Ast kam in zwei Stufen in den 2000er Jahren hinzu, erst bis King George V, womit der London City Airport direkt angeschlossen wurde, dann mit einer zweiten Themse-Unterquerung im Röhrentunnel bis Woolwich.

The first proposals for a rail link to the Docklands had included 'proper' light rail with some street-running to Mile End Underground station. The final decision, however, went in favour of a completely grade-separated system.

The success of the DLR soon led to the construction of several new branches, the first in 1994 from Poplar via Canning Town (then with connections to the North

LONDON Docklands Light Railway

35.5 km (~ 5 km unterirdisch | *underground*), 45 Bahnhöfe | *stations*

31-08-1987: Tower Gateway / Stratford – Island Gardens
29-07-1991: Bank – Shadwell
12-08-1991: + Canary Wharf
28-03-1994: Poplar – Beckton
16-01-1996: + Pudding Mill Lane
05-03-1998: + Canning Town
20-11-1999: Island Gardens – Lewisham
03-12-1999: + Cutty Sark
02-12-2005: Canning Town – King George V
09-12-2007: + Langdon Park
10-01-2009: King George V – Woolwich Arsenal
31-08-2011: Canning Town – Stratford International

Pudding Mill Lane

Als Teil der erfolgreichen Bewerbung für die Olympischen Sommerspiele 2012 wurde eine neue Strecke von Canning Town zum neuen Regionalbahnhof Stratford International gebaut. Dazu wurde zwischen Canning Town und Stratford die ehemalige Strecke der North London Line übernommen, während deren südlicher Abschnitt zwischen Canning Town und North Woolwich geschlossen wurde (die Trasse wird nun teilweise für den Crossrail-Ast nach Abbey Wood genutzt).

In den letzten Jahren wurden die meisten Bahnsteige für den Einsatz von 3-Wagen-Zügen verlängert, wozu auch die Verstärkung einiger Viadukte und Brücken notwendig war. An kürzeren Bahnsteigen können bei 3-Wagen-Betrieb nur gewisse Türen geöffnet werden. Außerdem wurde die Verzweigung nördlich von West India Quay 2009 entflochten, womit die Züge von Bank Richtung Lewisham an dieser Station normalerweise nicht mehr halten. Die letzte wesentliche Veränderung erfuhr das DLR-Netz am 28. April 2014, als die neue Station Pudding Mill Lane auf einer etwas nach Süden verschobenen, rund 500 m langen aufgeständerten Neubautrasse in Betrieb ging,

BN #41

London Line) to Beckton (8.4 km) providing service to the convention centre ExCel, various other attractions as well as access to the second depot. A few years later, the first crossing under the River Thames was completed, for which the original elevated station at Island Gardens had to be demolished and replaced by an underground station. In Greenwich and Lewisham, interchange is provided with many suburban lines serving the south of London. Another branch was added in two stages in the first decade of the new millennium, the first part to King George V, with a station right at the London City Airport, followed by a second Thames crossing in a tube tunnel to Woolwich.

As part of the successful bid to host the 2012 Olympic Games, a new route from Canning Town to Stratford International, a new mainline station for regional services on the Channel Tunnel Rail Link, was built. It replaced the former North London Line service between Stratford and Canning Town, while the remaining section to North Woolwich was abandoned (part of it is now being used for the Crossrail alignment to Abbey Wood).

In recent years, most platforms have been extended for 3-car operation, which required the strengthening of certain viaducts and bridges. A 'selective door close' system is used at the shorter platforms when 3-car trains are in operation. In addition, the junction north of West India Quay station was disentangled in 2009, with the result that trains from Bank

Bank

was auf der alten Trasse den Bau der Tunnelrampe für Crossrail ermöglichte.

Ein einst geplanter Ast mit vier Zwischenstationen von Gallions Reach auf dem Beckton-Ast bis Dagenham Dock wird nicht weiter verfolgt, da das Entwicklungsgebiet Barking Riverside stattdessen durch London Overground angeschlossen wird.

Bei der DLR sind insgesamt 149 Fahrzeuge im Einsatz, die zwei Generationen angehören. Die ursprünglichen Wagen des Typs P86 und P89 kann man heute bei der Stadtbahn in Essen sehen. Die älteren Wagen (die Typen B90, B92 und B2K) wurden Mitte der 2000er Jahre renoviert und bekamen wie die neueren Fahrzeuge vom Typ B2007 und B2009 einen rot dominierten Anstrich. Bei allen Fahrzeugen handelt es sich um hochflurige Gelenktriebwagen, bei einer Fußbodenhöhe von 1025 mm über Schienenoberkante ermöglichen sie stufenloses Einsteigen. Sie verkehren in Doppel- oder Dreifachtraktion. Die Stromversorgung erfolgt mit 750 V Gleichstrom über eine von unten bestrichene seitliche Stromschiene. Die Spurweite beträgt 1435 mm.

to Lewisham no longer stop at this station during normal service. The last major modification to the DLR system happened on 28 April 2014, when the new Pudding Mill Lane station opened on a new elevated route roughly 500 m long, moved slightly to the south to allow for the construction of a tunnel ramp for Crossrail.

Yet another planned branch, this time from Gallions Reach on the Beckton branch to Dagenham Dock with four intermediate stations, is no longer being pursued, as the redevelopment area now known as Barking Riverside will be linked by a London Overground extension.

The DLR fleet comprises 149 vehicles belonging to two generations. The original P86 and P89 stock can now be seen in service in Essen (Germany). The older cars (classes B90, B92 and B2K) were all refurbished in the mid-2000s and like the newer B2007 and B2009 vehicles, now boast a predominantly red livery. With a floor height of 1025 mm above the top of the rail, the high-floor articulated vehicles provide stepfree access. The trains are made up of two or three cars. The DLR is powered by 750 V DC via an aluminium third rail, with current being taken from the underside of the rail. The track gauge is the standard 1435 mm.

DLR > Fahrzeuge | *Rolling Stock* (750 V DC)

Nummer *Number*	Anzahl *Quantity*	Hersteller *Manufacturer*	Typ *Class*	Länge *Length*	Breite *Width*	Ausgeliefert *Delivered*
22-44	23	BN Construction Brugge	B90	28 m	2.65 m	1991-1992
45-91	47	BN Construction Brugge	B92	28 m	2.65 m	1992-1995
01-16, 92-99	24	Bombardier	B2K	28 m	2.65 m	2001
101-124	24	Bombardier	B2007	28 m	2.65 m	2007-2008
125-155	31	Bombardier	B2009	28 m	2.65 m	2009

West India Quay > Poplar (2011 mit Crossrail-Baustelle | *with Crossrail construction site*)

West India Quay (B2K - 2005 im Originalanstrich | *in original livery*)

Pontoon Dock

Stratford > Stratford International (mit | *with Olympic Stadium*)

Royal Victoria

Stratford International

Woolwich Arsenal

Stratford (2011 - oberer Bahnsteig | *upper platform*)

All Saints (B2K - 2005 im Originalanstrich | *in original livery*)

West Silvertown <> Canning Town (*feat. Emirates Air Line*)

Finchley Road (Metropolitan Line links | *left* – Jubilee Line rechts | *right*)

LONDON UNDERGROUND

London war die erste Stadt der Welt, in der unterirdische Bahnstrecken gebaut wurden. Die ersten Abschnitte des heutigen *Subsurface*-Netzes mit der *Metropolitan Railway* wurden bereits 1863 in Betrieb genommen, auch wenn diese Linien bis 1905 mit Dampf betrieben wurden. London war aber auch Pionier im Bereich der elektrischen Untergrundbahnen, denn die 1890 eröffnete *City & South London Railway* kann man als die erste richtige Metrolinie der Welt betrachten. Der Großteil der heutigen Strecken durch die Innenstadt wurde im ersten Jahrzehnt des 20. Jahrhunderts gebaut, nur die Victoria Line und die Jubilee Line entstanden später. Ab 1908 wurde für die meisten Linien, obwohl sie von verschiedenen Privatgesellschaften betrieben wurden, der Begriff **‚UndergrounD‘** an den Stationseingängen verwendet. 1933 wurden alle Linien verstaatlicht und als ‚London Underground‘ Teil von *London Passenger Transport Board*, oder kurz *London Transport*. Im Jahr 2002 wurde die Infrastruktur der U-Bahn nach dem Modell der *Public Private Partnership* an Privatfirmen übergeben, für den Betrieb war weiterhin *London Underground Ltd* zuständig. Bis 2032 sollte das Konsortium *Tube Lines* die Unterhaltung und die Erneuerung der Jubilee, Northern und Piccadilly Line übernehmen, die übrigen Linien gingen an *Metronet*. Doch bereits 2008 (*Metronet*) bzw. 2010 (*Tube Lines*) ging das gesamte Netz wieder in die öffentliche Hand zurück, nun an *Transport for London* (TfL).

Auf dem offiziellen Netzplan der Londoner U-Bahn (meist einfach ‚The Tube‘ - die Röhre - genannt) ist das Netz stark verzerrt dargestellt. Den ersten Plan dieser Art schuf Harry Beck im Jahre 1931, dabei bleiben die teils

London was the first city in the world to build urban underground railways. The first sections of the present subsurface network, including the original Metropolitan Railway, were brought into service in as early as 1863, although steam locomotives remained in service on these lines until 1905. However, London was also a pioneer in building electric underground lines, opening the first real metro line in the world, the 'City & South London Railway', in 1890. Most of today's lines in the central area were built in the first decade of the 20th century, with only the Victoria and Jubilee Lines having been added later. From 1908, most lines, although operated by various privately owned companies, started displaying the term ***'UndergrounD'*** *at station entrances. In 1933, all the lines were integrated into the newly formed public 'London Passenger Transport Board', or simply 'London Transport'. In 2002, the Underground infrastructure was transferred to two private companies under the Public Private Partnership scheme, although the operation of the lines remained with London Underground Ltd. Until 2032, 'Tube Lines' was supposed to maintain, renew and upgrade the Jubilee, Northern and Piccadilly Lines, including trains and stations, whereas 'Metronet' became responsible for the rest of the lines. In 2008 (Metronet) and 2010 (Tube Lines), however, the infrastructure returned to public ownership, now under the authority of 'Transport for London' (TfL).*

The official map of the Underground (or simply the 'Tube') is an extremely distorted representation of the network. The diagram design, which was created by

Barons Court (Piccadilly Line links | *left* – District Line rechts | *right*)

enormen Unterschiede bei den Stationsabständen im Zentralbereich im Vergleich zu den Vororten unberücksichtigt. Innerhalb des von der Circle Line begrenzten Bereichs liegen die Stationen durchschnittlich ca. 780 m voneinander entfernt (der kürzeste Abstand liegt mit 260 m zwischen Leicester Square und Covent Garden). Im äußeren Bereich hingegen ist der mittlere Abstand 1440 m (der längste ist mit 6,2 km zwischen Chalfont & Latimer und Chesham).

Während sich der Großteil des U-Bahn-Netzes auf der Nordseite der Themse erstreckt, wird die Südseite von einem dichten Netz von Vorortbahnen erschlossen, was neben den schwierigeren Bodenverhältnissen ein Grund war, warum die U-Bahn kaum in die südlichen Bezirke vorgedrungen ist. Seit 2014 ist eine Verlängerung der Bakerloo Line nach Süden wieder verstärkt im Gespräch.

Innerhalb des Zentralbereichs, Zone 1 im 9-Tarifzonen-System, ist die U-Bahn häufig stark überlastet. Das liegt einerseits an starken Pendlerströmen in bzw. aus der Innenstadt, andererseits aber auch am Mangel an durchgebundenen Vorortlinien, wodurch Millionen Fahrgäste gezwungen sind, an den zahlreichen Kopfbahnhöfen zur U-Bahn umzusteigen. Die einzige durchgehende Vorortbahn ist „Thameslink", die innerhalb der Zone 1 entlang ihrer Nord-Süd-Strecke sechs Bahnhöfe hat. Ähnlich dem Pariser RER wird „Crossrail" ab ca. 2019 die von Liverpool Street und Paddington ausgehenden Vorortbahnen über eine innerstädtische Tunnelstrecke direkt miteinander verknüpfen (siehe S. 115). Während eine zweite Crossrail-Strecke vorbereitet wird, sind für die U-Bahn neben der erwähnten Verlängerung der Bakerloo Line und kurzen Ergänzungen der Metropolitan und Northern Line in den nächsten Jahrzehnten keine wesentlichen Erweiterungen zu erwarten.

Harry Beck in 1931, ignores the significant differences in distance between stations in the central area and those in the suburbs. In the area confined by the Circle Line, the average distance between stations is approx. 780 m (the shortest is 260 m between Leicester Square and Covent Garden). Outside this area, the average is 1440 m between stations (the longest being between Chalfont & Latimer and Chesham at 6.2 km).

Most of the Underground network lies north of the River Thames, the southern side being dominated by suburban railways. More complicated ground conditions were another reason why no further plans have been made to extend the Underground to the southern boroughs. However, since 2014, a southern extension of the Bakerloo Line has once again come under consideration.

The Tube gets very busy in the central area, labelled Zone 1 in the 9-zone fare system. This is partly due to heavy peak-hour traffic to and from the centre, but is mostly caused by a lack of direct cross-city routes for the suburban railways. Millions of passengers are thus forced to change from suburban trains at a number of termini to continue their journey into the centre proper on one of the Tube lines. The only suburban service through the central area is Thameslink, with six stations within Zone 1 along its through-running north-south route. Like the Paris RER, Crossrail will provide direct connections for suburban trains currently starting at Paddington and Liverpool Street via a central underground link (see p. 115). While a second Crossrail link is also in the pipeline, no major extensions to the Tube network can be expected besides the aforementioned Bakerloo Line extension, and two short branches for the Metropolitan and Northern Lines.

Watford (Metropolitan Line – S8 stock)

Subsurface Lines

Die ältesten Untergrundbahnstrecken wurden in London in geringer Tiefe (ca. 5-10 m) in offener Bauweise gebaut, sie werden deshalb als *Subsurface Lines* (Unterpflasterbahnen) bezeichnet, im Gegensatz zu den *Tube Lines* (Röhrenbahnen). Dabei wird erst ein Graben geöffnet, dann die Tunnelsohle und die Seitenwände errichtet, das Ganze abgedeckt und schließlich die Oberfläche wiederhergestellt. Diese Bauweise ist gut für Strecken entlang breiter Straßen geeignet (und wurde in abgewandelter Form meist bei der Berliner U-Bahn angewandt), allerdings mussten bei der Londoner U-Bahn auch sehr viele Gebäude abgerissen und nach Fertigstellung des Tunnels wieder aufgebaut werden. Obwohl diese Bauweise etwas billiger ist, wird sie heute weltweit immer weniger angewandt, weil die Beeinträchtigungen an der Oberfläche zu groß sind.
Zu den Londoner *Subsurface Lines* gehören die folgenden Linien:

- Circle Line
- Hammersmith & City Line
- Metropolitan Line
- District Line

Bis Dezember 2007 gehörte auch die East London Line zu den Subsurface-Linien, sie wurde dann umgebaut und ist seit 2010 Teil des London Overground-Netzes (siehe S. 110).

Die Subsurface-Linien sind über die Circle Line miteinander verflochten und teilen sich abschnittsweise die

The oldest lines on today's London Underground network were built at a low depth (about 5-10 m) by the cut-and-cover method, and are therefore referred to as the 'subsurface lines'. With this method, a trench is first dug from the surface, the tunnel floor and walls are then built, before finally the route is covered and the surface reinstated. It is mostly used for tunnels running under major roads, although for the first underground routes through London many properties had to be demolished, and after the completion of the tunnel, reconstructed. This method, though cheaper, has become less popular worldwide as it causes long disruptions at the surface. The following lines constitute the London Underground subsurface network:

- *Circle Line*
- *Hammersmith & City Line*
- *Metropolitan Line*
- *District Line*

Until December 2007, the East London Line had also formed part of the subsurface network, but it was then upgraded and integrated into the London Overground network in 2010 *(see p. 110)**.*

All the subsurface lines are interconnected by means of the Circle Line, sharing the same tracks on some sections. The tunnel profile is similar to that of mainline railways, and the rolling stock used is notably larger than that on the tube lines. By 2016, all the older train

Gleise. Das Tunnelprofil ist ähnlich wie bei einer richtigen Eisenbahn, wodurch auch wesentlich geräumigere Fahrzeuge als auf den *Tube Lines* eingesetzt werden können. Die neuen S-Züge, die bis 2016 sämtliche ältere Baureihen auf diesen Linien ersetzt haben werden, sind 2,92 m breit und 3,69 m hoch. Im Gegensatz dazu sind die *Tube*-Züge nur 2,63 m breit und 2,88 m hoch. Auf der Metropolitan Line fahren 133,7 m lange, durchgehend begehbare 8-Wagen-Züge (S8), auf den anderen Linien 117,5 m lange 7-Wagen-Züge (S7). Außerhalb der Tunnelstrecken sind die Fahrzeuge beider Profile in einem gewissen Maß miteinander kompatibel, so dass auf einigen Strecken auch ein Mischbetrieb stattfindet (Rayners Lane – Uxbridge sowie im Bereich Ealing Common). Da die Fußbodenhöhe der *Subsurface*-Züge bei 980 mm, die der *Tube*-Züge aber nur bei 610 mm liegt, musste an gemeinsam bedienten Bahnhöfen eine mittlere Bahnsteighöhe gewählt werden.

Beide Teilnetze haben eine Spurweite von 1435 mm. Die Stromzufuhr mit 630 V Gleichstrom erfolgt über ein 2-Stromschienen-System, eine außenliegende Stromschiene als Hinleiter (+) und eine zwischen den Gleisen liegende als Rückleiter (–).

Mit einer Länge von rund 140 km (ab 2018 144 km; davon etwa 20% unterirdisch) stellt das *Subsurface*-Netz etwa ein Drittel des gesamten Londoner U-Bahn-Netzes dar.

types will have been replaced by the new S stock, which are 2.92 m wide and 3.69 m high, compared to a width of 2.63 m and a height of just 2.88 m for the average tube stock. The Metropolitan Line is served by 133.7 m eight-car trains (S8), while the other lines have 117.5 m seven-car trains (S7). All the new cars are interconnected via gangways. To a certain extent, subsurface and tube stock is compatible outside tunnels, and shared service is provided on the Rayners Lane – Uxbridge section as well as on a short stretch around Ealing Common. With the floor height of subsurface trains being 980 mm and that of tube trains just 610 mm, a compromise platform height had to be chosen at the shared stations.

Both systems have 1435 mm standard gauge and use two power rails, the positive rail lying on the outside and the negative between the tracks; the traction voltage is 630 V DC.

With a total length of approx. 140 km (from 2018, 144 km; and only some 20 % lying underground), the subsurface network makes up about a third of the entire London Underground network.

LU Subsurface Lines > Fahrzeuge | *Rolling Stock* (630 V DC)

Nummer *Number*	Anzahl *Quantity*	Einsatz *In service*	Hersteller *Manufacturer*	Typ *Class*	Länge *Length*	Breite *Width*	Ausgeliefert *Delivered*
7000...8129, 17000...17538	*	DIS	Metro-Cammell	D stock	18.3 m	2.85 m	1979-1983
21001-21116, 22001-24116	58 (x8)	MET	Bombardier	S8 stock	16.7 m	2.92 m	2010-2012
21301-21566, 22301-25566	133 (x7)	CIR, H&C, DIS	Bombardier	S7 stock	16.7 m	2.92 m	2012-2016

* bis 2016 durch Baureihe S7 ersetzt | *to be replaced by S7 stock by 2016*

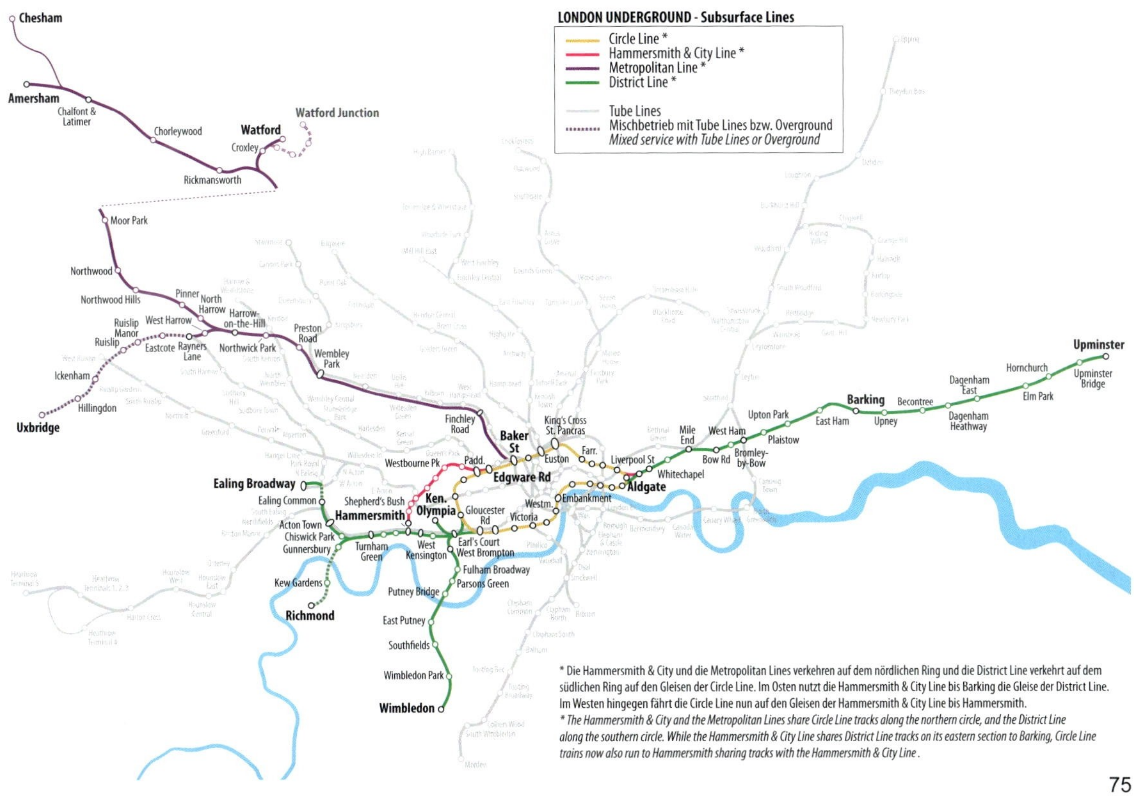

* Die Hammersmith & City und die Metropolitan Lines verkehren auf dem nördlichen Ring und die District Line verkehrt auf dem südlichen Ring auf den Gleisen der Circle Line. Im Osten nutzt die Hammersmith & City Line bis Barking die Gleise der District Line. Im Westen hingegen fährt die Circle Line nun auf den Gleisen der Hammersmith & City Line bis Hammersmith.

** The Hammersmith & City and the Metropolitan Lines share Circle Line tracks along the northern circle, and the District Line along the southern circle. While the Hammersmith & City Line shares District Line tracks on its eastern section to Barking, Circle Line trains now also run to Hammersmith sharing tracks with the Hammersmith & City Line .*

Hammersmith (S7 stock)

Circle Line + Hammersmith & City Line

Die **Circle Line** (Ringlinie) erschien als solche erst 1949 auf dem Netzplan der Londoner U-Bahn, obwohl sie durch die ältesten U-Bahn-Tunnel der Welt fährt. Bis zum 13. Dezember 2009 handelte es sich um eine wirkliche, 20,5 km lange Ringlinie, doch seither fährt sie etwa alle 10 Minuten von Hammersmith kommend über den Nord- und Südring und endet schließlich am Bahnhof Edgware Road. Sie teilt sich die Gleise mit der Hammersmith & City Line im Norden und mit der District Line im Süden. Auch die Metropolitan Line verkehrt zwischen Baker Street und Aldgate auf denselben Gleisen. Alle sechs Verzweigungen entlang der Ringstrecke sind niveaugleich, so dass es bei vier ineinander verflochtenen Linien immer wieder zu Behinderungen und Verspätungen kommen kann. Die Circle Line verbindet alle wichtigen Fernbahnhöfe, außer Waterloo und London Bridge, die auf der Südseite der Themse liegen. Eine Fahrt auf dem gesamten Ring dauert etwa eine Stunde.

Noch bis 1990 war die **Hammersmith & City Line** auf den Netzplänen als Teil der Metropolitan Line dargestellt. Mit Pink als Linienkennfarbe verkehrt sie seither etwa alle 10 Minuten zwischen Hammersmith und Barking entlang des Nordrings und auf dem östlichen Abschnitt auf den Gleisen der District Line.

Der nördliche Teil der Ringstrecke wurde bereits 1863 eröffnet. Damals fuhren Dampfzüge von Paddington im Westen bis nach Farringdon in der City. Die als *Metropolitan Railway* bezeichnete Strecke wurde bald an beiden Enden verlängert und bekam mehrere Äste. Wenig später

*The **Circle Line** as such only appeared on the London Underground map in 1949, although the route it serves includes the first underground sections ever built. Until 13 December 2009, the Circle Line was an actual continuously operated 20.5 km ring line, but now it departs from Hammersmith every 10 minutes and runs via the northern and then the southern ring to terminate at Edgware Road. The tracks on its northern segment are shared with the Hammersmith & City Line and partly with the Metropolitan Line, too, while those on its southern segment are shared with the District Line. All six junctions along the circle are flat, which inevitably makes the operation of four interconnected lines very complicated, and often results in delays. The Circle Line links all the mainline termini spread around Central London except Waterloo and London Bridge, which lie on the south bank of the River Thames. A trip around the full circle takes about an hour.*

*Until 1990, the **Hammersmith & City Line** was shown on maps as being part of the Metropolitan Line. Now shown in pink, it runs every 10 minutes between Hammersmith and Barking along the northern part of the Circle Line, sharing tracks with the District Line on the eastern branch.*

The northern part of the circular route dates back to 1863, when the first steam-powered trains began running under London roads from Paddington in the west to Farringdon in the City. This route became known as the 'Metropolitan Railway', and it was subsequently

Wood Lane

begann die *Metropolitan District Railway* mit dem Bau einer Strecke zwischen South Kensington und Westminster, und von dort entlang der Themse weiter in Richtung City. Beide Bahngesellschaften sollten sich bald darauf zusammenschließen, stattdessen wurden sie immer mehr zu Konkurrenten, vor allem nachdem 1884 der gemeinsame Betrieb auf der Ringstrecke begonnen hatte.

Die ursprüngliche, völlig an der Oberfläche errichtete *Hammersmith & City Railway* wurde 1864 eröffnet. Wie auf den ersten Tunnelstrecken zwischen Paddington und

extended with several branches at each end. Soon afterwards, the 'Metropolitan District Railway' began building its first route, which ran from South Kensington to Westminster and then along the north shore of the River Thames. Both companies were to be merged soon after, but this never happened. Instead, they were actually competing when shared operation along the full circle began in 1884.

The original 'Hammersmith & City Railway', which was built completely on the surface, dates back to 1864.

Circle Line + Hammersmith & City Line

Circle Line: 27.2 km (~ 19 km unterird. | *underground*), 36 Bhf. | *stations*
H&C Line: 25.4 km (~ 12 km unterird. | *underground*), 29 Bhf. | *stations*

10-01-1863: Paddington – Farringdon
13-06-1864: Paddington – Hammersmith
23-12-1865: Farringdon – Moorgate
01-02-1866 + Westbourne Park
01-10-1868: Edgware Road – Gloucester Road
16-12-1868 + Latimer Road
24-12-1868: Gloucester Road – Westminster
30-05-1870: Westminster – Blackfriars
03-07-1871: Blackfriars – Mansion House
30-10-1871 + Royal Oak
12-07-1875: Moorgate – Liverpool Street
18-11-1876: Liverpool Street – Aldgate
25-09-1882: Aldgate – Tower Hill
06-10-1884: Tower Hill – Mansion House
06-10-1884: Liverpool Street – Whitechapel
02-06-1902: Whitechapel – Bromley-by-Bow – Barking
11-06-1902: + Bow Road
23-06-1902: + Stepney Green
01-04-1914: + Goldhawk Road
12-10-2008: + Wood Lane

1905/06 elektrischer Betrieb | *electric service*

Edgware Road

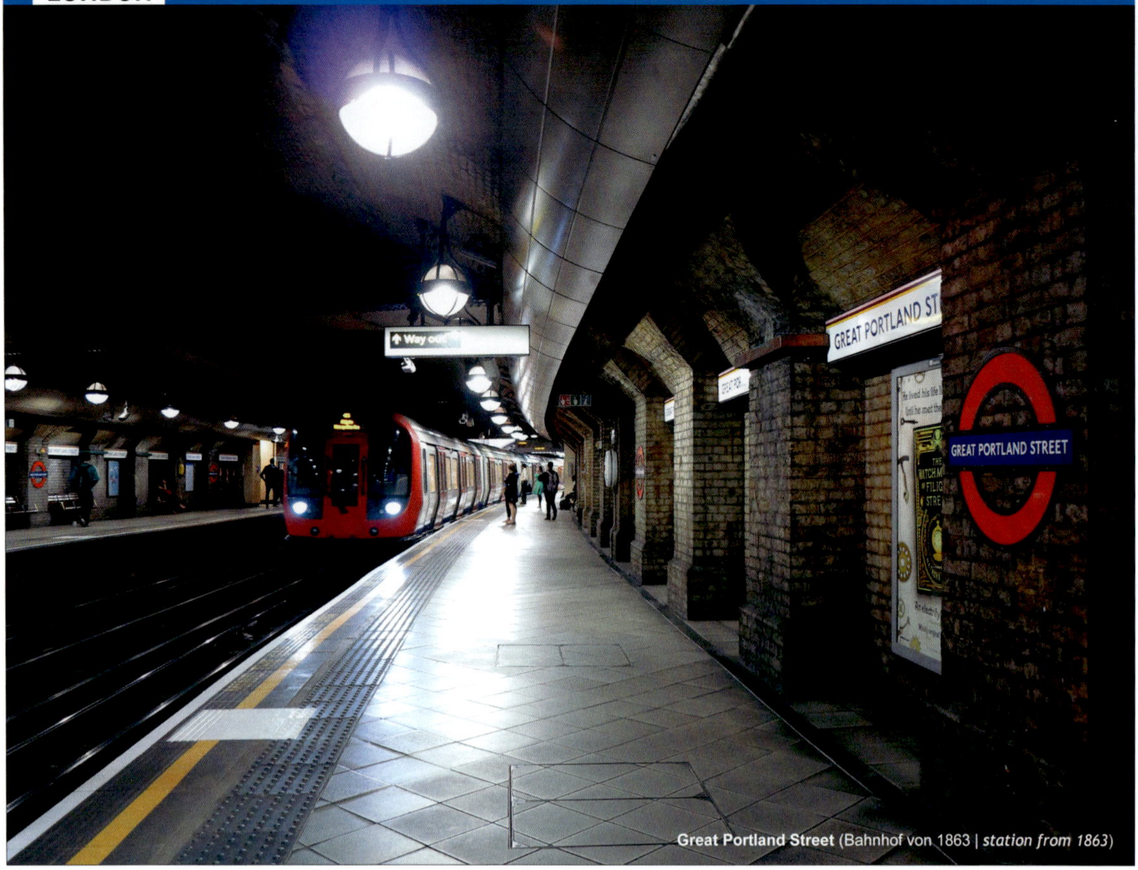

Great Portland Street (Bahnhof von 1863 | *station from 1863*)

Farringdon lag hier damals ein 3-Schienen-Gleis, um durchgehenden Verkehr auf der früher breitspurigen *Great Western Railway* zu ermöglichen.

Während der Hammersmith-Ast meist auf einem gemauerten Viadukt und teils ebenerdig verläuft, ist der Ring bis auf kurze Abschnitte südlich vom Bahnhof High Street Kensington und im Bereich von Farringdon fast völlig unterirdisch. Mehrere Stationen, wie z.B. Paddington, Sloane Square oder South Kensington, liegen in einem offenen Einschnitt. Entlang der Strecke gibt es außerdem bis heute zahlreiche Öffnungen, die ursprünglich zum Dampfablassen nötig waren. Während die Circle Line im Norden hauptsächlich unter breiten Straßenzügen und im Südosten entlang

As with the first tunnel section between Paddington and Farringdon, the western extension was built to standard and broad gauge to allow through service on the broad-gauge Great Western Railway.

While the Hammersmith branch was built mostly on a brick viaduct and partly at grade, the Circle Line is mostly underground, except for some short stretches south of High Street Kensington station and in the Farringdon area. Several stations lie in a partly open cutting (e.g. Paddington, Sloane Square and South Kensington). The numerous openings still found along the route were initially necessary to allow the steam produced by the locomotives to escape. Whereas the

Farringdon

Baker Street

Blackfriars (kürzlich renoviert | *recently refurbished*)

der Themse verläuft, ist die Streckenführung auf anderen Abschnitten weniger leicht nachvollziehbar, da die Trasse an vielen Stellen überbaut wurde.

Auf dem Hammersmith-Ast wurde am 12. Oktober 2008 die Station Wood Lane in Betrieb genommen, etwa an derselben Stelle existierte bereits von 1908 bis 1959 ein Bahnhof.

northern part of the Circle Line runs along major roads and the southeastern along the River Thames, other parts were later built over and the alignment is not clearly visible from the surface.

On the Hammersmith branch, an in-fill station called Wood Lane was opened on 12 October 2008 near the site where a station had once existed between 1908 and 1959.

Edgware Road

Paddington (kürzlich renoviert | *recently refurbished*)

Baker Street
(westliches Stumpfgleis | *western bay track*)

Metropolitan Line

Tagsüber werden auf der Metropolitan Line folgende Linienführungen angeboten:
① Aldgate/Baker Street – Uxbridge: 8 Züge pro Stunde
② Baker Street – Watford: 4 Züge pro Stunde
③ Aldgate – Amersham: 2 Züge pro Stunde
④ Aldgate – Chesham: 2 Züge pro Stunde
Zusätzliche Züge in der Hauptverkehrszeit von/nach Chesham bzw. Amersham verkehren teils als Express zwischen Moor Park und Harrow-on-the-Hill sowie zwischen Harrow-on-the-Hill und Finchley Road. Zwischen Wembley Park und Harrow-on-the-Hill stehen der Metropolitan Line vier Gleise exklusiv zur Verfügung.

Die heutige Metropolitan Line umfasst den Großteil der Strecken, die einst von der *Metropolitan Railway* befahren wurden. Darunter war die erste städtische Untergrundbahn der Welt (1863) zwischen Paddington und Farringdon (siehe Circle Line). Die *Metropolitan Railway* wurde schnell in alle Richtungen verlängert, in den siebziger Jahren des 19. Jahrhunderts vor allem Richtung Nordwesten durch damals größtenteils unbebautes Gebiet. Bereits 1889 fuhren die Züge bis Chesham und 1892 bis Aylesbury (ca. 60 km von Baker Street). Das Gebiet entlang der *Metropolitan Railway* wurde bald als ‚Metroland' bekannt, denn viele Siedlungsprojekte wurden direkt von der Bahngesellschaft vorangetrieben. Bis 1935/36 fuhren die Dampfzüge der *Metropolitan Railway* zu weit entfernten Zielen wie Brill oder Verney Junction, beide etwa 20 km westlich von Aylesbury.

Der 11 km lange Abzweig von Harrow nach Uxbridge wurde 1904 eröffnet. Mehrere Stationen wurden erst später

During daytime off-peak hours, the Metropolitan Line offers the following services:
① Aldgate/Baker Street – Uxbridge: 8 trains per hour
② Baker Street – Watford: 4 trains per hour
③ Aldgate – Amersham: 2 trains per hour
④ Aldgate – Chesham: 2 trains per hour
Some of the additional rush-hour trains to/from Chesham and Amersham run express between Moor Park and Harrow-on-the-Hill and between Harrow and Finchley Road. Between Wembley Park and Harrow, the Metropolitan Line has four exclusive tracks.

Today's Metropolitan Line covers most of the routes formerly served by the 'Metropolitan Railway', which began operating along the world's first urban underground route between Paddington and Farringdon in 1863 (see Circle Line). The original Metropolitan Railway quickly began to grow in all directions, notably in the 1870s, when it was extended as a surface railway towards the northwest, running mainly through then still sparsely populated areas. By 1889, it had reached Chesham, and in 1892, Aylesbury (about 60 km from Baker Street). The area along the Metropolitan Railway soon became known as Metro-Land, with many housing estates being promoted directly by the railway company. Until 1935/36, Metropolitan steam trains used to serve such remote destinations as Brill and Verney Junction, each about 20 km west of Aylesbury.

In 1904, an 11 km branch was opened from Harrow to Uxbridge, and several stations were added at a later date

Watford (zur Schließung vorgesehener Bahnhof | *station to be abandoned*)

eingefügt, nachdem die Bebauung dichter geworden war. Diese Strecke war eigentlich ein Projekt der *District Railway*, als Teil des Astes von Ealing, der jetzt von der Piccadilly Line befahren wird. Ab 1910 fuhren Züge beider Gesellschaften nach Uxbridge.

Der elektrische Betrieb begann auf der innerstädtischen Tunnelstrecke und oberirdisch bis nach Uxbridge im Jahr 1905. Während auf diesem Ast elektrische Triebwagen eingesetzt wurden, verkehrten Richtung Aylesbury weiterhin lokbespannte Züge mit Abteilwagen, bis Harrow nun allerdings mit Elektrolokomotiven.

Der Abschnitt von Finchley Road bis Wembley Park wurde zwischen 1913 und 1915 viergleisig ausgebaut. Während der 1920er Jahre wurde die *Metropolitan Railway* bis Rickmansworth elektrifiziert und 1925 ein 3 km langer

as the population grew in the area. This branch was actually promoted by the District Railway as an extension of their line from Ealing (now served by the Piccadilly Line); from 1910 it was served by both companies.

In 1905, electric service began on both the original underground line and the surface route to Uxbridge. Whereas EMUs with open saloon cars began operating to Uxbridge, destinations northwest of Harrow were served by loco-hauled trains with compartment carriages, the electric locomotives being swapped for steam ones at Harrow.

As service frequencies increased, the section between Finchley Road and Wembley Park was quadrupled in 1913/15. During the 1920s, electric operation was extended to Rickmansworth, and the 3 km branch to

Metropolitan Line

65.3 km (~ 9.5 km unterirdisch | *underground*), 34 Bahnhöfe | *stations*

6.4 km gemeinsam mit | *shared with* Circle and Hammersmith & City Lines
8.6 km gemeinsam mit | *shared with* Piccadilly Line

10-01-1863: Baker Street – Farringdon
23-12-1865: Farringdon – Moorgate
13-04-1868: Baker Street – Swiss Cottage
12-07-1875: Moorgate – Liverpool Street
18-11-1876: Liverpool Street – Aldgate
30-06-1879: Swiss Cottage – West Hampstead
24-11-1879: West Hampstead – Willesden Green
02-08-1880: Willesden Green – Harrow-on-the-Hill
25-05-1885: Harrow-on-the-Hill – Pinner
01-09-1887: Pinner – Rickmansworth
08-07-1889: Rickmansworth – Chesham
01-09-1892: Chalfont & Latimer – Amersham (– Aylesbury)
14-10-1893: + Wembley Park
04-07-1904: Harrow-on-the-Hill – Uxbridge
25-09-1905: + Ickenham
26-05-1906: + Rayners Lane, Eastcote
21-05-1908: + Preston Road
09-05-1910: + Moor Park
05-08-1912: + Ruislip Manor
17-11-1913: + West Harrow
22-03-1915: + North Harrow
28-06-1923: + Northwick Park
10-12-1923: + Hillingdon
02-11-1925: Moor Park – Watford
13-11-1933: + Northwood Hills

Elektrischer Betrieb | *Electric service:*
1905 Aldgate – Uxbridge
1925 Harrow-on-the-Hill – Rickmansworth
1960 Rickmansworth – Amersham / Chesham

Preston Road

Abzweig von Moor Park nach Watford in Betrieb genommen. Kurz darauf erfolgte der viergleisige Ausbau bis nach Harrow.

1932 erhielt die *Metropolitan Railway* schließlich noch einen weiteren Ast von Wembley Park nach Stanmore zur Erschließung eines Neubaugebiets. Ein Jahr später ging die Bahngesellschaft im öffentlichen Betrieb *London Transport* auf und wurde fortan als **Metropolitan Line** bezeichnet. Bald darauf wurde der Betrieb westlich von Aylesbury eingestellt. Zur Beseitigung des Engpasses zwischen Finchley Road und Baker Street wurden zwei weitere Röhrentunnel gebaut und der Ast nach Stanmore sowie zwei der vier Gleise zwischen Finchley Road und Wembley Park 1939 am U-Bahnhof Baker Street an die Bakerloo Line angeschlossen (siehe Jubilee Line).

Die Metropolitan Line wurde erst 1960 bis Amersham und Chesham elektrifiziert, der Betrieb auf dem Abschnitt Amersham – Aylesbury wurde an British Rail übergeben. Bis 1962 wurde die Strecke bis zum Abzweig Watford South viergleisig ausgebaut. Die Express-Gleise zwischen Harrow und diesem Abzweig sowie die zweigleisige Strecke westlich davon werden von den halbstündlichen Dieseltriebwagen der *Chiltern Railway* von/nach Marylebone mitbenutzt.

Mittelfristig ist für die Metropolitan Line eine 3 km lange Verbindung zwischen Croxley und Watford High Street unter Nutzung einer ehemaligen Eisenbahntrasse geplant. Der heutige Endpunkt Watford wird dann aufgegeben, die Metropolitan-Züge werden ab ca. 2020 bis Watford Junction im Mischbetrieb mit London Overground fahren. [www.croxleyraillink.com]

Watford opened in 1925. Soon after, another pair of tracks was added to the Wembley Park – Harrow section.

In 1932, yet another branch was built, this time from Wembley Park to Stanmore, running mainly through open countryside to serve future housing estates. A year later, in 1933, the Metropolitan Railway was integrated into the publicly owned 'London Transport' and became the ***Metropolitan Line****. As a consequence, services beyond Aylesbury were withdrawn soon afterwards. To eliminate the bottleneck between Finchley Road and Baker Street, two tube tunnels were excavated, and the Stanmore branch plus the slow tracks between Wembley Park and Finchley Road were linked to the Bakerloo Line at Baker Street in 1939 (see Jubilee Line).*

The Metropolitan Line was eventually electrified from Rickmansworth to Amersham and Chesham in 1960, and services beyond Amersham were transferred to British Railways. By 1962, the route had become 4-track up to the Watford South Junction. The express tracks between Harrow-on-the-Hill and this junction, just like the two existing tracks beyond that point, are shared with half-hourly Chiltern Railway diesel services to/from Marylebone.

In the mid-term future, a link for the Metropolitan Line will be built from Croxley to Watford High Street by taking advantage of a former railway alignment. The present Watford terminus will be abandoned, and Metropolitan Line trains will instead continue on London Overground tracks to Watford Junction from around 2020. [www.croxleyraillink.com]

Preston Road > Wembley Park

Moor Park

Kilburn (Jubilee Line Bahnsteig | *platform*)

Farringdon

Harrow-on-the-Hill

Earl's Court (District Line-Knoten | *District Line hub*)

District Line

Mit acht verschiedenen Endpunkten stellt die District Line ein eigenes Netz (64,5 km) innerhalb des U-Bahn-Netzes dar. Außerhalb der Hauptverkehrszeiten gibt es folgende Linienführungen, die alle über Earl's Court führen:

① Ealing Broadway – Upminster: 6 Züge pro Stunde
② Richmond – Upminster: 6 Züge pro Stunde
③ Wimbledon – Tower Hill/Barking: 6 Züge pro Stunde
④ Wimbledon – Edgware Road: 6 Züge pro Stunde
⑤ Kensington Olympia – High Street Kensington: 3 Züge pro Stunde am Wochenende und 2 bei Messen.

Die *Metropolitan District Railway* wurde kurz nach Eröffnung der ersten Untergrundbahn 1863 von Paddington nach Farringdon gegründet. Die neue Gesellschaft wollte von Kensington in die City eine eigene Strecke bauen, die dann gemeinsam mit der *Metropolitan Railway* eine Ringlinie bilden sollte. Die Strecke entlang der Themse wurde bis 1871 zusammen mit dem Victoria Embankment, einer Uferpromenade, errichtet. Die *District Railway* wurde in den folgenden Jahren vor allem Richtung Westen verlängert, so 1874 bis Hammersmith und von dort dann weiter über die bereits bestehende Strecke der L&SWR (*London & South Western Railway*) nach Richmond. 1879 wurde auch der Ast nach Ealing Broadway fertiggestellt. Wie bei der *Metropolitan Railway* brachten auch die neuen District-Strecken eine rege Bautätigkeit entlang der Bahn mit sich. 1880 erreichte der südliche Ast das Themse-Ufer an der Putney Bridge. Als nächstes folgte 1883 der Ast von Acton Town nach Hounslow (heute Teil der Piccadilly

With eight different termini, the District Line represents a network of its own (64.5 km) within the London Underground system. During off-peak hours, the following services, all running through Earl's Court, are operated:

① Ealing Broadway – Upminster: 6 trains per hour
② Richmond – Upminster: 6 trains per hour
③ Wimbledon – Tower Hill/Barking: 6 trains per hour
④ Wimbledon – Edgware Road: 6 trains per hour
⑤ Kensington Olympia – High Street Kensington: 3 trains per hour on weekends and 2 during exhibitions.

The 'Metropolitan District Railway' was founded soon after the opening of the first underground route from Paddington to Farringdon in 1863. The new company intended to build a line from Kensington to the City, which would then form a circular line with the Metropolitan Railway's routes. The southern side of the circle was developed together with the Victoria Embankment along the River Thames, and completed in stages by 1871. In the following years, the District Railway mainly expanded towards the west, e.g. to Hammersmith in 1874, and then on to Richmond over L&SWR tracks (London & South Western Railway). In 1879, a branch to Ealing Broadway was added to the District network. As with the Metropolitan Railway, the building of new railways brought about a rapid increase in housing development in the newly served areas. In 1880, the southern branch reached the Thames riverside at Putney Bridge. The next branch to follow was in 1883 from Acton Town to Hounslow (now

Southfields (während des Wimbledon-Tennis-Turniers | *during Wimbledon Championships*)

Line). Die Verlängerung über die Themse von Putney Bridge bis Wimbledon wurde von der L&SWR gebaut, aber ab 1889 von der District befahren. Anfang des 20. Jahrhunderts ging der Netzausbau im Westen Londons weiter. Der Ast nach South Harrow wurde 1903 eröffnet, weiter nach Uxbridge ging es 1910 auf der Strecke der *Metropolitan Railway* (heute von der Piccadilly Line befahren).

Der Ausbau im Osten der Stadt schritt langsamer voran. Gleichzeitig mit der Vollendung der Ringlinie 1884 wurde auch eine Verlängerung nach Whitechapel mit einem Verbindungstunnel zur East London Line in Betrieb genommen. Kurz vor der Jahrhundertwende begann die District mit dem Bau einer weiteren, 3 km langen unterirdischen Strecke, um in Bromley-by-Bow einen Anschluss an die LT&SR (*London, Tilbury & Southend Railway*) zu schaffen, über deren Gleise sie dann weiter Richtung Barking und Upminster fahren konnte.

part of the Piccadilly Line). The extension across the River Thames from Putney Bridge to Wimbledon was actually built by the L&SWR (1889), but the District Railway was granted running powers on it. The District's expansion into the western suburbs continued into the early 20th century, with a branch to South Harrow opening in 1903. Trains started running through to Uxbridge on the Metropolitan Railway in 1910 (now served by the Piccadilly Line).

The expansion of the District Railway was less dynamic at the eastern end. The completion of the missing section of the Circle Line was not achieved until 1884, when an extension to Whitechapel with a link to the East London Railway was also opened. Just before the turn of the century, the District began to construct another 3 km underground route to link its own lines to the LT&SR (London Tilbury & Southend Railway) west of Bromley-by-

District Line

64.5 km (~ 14 km unterirdisch | *underground*), 60 Bahnhöfe | *stations*

20.8 km gemeinsam mit | *shared with* Circle and Hammersmith & City Lines
1.5 km gemeinsam mit | *shared with* Piccadilly Line

{31-03-1858: Bromley-by-Bow – Barking}
01-10-1868: Edgware Road – Gloucester Road
24-12-1868: Gloucester Road – Westminster
{01-01-1869: Hammersmith Grove Rd – Richmond}
12-04-1869: Gloucester Road – West Brompton
30-05-1870: Westminster – Blackfriars
03-07-1871: Blackfriars – Mansion House
30-10-1871: + Earl's Court
{01-02-1872: Earl's Court – Kensington Olympia}
{01-04-1873: + Ravenscourt Park}
09-09-1874: Earl's Court – Hammersmith
01-06-1877: Hammersmith – Richmond
01-07-1879: Turnham Green – Ealing Broadway
01-03-1880: West Brompton – Putney Bridge
06-10-1884: Mansion House – Whitechapel
{01-05-1885: Barking – Upminster}
03-06-1889: Putney Bridge – Wimbledon
02-06-1902: Whitechapel – Bromley-by-Bow (– Upminster)
11-06-1902: + Bow Road
23-06-1902: + Stepney Green
09-10-1905: + Barons Court
01-02-1912: + Stamford Brook
17-12-1934: + Upminster Bridge
13-05-1935: + Elm Park

1905 elektrischer Betrieb außer | *electric service except*
1908 East Ham – Barking
1932 Barking – Upminster
1946 Earl's Court – Kensington Olympia

Sloane Square (kürzlich modernisierter Bahnhof | *recently refurbished station*)

Ende des 19. Jahrhunderts, als die ersten elektrischen Röhrenbahnen ihren Betrieb aufnahmen, war es immer deutlicher geworden, dass sowohl die District als auch die Metropolitan etwas tun mussten, um den Komfort für die Fahrgäste vor allem auf den mit Rauch verschmutzten unterirdischen Strecken zu verbessern. Die Elektrifizierung der District-Strecken war 1905 abgeschlossen.

Bis 1932 bekam die District eigene Gleise bis Upminster. Gleichzeitig übernahm die Piccadilly Line einige Fahrten auf dem Hounslow-Ast (die District fuhr dort noch bis 1964), den Ast nach Uxbridge übernahm die Piccadilly Line 1933.

Der Richmond-Ast gehört bis heute zum staatlichen Bahnnetz von Network Rail. Dieser Abschnitt wird gemeinsam mit der North London Line, die seit 2007 Teil des London Overground-Netzes ist, befahren.

Plaistow

Bow, and share tracks from there onwards to Barking and Upminster.

Towards the end of the 19th century, when the first electrically operated tube lines were being brought into service, it became evident that the District as well as the Metropolitan Railway had to do something to improve travel conditions for passengers, especially in the still smoke-filled tunnels. As a result, by late 1905, most of the District routes had been electrified.

By 1932, two separate tracks had been laid for the District Railway all the way to Upminster. At the same time, some services on the Hounslow branch were transferred to the Piccadilly Line, the District Line sharing that route until 1964. In 1933, the Uxbridge branch also became part of the Piccadilly Line in lieu of the District Line.

The national infrastructure company Network Rail is still responsible for the Richmond branch, which the District Line shares with North London Line trains, which are now part of the London Overground network.

Chiswick Park (Eingangsgebäude von Charles Holden | *station building designed by Charles Holden*)

Bombardier S7 stock

Upminster Bridge

West Brompton
(Metro-Cammell D stock)

Barons Court

Finchley Central (Northern Line)

Tube Lines

Nachdem die *Subsurface*-Strecken (Unterpflasterbahnen) für dampfbetriebene Züge während der sechziger und siebziger Jahre des 19. Jahrhunderts in offener Bauweise gebaut worden waren, wurde klar, dass diese Bauweise in der Innenstadt nicht angewandt werden kann, da die Beeinträchtigungen an der Oberfläche zu erheblich wären. Der erste tief liegende Tunnel wurde unter der Themse bereits 1843 errichtet und später in die *East London Railway* integriert. Mit der von James Henry Greathead entwickelten Schildvortriebsmethode entstand 1890 die erste elektrische ‚Röhrenbahn' (*Tube*) von der City bis Stockwell (siehe S. 90) und erfreute sich großer Beliebtheit, so dass im Laufe des folgenden Jahrzehnts zahlreiche Pläne für weitere *Tube*-Linien kreuz und quer durch die Innenstadt erarbeitet wurden. Sowohl Tunnel als auch Stationen wurden von vertikalen Schächten aus gegraben, so dass an der Oberfläche von den Bauarbeiten wenig zu merken war. Der Durchmesser der Streckentunnel wurde mit nur 3,55 m festgelegt (der heutige weltweite Standard bei eingleisigen Röhrentunneln liegt bei 5-6 m), in den Stationen mit 6,5 m. Die Strecken verlaufen in einer durchschnittlichen Tiefe von 20 m meist durch eine Tonschicht, welche sich besonders gut für derartige unterirdische Bauarbeiten eignet.

Auch wenn der Begriff *Tube* heute für das gesamte U-Bahn-Netz sogar offiziell benutzt wird, besteht das eigentliche *Tube*-Netz aus folgenden Linien:

- Northern Line
- Central Line
- Bakerloo Line
- Piccadilly Line
- Victoria Line
- Jubilee Line
- Waterloo & City Line

Once most of the subsurface underground routes for steam-powered trains had been built during the 1860s and 1870s, it became clear that the cut-and-cover method could not be used for lines penetrating the central area of the city, as this method of construction had caused too much disruption at the surface. The first deep-level tunnel under the River Thames had already opened in 1843, and was later incorporated into the East London Railway. Later, James Henry Greathead developed a new method which used an iron shield, resulting in the first electric 'tube' line, opened in 1890 to link the City to Stockwell (see p. 90). It gained immediate popularity, and during the following decade many similar lines were designed all across central London. Tunnels as well as stations were excavated from shafts, thus causing as little disturbance at the surface as possible. The diameter of the running tunnels was eventually fixed at approximately 3.55 m (the modern worldwide standard for single-track bored tunnels being 5-6 m), and the station tunnels at 6.5 m. The tube tunnels run at an average depth of 20 m and mostly through clay, ideal for subterranean excavation.

Although the term 'Tube' is now loosely used for any line forming part of the London Underground network, the proper tube network comprises the following lines:

- *Northern Line*
- *Central Line*
- *Bakerloo Line*
- *Piccadilly Line*
- *Victoria Line*
- *Jubilee Line*
- *Waterloo & City Line*

Aufgrund des stark eingeschränkten Tunnelprofils ist auch der Wagenpark dementsprechend beengt. Die Fahrzeuge sind zwar 2,62-2,64 m breit und 16,09-17,77 m lang, aber nur 2,88 m hoch (die *Subsurface*-Züge sind 80 cm höher). Die Fußbodenhöhe liegt bei 60 cm über Schienenoberkante, einen stufenlosen Einstieg gibt es aber nur an den neueren Stationen der Jubilee Line und manchen Stationen der Victoria Line. An Bahnsteigen, die sowohl von *Tube*- als auch von *Subsurface*- (im Fall der Piccadilly Line) bzw. London Overground-Zügen (im Fall der Bakerloo Line) benutzt werden, muss man etwa 15 cm in den Zug hinuntersteigen, sonst meist eine Stufe hinauf.

Mit einer Länge von 263,5 km (+ 21 km gemeinsam mit anderen Strecken) stellen die *Tube*-Linien etwa zwei Drittel des Gesamtnetzes der Londoner U-Bahn dar. Davon sind etwa 154 km unterirdisch. Mit der geplanten Verlängerung der Northern Line nach Battersea wird sich das *Tube*-Netz bis Ende des Jahrzehnts um rund 3 km vergrößern.

Due to the small profile of the running tunnels, the rolling stock used on these lines is also of limited size. Although the trains are 2.62-2.64 m wide and 16.09-17.77 m long, they are just 2.88 m high (the subsurface stock is 800 mm higher). The floor height is approximately 600 mm above the top of the rails, level access into the cars only being provided at the new Jubilee Line and some Victoria Line stations. At stations served by both tube and subsurface stock (as on the Piccadilly Line) or by tube and London Overground stock (as on the Bakerloo Line), an approximately 150 mm step down is required, while at most standard tube stations an equally high step upwards is necessary for boarding.

With a total length of 263.5 km (+ 21 km of shared routes), the tube lines represent about two thirds of the entire London Underground network, with approx. 154 km actually lying underground. With the planned extension of the Northern Line to Battersea, the Tube network will grow by approximately 3 km by the end of the decade.

LU Tube Lines > Fahrzeuge | *Rolling Stock* (630 V DC)

Nummer *Number*	Anzahl *Quantity*	Einsatz *In service*	Hersteller *Manufacturer*	Typ *Class*	Länge *Length*	Breite *Width*	Ausgeliefert *Delivered*
3231...3567, 4231...4567	36 (x7)	BAK	Metro-Cammell	1972 stock	16.0 m	2.64 m	1972
100...253,300...453, 500...696, 854...897	86½ (x6)	PIC	Metro-Cammell	1973 stock	17.5 m	2.63 m	1973
91001-91349, 92001...93464	85 (x8)	CEN	ASEA/Adtranz	1992 stock	16.3 m	2.62 m	1992
65501-65510, 67501-67510	5 (x4)	W&C	ASEA/Adtranz	1992 stock	16.3 m	2.62 m	1992
51501-51726, 52501...53726	106 (x6)	NOR	Alstom	1995 stock	17.8 m	2.63 m	1996-1997
96001-96126, 96201...96725	63 (x7)	JUB	Alstom	1996 stock	17.8 m	2.63 m	1996
11001-11094, 12001...14094	47 (x8)	VIC	Bombardier	2009 stock	13.3 m	2.62 m	2009

Kentish Town

Northern Line

Die Northern Line hat nicht nur mehrere Außenäste, sondern auch zwei Innenstadtstrecken, eine über das West End (Charing Cross) und eine über die City (Bank), die von den Zügen der beiden nördlichen Hauptäste abwechselnd alle 3-4 Minuten befahren werden. Manche Züge über Charing Cross enden in Kennington und werden in einigen Jahren bis Battersea weitergeführt. Der Ast nach Mill Hill East wird außerhalb der Hauptverkehrszeiten als Shuttle betrieben. Seit 2014 wird auf der Northern Line weitgehend automatisch (ATO) gefahren.

Auch wenn die Northern Line unter diesem Namen erst im Jahre 1937 auf dem Londoner U-Bahn-Netzplan erschien, so gehen ihre Anfänge auf das Jahr 1890 zurück, als Londons erste elektrische Untergrundbahn, die 5,6 km lange *City & South London Railway*, zwischen King William Street (in der Nähe der heutigen Station Monument) und Stockwell in Betrieb ging. Zehn Jahre später wurden die Tunnel unter der Themse neu gebaut, die übrigen erweitert und die Linie an beiden Enden verlängert.

In der Zwischenzeit hatte ein regelrechter U-Bahn-Bauboom in ganz London eingesetzt, unter anderem wurde 1907 die *Charing Cross, Euston & Hampstead*

The Northern Line has not only several outer branches, but also two alternative routes through central London, the Bank or City branch and the Charing Cross or West End branch, with each branch served alternately every 3-4 minutes by trains from the two main northern legs. Most trains via Charing Cross terminate at Kennington, but in a few years they will continue to Battersea. The branch to Mill Hill East is served by a shuttle train during off-peak hours. Since 2014, automatic train operation (ATO) has been available on the Northern Line.

Although the Northern Line only appeared on the London Underground map with this name in 1937, its origins go back to 1890, when the first electrically powered underground line opened in London between King William Street (near the present Monument station) and Stockwell: the 5.6 km 'City & South London Railway'. Ten years later, new tunnels were built under the River Thames, the other tunnels were widened, and the line was extended in both directions.

In the meantime, a real construction boom for further tube lines had begun all over London, and the 'Charing Cross, Euston

Embankment

East Finchley

Railway, später einfach als *Hampstead Tube* bezeichnet, von Charing Cross bis Golders Green mit einem Abzweig bis Archway in Betrieb genommen. Bis 1924 wurde diese Linie Richtung Edgware durch größtenteils unbebautes Gebiet verlängert. Bald darauf wurde die *City & South London Railway* mit der *Hampstead Tube* zu einem Linienbündel verknüpft und 1926 nach Süden bis Morden verlängert.

Ende der 1930er Jahre, nachdem 1933 alle U-Bahn-Strecken von *London Transport* übernommen worden

& Hampstead Railway', later simply referred to as the 'Hampstead Tube', opened from Charing Cross to Golders Green and Archway in 1907. By 1924, this line had been extended north to Edgware through mostly undeveloped areas. Soon after, the City & South London Railway was connected to the Hampstead Tube for joint operation and extended south to Morden in 1926.

Towards the end of the 1930s, with all the Underground lines having been taken over by London Transport

Northern Line

59.1 km (~ 40.4 km unterirdisch | *underground*), 50 Bahnhöfe | *stations*

{22-08-1867: [Finsbury Park –] East Finchley – Mill Hill East [– Edgware]}
{01-04-1872: Finchley Central – High Barnet}
18-12-1890: Stockwell – King William Street
24-02-1900: [X] Borough – King William Street
25-02-1900: Borough – Moorgate
03-06-1900: Stockwell – Clapham Common
17-11-1901: Moorgate – Angel
12-05-1907: Angel – Euston
22-06-1907: Charing Cross – Archway
22-06-1907: Camden Town – Golders Green
06-04-1914: Charing Cross – Embankment
19-11-1923: Golders Green – Hendon Central
20-04-1924: Euston (Bank branch) – Camden Town
18-08-1924: Hendon Central – Edgware
27-10-1924: + Burnt Oak
13-09-1926: Embankment – Kennington
13-09-1926: Clapham Common – Morden
06-12-1926: + Balham
{01-03-1933: + West Finchley}
03-07-1939: Archway – East Finchley
14-04-1940: East Finchley – High Barnet
19-01-1941: + Highgate
18-05-1941: Finchley Central – Mill Hill East
2020: Kennington – Battersea

Oval

Kentish Town

waren, bekam die Northern Line eine Verlängerung von Archway Richtung Norden hauptsächlich über bestehende Vorortbahnstrecken. Mit Erreichen von High Barnet 1940 und Mill Hill East 1941 war die heutige Northern Line vollendet.

Zu Erschließung eines Entwicklungsgebiets am Südufer der Themse ist derzeit eine rund 3 km lange Verlängerung von Kennington bis Battersea geplant. Die zu bauenden Tunnelröhren werden von der bestehenden Schleife am Bahnhof Kennington ausfädeln. Die Eröffnung des Neubauabschnitts könnte 2020 erfolgen.

Bis Mitte der 2020er Jahre soll die Northern Line in zwei voneinander unabhängige Linien getrennt werden.

in 1933, the Northern Line was extended north from Archway, mostly over existing railways. It reached High Barnet in 1940 and Mill Hill East in 1941, completing the present layout of the Northern Line.

Currently, a 3 km extension from Kennington to Battersea is planned to serve a redevelopment area on the south bank of the River Thames. The tube tunnels will be linked to the existing loop at Kennington. This new section may open in 2020.

By the mid-2020s, the Northern Line may have been split into two completely separate lines.

Balham

Charing Cross

Tottenham Court Road

Northern Line stock

Clapham North

Tottenham Court Road

Tottenham Court Road

White City

Central Line

Auf dem zentralen Abschnitt der Central Line, Londons wichtigster Ost-West-Verbindung, welche sowohl die Einkaufsstraße Oxford Street als auch das Bankenviertel in der City of London erschließt, fahren die Züge im 2½-Minuten-Takt: je 9 Züge pro Stunde zwischen West Ruislip und Epping sowie zwischen Ealing Broadway und Hainault (drei davon weiter bis Woodford), dazu kommen je 3 Züge pro Stunde zwischen Northolt und Loughton sowie drei zwischen White City und Newbury Park. Der mittlere, unterirdische Abschnitt stellt eine typische *Tube*-Linie dar, die Außenstrecken verlaufen größtenteils an der Oberfläche. Im Anschluss an die Auslieferung der neuen Fahrzeuge wurde Ende der 1990er Jahre auf der Central Line der halbautomatische Betrieb (ATO) eingeführt.

Die *Central London Railway* wurde am 30. Juli 1900 von Shepherd's Bush bis Bank (9,3 km) in Betrieb genommen. Bis 1903 wurden die Waggons von elektrischen Lokomotiven gezogen, dann jedoch durch Triebwagen ersetzt. 1912 kam ein kurzer Abschnitt bis zum Fernbahnhof Liverpool Street dazu. Ab 1920 konnte über Gleise der *Great Western Railway* bis Ealing gefahren werden. Wesentliche Erweiterungen geschahen erst Mitte der 1940er Jahre, teils unterirdisch, teils durch Übernahme bestehender Vorortbahnen, so nach West Ruislip 1948. Der 1949 aufgenommene Betrieb auf den Gleisen der *Great Eastern* Richtung Epping wurde von 1957 bis 1994 bis Ongar (9,7 km) ausgedehnt. Auf einem langen Abschnitt der Strecke Epping – Ongar findet heute ein Museumsbetrieb mit Dampf- und Dieselzügen statt [www.eorailway.co.uk].

The Central Line is London's most important east-west link, serving both the shopping area around Oxford Street as well as the business district in the City of London, and on the central section there is a train every 2½ minutes: 9 trains per hour between West Ruislip and Epping as well as between Ealing Broadway and Hainault (with three continuing to Woodford); and in addition, 3 trains per hour between Northolt and Loughton as well as between White City and Newbury Park. The central underground section is a typical tube line, but most of the outer sections lie above ground. Following the arrival of new rolling stock, automatic train operation (ATO) was introduced on the Central Line in the late-1990s.

The 'Central London Railway' was opened on 30 July 1900 from Shepherd's Bush to Bank (9.3 km). The passenger carriages were hauled by electric locomotives until 1903, when they were replaced with motorised cars. In 1912, the line was extended to Liverpool Street to provide a link to the mainline rail services towards the eastern suburbs. In 1920, trains started to run to Ealing over tracks belonging to the 'Great Western Railway'. Large-scale expansion, however, only took place in the mid-1940s, partly underground and partly by taking over existing suburban rail lines, e.g. to West Ruislip in 1948. Service on Great Eastern tracks to Epping started in 1949, and between 1957 and 1994, Central Line trains even continued to Ongar (9.7 km). Much of the Epping to Ongar line is now a heritage line with steam and diesel operation [www.eorailway.co.uk].

Ealing Broadway

South Woodford

Central Line

73.3 km (~ 26 km unterirdisch | *underground*), 49 Bahnhöfe | *stations*

{22-08-1856: [Stratford –] Leyton – Loughton}
{24-04-1865: Loughton – Epping [– Ongar]}
30-07-1900: Shepherd's Bush – Bank
24-09-1900: + Bond Street
{01-05-1903: [Ilford –] Newbury Park – Woodford}
{15-06-1903: North Acton – *Greenford East Junction*}
{01-10-1904: *Greenford East Junction* – Greenford}
{02-04-1906: Greenford – West Ruislip}
14-05-1908: Shepherd's Bush – Wood Lane (> White City)
28-07-1912: Bank – Liverpool Street
03-08-1920: Wood Lane – Ealing Broadway
05-11-1923: + North Acton, West Acton
04-12-1946: Liverpool Street – Stratford
05-05-1947: Stratford – Leytonstone
30-06-1947: North Acton – Greenford
14-12-1947: Leytonstone – Woodford
14-12-1947: Leytonstone – Newbury Park
31-05-1948: Newbury Park – Hainault
21-11-1948: Greenford – West Ruislip
21-11-1948: Woodford – Loughton
21-11-1948: Woodford – Hainault
25-09-1949: Loughton – Epping

Bank

Shepherd's Bush

White City

Central Line stock

Epping

Gants Hill

Lancaster Gate

Waterloo & City Line

Die Waterloo & City Line wurde 1898 als eine der ersten elektrischen U-Bahnen der Welt von der *London & South Western Railway* eröffnet, um deren Kopfbahnhof Waterloo mit der City zu verbinden. Sie wurde erst 1994 von der ehemaligen *British Rail* an London Underground übergeben, der blau geprägte Anstrich von Network Southeast blieb jedoch noch bis 2006 erhalten. Heute pendeln die 4-Wagen-Züge im 5-Minuten-Takt. Sonntags ist diese Linie geschlossen.

The Waterloo & City Line was built by the 'London & South Western Railway' to link their terminus at Waterloo to the City of London. When it opened in 1898, it was one of the first electric metro lines in the world. It was only handed over from British Rail to London Underground in 1994, though the trains' blue-dominated Network Southeast livery was maintained until 2006. Today it is served every five minutes by 4-car shuttle trains. There is no Sunday service on this line.

Waterloo

Bank

Waterloo & City Line

2.4 km (völlig unterirdisch | *completely underground*)

2 Bahnhöfe | *Stations*

{08-08-1898 Waterloo – Bank}

05-04-1994 Waterloo – Bank [London Underground]

Paddington

Bakerloo Line

Die Bakerloo Line kann in zwei Abschnitte unterteilt werden: 1) die eigentliche *Tube* von Elephant & Castle bis Queen's Park (10,9 km) und 2) die oberirdische Verlängerung auf den Network Rail-Gleisen von Queen's Park bis Harrow & Wealdstone (12,7 km) im Mischbetrieb mit London Overground-Zügen, die alle 20 Minuten Euston mit Watford Junction verbinden. Die Bakerloo Line fährt alle drei Minuten vom südlichen Endpunkt ab. Drei Züge pro Stunde fahren über Queen's Park hinaus bis Stonebridge Park, sechs bis Harrow & Wealdstone.

Die *Baker Street & Waterloo Railway* wurde 1906/07 zwischen Elephant & Castle und Edgware Road in Betrieb genommen. 1915 erreichte sie Queen's Park, wo sie an die Vorortgleise der *London & North Western Railway* (LNWR) nach Watford angeschlossen wurde. 1982 wurde der 1917 bis Watford Junction ausgedehnte Betrieb nach Stonebridge Park verkürzt, seit 1984 fahren die Züge nun bis Harrow & Wealdstone.

Im Norden bekam die Bakerloo Line 1939 einen Ast von Baker Street nach Stanmore, nachdem für die Metropolitan Line zwischen Baker Street und Finchley Road eine Entlastungsstrecke gebaut worden war. 1979 wurde daraus die neue Jubilee Line (siehe S. 106).

Eine Verlängerung der Bakerloo Line Richtung Süden nach Camberwell und weiter erschien immer wieder in den Planungen, auch derzeit ist sie wieder im Gespräch, entweder über Peckham Rye oder über die Old Kent Road nach Lewisham, um dort gegebenenfalls die Vorortbahn nach Hayes zu übernehmen.

The Bakerloo Line can be divided into two sections: 1) the proper tube line from Elephant & Castle to Queen's Park (10.9 km), and 2) the shared surface section running over Network Rail tracks from Queen's Park to Harrow & Wealdstone (12.7 km), where London Overground trains run every 20 minutes between Euston and Watford Junction. The Bakerloo Line departs from its southern terminus every three minutes, with three trains per hour continuing beyond Queen's Park to Stonebridge Park, and six to Harrow & Wealdstone.

The 'Baker Street & Waterloo Railway' was opened between Elephant & Castle and Edgware Road in 1906/07. In 1915, it reached Queen's Park, where it was linked to the suburban tracks of the 'London & North Western Railway' (LNWR) to Watford. In 1982, the through service to Watford Junction, introduced in 1917, was curtailed at Stonebridge Park, but it was extended to Harrow & Wealdstone in 1984.

In 1939, the Bakerloo Line received a northern branch from Baker Street to Stanmore after two relief tunnels had been built for the Metropolitan Line between Baker Street and Finchley Road. This branch became part of the new Jubilee Line in 1979 (see p. 106).

A southern extension of the Bakerloo Line from Elephant & Castle to Camberwell and beyond has reappeared on the table time and again, and the idea has once again recently been revived. Either via Peckham Rye or along Old Kent Road the line may reach Lewisham, from where it could take over the suburban line to Hayes.

Kensal Green
(links Zug der London Overground
London Overground train on the left track)

Harlesden

Harlesden

Bakerloo Line

23.6 km (~ 10.6 km unterirdisch | *underground*), 25 Bahnhöfe | *stations*

12.7 km gemeinsam mit | *shared with* London Overground

{20-07-1837: [Euston –] Queen's Park – Harrow & Wealdstone [– Watford]}
10-03-1906: Baker Street – Lambeth North
05-08-1906: Lambeth North – Elephant & Castle
27-03-1907: Baker Street – Marylebone
15-06-1907: Marylebone – Edgware Road
01-12-1913: Edgware Road – Paddington
31-01-1915: Paddington – Kilburn Park
11-02-1915: Kilburn Park – Queen's Park
10-05-1915: Queen's Park – Willesden Junction
06-06-1915: + Maida Vale
01-10-1916: + Kensal Green
16-04-1917: Willesden Junction – Harrow & Wealdstone [– Watford Jctn]
01-08-1917: + Stonebridge Park
03-07-1933: + South Kenton

Baker Street

Arnos Grove

Piccadilly Line

Außerhalb der Hauptverkehrszeiten fahren die Piccadilly-Züge von Cockfosters alle 5 Minuten zum Flughafen Heathrow, nämlich abwechselnd zum Terminal 5 und um die Schleife über Terminal 4. Der Ast nach Rayners Lane wird alle 10 Minuten bedient, wobei jeder zweite Zug nach Uxbridge weiterfährt. Auf der östlichen Strecke fahren die Züge im Abstand von wenigen Minuten bis Cockfosters, manche enden auch in Arnos Grove.

Die Piccadilly Line wurde 1906 als tief liegende Tunnelstrecke von Hammersmith bis Finsbury Park (14 km) teils zur Entlastung der District Line eröffnet. Eine kurze Zweiglinie von Holborn bis Aldwych kam 1907 hinzu, die 1994 geschlossen wurde. Bis in die frühen 1930er Jahre blieb die Linienführung der Piccadilly Line unverändert. 1933 erreichte sie im Norden Cockfosters (12 km). Im Westen hingegen wuchs die Piccadilly Line auf Kosten der District Line, indem sie 1932/33 die Strecke von 1884 nach Hounslow (bis 1964 Mischbetrieb) und die von 1910 nach Rayners Lane übernahm. Der Abschnitt von Hammersmith bis Turnham Green war bereits viergleisig.

Nach dieser großen Erweiterung veränderte sich die Streckenführung der Piccadilly Line erst wieder 1975, als eine unterirdische Verlängerung von Hounslow West bis Hatton Cross und 1977 weiter zum Flughafen Heathrow fertiggestellt war. 1986 wurde auch der Terminal 4 über eine 6 km lange eingleisige Schleife angeschlossen, am 27. März 2008 kam schließlich noch ein 2 km langer Abzweig zum Terminal 5 hinzu.

During off-peak hours, the Piccadilly Line runs to Heathrow Airport every five minutes, with trains alternating between Terminal 5 and the Terminal 4 loop. The route to Rayners Lane is served every 10 minutes, with every other train continuing to Uxbridge. At the eastern end, there is a train every few minutes to Cockfosters, with some services terminating at Arnos Grove.

The Piccadilly Line was opened in 1906 as a deep-level tube line between Hammersmith and Finsbury Park (14 km), partly to relieve the District Line. A short branch from Holborn to Aldwych was added in 1907, but it was permanently closed in 1994. The Piccadilly Line's layout remained unaltered until expansion began in the early 1930s. The 12 km northern extension reached Cockfosters in 1933. The western extensions, however, were realised by taking over two of the District Line branches in 1932/33, the 1884 route to Hounslow (which had mixed service until 1964) and the 1910 route to Rayners Lane. The section from Hammersmith to Turnham Green had already been equipped with four tracks.

After this massive expansion, the Piccadilly Line remained unchanged until it was extended 5 km underground from Hounslow West to Hatton Cross (1975) and Heathrow Airport (1977). In 1986, a 6 km single-track loop was added to serve the new Terminal 4, and finally on 27 March 2008, a 2 km branch to the new Terminal 5 completed the present line.

Earl's Court

LONDON Underground - Piccadilly Line

71 km (~ 38 km unterirdisch | *underground*), 53 Bahnhöfe | *stations*
8.6 km gemeinsam mit | *shared with* Metropolitan Line
1.5 km gemeinsam mit | *shared with* District Line

{01-06-1877: Hammersmith – Turnham Green} [District Railway]
{01-07-1879: Turnham Green – Ealing Broadway} [District Railway]
{01-05-1883: Acton Town – Hounslow Town} [District Railway]
{21-07-1884: Osterley – Hounslow West} [District Railway]
{01-04-1886: + Hounslow Central} [District Railway]
{23-06-1903: Ealing Common – South Harrow} [District Railway]
{04-07-1904: Rayners Lane – Uxbridge} [Metropolitan Railway]
{25-09-1905: + Ickenham} [Metropolitan Railway]
{26-05-1906: + Rayners Lane, Eastcote} [Metropolitan Railway]
15-12-1906: Hammersmith – Finsbury Park
08-01-1907: + South Kensington
11-04-1907: + Covent Garden
{16-04-1908: + Northfields} [District Railway]
{01-03-1910: South Harrow – Rayners Lane – Uxbridge} [District Railway]
{05-08-1912: + Ruislip Manor} [Metropolitan/District Railway]
{10-12-1923: + Hillingdon} [Metropolitan/District Railway]
04-07-1932: Hammersmith – South Harrow
19-09-1932: Finsbury Park – Arnos Grove
09-01-1933: Acton Town – Northfields
13-03-1933: Northfields – Hounslow West
13-03-1933: Arnos Grove – Oakwood
31-07-1933: Oakwood – Cockfosters
23-10-1933: South Harrow – Uxbridge
19-07-1975: Hounslow West – Hatton Cross
16-12-1977: Hatton Cross – Heathrow Terminals 1-2-3
12-04-1986: Hatton Cross – Heathrow Terminal 4 – Heathrow T1-2-3
27-03-2008: Heathrow T1-2-3 – Heathrow Terminal 5

Piccadilly Circus

Hammersmith

Acton Town

Covent Garden

Heathrow Terminals 1, 2, 3

Finsbury Park

South Kensington

Hounslow West

King's Cross St. Pancras

Covent Garden

Holborn

Oxford Circus

Victoria Line

Die Victoria Line verkehrt alle 2-3 Minuten, wobei im Norden manche Züge statt in Walthamstow Central bereits in Seven Sisters enden.

Die Victoria Line war 1968 die erste neue U-Bahn-Linie durch die Londoner Innenstadt seit dem Bauboom Anfang des 20. Jahrhunderts. Als komplette Neubaustrecke hat sie die einfachste Entstehungsgeschichte aller U-Bahn-Linien. Sie wurde in vier Stufen zwischen 1968 und 1971 in Betrieb genommen, die Station Pimlico folgte erst 1972. Auch wenn anfangs ein größeres Tunnelprofil in Erwägung gezogen worden war, entschied man sich schließlich für Standard-Röhrentunnel mit nur 3,55 m Durchmesser. Ursprünglich sollte auch diese Linie über bestehende Vorortbahnen in die Außenbezirke geführt werden, wovon später jedoch Abstand genommen wurde. Die Victoria Line verbindet mehrere Fernbahnhöfe und bietet an sechs Stationen eine bahnsteiggleiche Umsteigemöglichkeit zu anderen Linien. Sie ist außer der kurzen Waterloo & City Line die einzige vollkommen unterirdische Linie in London und wurde von Anfang an halbautomatisch im ATO-Modus betrieben.

The Victoria Line runs every 2-3 minutes, with some trains terminating at Seven Sisters instead of Walthamstow Central.

In 1968, the Victoria Line became the first new underground line to be opened across central London since the tube construction boom of the first decade of the 20th century. As the entire line was newly-built, its history is far less complex than that of the other lines. The Victoria Line was brought into service in four stages between 1968 and 1971, with Pimlico station following in 1972. Although a larger tunnel profile was initially considered, the final choice was for the standard tube tunnels with a diameter of just 3.55 m. Some early plans envisaged extensions over existing suburban rail routes to the outer districts, but none of them materialised. The Victoria Line connects several mainline termini and provides cross-platform interchange with other lines in six of its stations. Apart from the short Waterloo & City Line, the Victoria Line is the only line in London which lies completely underground. It was designed to be operated semi-automatically in ATO mode from its opening day.

Victoria Line stock

Highbury & Islington

Stockwell

Warren Street

Warren Street

Victoria Line

21.3 km (völlig unterirdisch | *totally underground*), 16 Bahnhöfe | *stations*

01-09-1968: Walthamstow Central – Highbury & Islington
01-12-1968: Highbury & Islington – Warren Street
07-03-1969: Warren Street – Victoria
23-07-1971: Victoria – Brixton
14-09-1972: + Pimlico

London Bridge

Jubilee Line

Außerhalb der Hauptverkehrszeiten verlässt die Jubilee Line wochentags den östlichen Endpunkt Stratford alle 3-4 Minuten. Etwa 12 von 20 Zügen pro Stunde fahren durch bis Stanmore, die anderen enden in Willesden Green oder Wembley Park.

Die Jubilee Line ist auf dem Netzplan der Londoner U-Bahn erst seit 1979 zu sehen. Ihre Strecke kann man in fünf Abschnitte einteilen, die jeweils einen anderen geschichtlichen Hintergrund haben:
1) Der nördlichste Abschnitt von Wembley Park bis Stanmore wurde 1932 als ein weiterer Ast der *Metropolitan Railway* eröffnet.
2) Der oberirdische Abschnitt von Finchley Road bis Wembley Park ist Teil der Verlängerung der ursprünglichen *Metropolitan Railway* nach Harrow-on-the-Hill von 1879-1880 (1913-1915 viergleisig ausgebaut). Die Jubilee Line bedient nun alle Zwischenbahnhöfe, während die Metropolitan Line als Express durchfährt.
3) Der unterirdische Abschnitt Baker Street – Finchley Road entstand 1939 als Entlastungsstrecke für die Metropolitan Line und wurde zusammen mit 1) und 2) an die Bakerloo Line übergeben.
4) Zur Entlastung der Bakerloo Line wurde der Abschnitt Baker Street – Green Park und weiter bis Charing Cross als Teil der geplanten *Fleet Line* errichtet. Diese wurde 1977 zum 25-jähriges Kronjubiläum von Queen Elizabeth II in Jubilee Line umbenannt und als solche 1979 von Charing Cross bis Stanmore eröffnet.

During off-peak hours on Mondays to Fridays, Jubilee Line trains leave the eastern terminus at Stratford every 3-4 minutes, with some 12 out of 20 trains running through to Stanmore, and the rest terminating at Willesden Green or Wembley Park.

The Jubilee Line only appeared on the London Underground map in 1979. Its present layout can be divided into five sections, each of which has a different history:
1) The northern section from Wembley Park to Stanmore opened in 1932 as another of several branches built by the Metropolitan Railway.
2) The surface Finchley Road – Wembley Park section is part of the original Metropolitan Railway extension to Harrow-on-the-Hill opened between 1879 and 1880 (and quadrupled between 1913 and 1915). The Jubilee Line now serves all intermediate stations, whereas the Metropolitan Line runs non-stop as an express metro line.
3) The underground Baker Street – Finchley Road section was opened in 1939 to relieve the Metropolitan Line, and together with 1) and 2) became a branch of the Bakerloo Line.
4) In order to reduce capacity constraints on the Bakerloo Line, the section from Baker Street to Green Park and further on to Charing Cross was built as part of the new Fleet Line, which was renamed the Jubilee Line when Queen Elizabeth II celebrated her silver jubilee in 1977. It opened from Charing Cross to Stanmore in 1979.

West Hampstead

5) In den 1990er Jahren wurde die 16 km lange Verlängerung der Jubilee Line über das Südufer der Themse und das damalige Entwicklungsgebiet Docklands in Angriff genommen. Der Abschnitt Green Park – Charing Cross ist seit Eröffnung der Verlängerung 1999 bis Stratford außer Betrieb. Auch wenn die auf der Jubilee Line eingesetzten Züge denen der anderen Tube-Linien entsprechen, wurden die Tunnel mit Schildvortriebsmaschinen mit einem Durchmesser von 4,35 m etwas großzügiger errichtet. Die unterirdischen Stationen wurden mit Bahnsteigtüren ausgestattet. Seit 2011 wird die Jubilee Line mit ATO betrieben.

5) In the 1990s, the 16 km 'Jubilee Line Extension' project from Green Park to Stratford was launched, taking the line to the south bank and the emerging Docklands area. Upon opening in 1999, the Green Park – Charing Cross section was closed. Although the trains in service on the Jubilee Line are similar to other Tube rolling stock, the deep-level tube tunnels were built slightly larger with a diameter of 4.35 m. The new underground stations were equipped with platform screen doors. Since 2011, the Jubilee Line has been operated in ATO (Automatic Train Operation) mode.

Canning Town (DLR darüber | *DLR on top*)

Foto Brendan Fox

Jubilee Line

37.2 km (~ 19 km unterirdisch | *underground*), 27 Bahnhöfe | *stations*

{30-06-1879: Finchley Road – West Hampstead} [Metropolitan]
{24-11-1879: West Hampstead – Willesden Green} [Metropolitan]
{02-08-1880: Willesden Green – Harrow-on-the-Hill} [Metropolitan]
{02-08-1880: + Neasden} [Metropolitan]
{12-05-1894: + Wembley Park} [Metropolitan]
{01-10-1909: + Dollis Hill} [Metropolitan]
{10-12-1932: Wembley Park – Stanmore} [Metropolitan]
{16-12-1934: + Queensbury} [Metropolitan]
{20-11-1939: Baker Street – Stanmore} [Bakerloo]
01-05-1979: (Charing Cross –) Green Park – Stanmore
14-05-1999: Stratford – North Greenwich
17-09-1999: North Greenwich – Bermondsey
24-09-1999: Bermondsey – Waterloo
07-10-1999: + London Bridge
20-11-1999: Waterloo – Green Park
20-11-1999: + Southwark
22-12-1999: + Westminster

Kilburn

Canary Wharf

Baker Street

Bond Street

Jubilee Line stock

Canary Wharf (Blick von der Docklands Light Railway | *view from Docklands Light Railway*)

North Greenwich

Gospel Oak (rechts Dieseltriebwagen nach Barking | *on the right, diesel unit to Barking*)

London Overground

Die Marke ‚London Overground' wurde am 11. November 2007 eingeführt, als *Transport for London* (TfL) begann, die Kontrolle einzelner Vorortbahnstrecken direkt zu übernehmen. Die Infrastruktur gehört weiterhin größtenteils zum staatlichen Netz von *Network Rail*, auf einigen Strecken herrscht Mischbetrieb mit anderen ‚Train Operating Companies' (TOC). Der Betrieb des Overground-Netzes wird derzeit von *London Overground Rail Operations* (LOROL) durchgeführt, einem Konsortium aus *Arriva UK Trains*, einer Tochterfirma der Deutschen Bahn, und *MTR Corporation* aus Hong Kong.

Das ursprüngliche London Overground-Netz umfasste die ehemalige Silverlink-*Franchise*, d.h. die Strecke Euston – Watford Junction sowie die North London Line (Richmond – Stratford) und die West London Line (Clapham Junction – Willesden Junction), außerdem die bislang nicht elektrifizierte Strecke Gospel Oak – Barking. Gleichzeitig wurde die East London Line (Shoreditch – New Cross/New Cross Gate) vom U-Bahn-Netz getrennt, für ihre Integration in das Overground-Netz modernisiert und im Norden über Dalston Junction bis Highbury & Islington auf einer Neubaustrecke teils auf alter Bahntrasse verlängert. Der moderne S-Bahn-Betrieb zwischen Dalston Junction und New Cross bzw. New Cross Gate wurde am 27. April 2010 aufgenommen. Im Süden wurde der Overground-Betrieb am 23. Mai 2010 auf dem bestehenden Netz bis Crystal Palace bzw. West Croydon ausgedehnt, im Norden erreichte die East London Line am 28. Feb. 2011 Highbury & Islington. Eine Art S-Bahn-Ring besteht schließlich seit dem 9. Dez. 2012,

The brand 'London Overground' was introduced on 11 November 2007, when Transport for London (TfL) began to take direct control of several suburban railway lines. Most of the infrastructure continues to be part of the national Network Rail, and on some routes, the Overground trains share tracks with other train operating companies (TOC). The actual operation of the Overground network is currently in the hands of London Overground Rail Operations (LOROL), a consortium of Arriva Trains UK (a subsidiary of Deutsche Bahn) and MTR Corporation of Hong Kong.

The initial London Overground network included the former Silverlink franchise, i.e. the Euston – Watford Junction route, the North London Line (Richmond – Stratford) as well as the West London Line (Clapham Junction – Willesden Junction), plus the Gospel Oak – Barking line, which is not yet electrified. At the same time, the East London Line (Shoreditch – New Cross/New Cross Gate) was separated from the London Underground network and modernised for its integration into the Overground network, while a northern extension via Dalston Junction to Highbury & Islington was added, partly reusing an old railway formation. The modern S-Bahn-style operation from Dalston Junction to New Cross and New Cross Gate was launched on 27 April 2010. In the south, Overground services were extended over existing tracks to Crystal Palace and West Croydon on 23 May 2010, and in the north, to Highbury & Islington on 28 February 2011. A kind of S-Bahn ring was completed on

Finchley Road & Frognal (North London Line)

als auch die Strecke Clapham Junction – Surrey Quays in das Overground-Netz integriert wurde. Dazu musste zuvor eine rund 1,5 km lange Spange zwischen Surrey Quays und Queens Road Peckham errichtet werden, auf der noch eine Zwischenstation vorgesehen ist. Für eine Fahrt auf der gesamten Ringstrecke muss allerdings mindestens zweimal umgestiegen werden, in Clapham Junction und Highbury & Islington. Von Stratford fahren die Züge alle 10 Minuten nach Willesden Junction, vier Züge fahren weiter nach Richmond und zwei nach Clapham Junction. Während der südliche Teil des Richmond-Astes durch die District Line verstärkt wird, gibt es zwischen Willesden Junction und Clapham Junction zwei weitere Overground-Züge sowie ab Shepherd's Bush zusätzliche Züge von Southern. Zwischen

9 December 2012, when the Clapham Junction – Surrey Quays route was integrated into the Overground network. To achieve this, a 1.5 km link between Surrey Quays and Queens Road Peckham had to be built, including the option for a future intermediate station. To travel on the entire orbital route, however, passengers have to change trains at least twice, at Clapham Junction and at Highbury & Islington. Overground trains leave Stratford every 10 minutes for Willesden Junction, with four trains per hour continuing to Richmond and two to Clapham Junction. The southern part of the Richmond branch is also served by the District Line, while between Willesden Junction and Clapham Junction, there are two additional Overground trains and from Shepherd's Bush, some more

Rotherhithe (East London Line)

Liverpool Street (Lea Valley Lines)

Hoxton (East London Line)

Dalston Junction und Surrey Quays verkehrt London Overground alle 3-5 Minuten, die Züge fahren abwechselnd zu den vier verschiedenen Endpunkten im Süden weiter, im Norden jeder zweite bis Highbury & Islington. Auf der Linie Euston – Watford Junction, die abschnittsweise auch von der Bakerloo Line befahren wird, herrscht ein 20-Minuten-Takt, zwischen Gospel Oak und Barking mit Dieseltriebwagen ein 15-Minuten-Takt.

Eine wesentliche Erweiterung erfuhr das London Overground-Netz am 31. Mai 2015, als die sogenannten Lea Valley Lines von Liverpool Street nach Enfield Town bzw. Cheshunt über Seven Sisters (jeweils alle 30 Minuten) sowie nach Chingford (alle 15 Minuten) übernommen wurden. Dazu kam noch die Spange zwischen Romford und Upminster. Die Gesamtstreckenlänge von London Overground hat somit 165 km erreicht. Bis Ende des Jahrzehnts soll die Linie Gospel Oak – Barking elektrifiziert und bis Barking Riverside verlängert werden.

Auf dem London Overground-Netz verkehren moderne Elektrotriebwagen der Baureihe 378 (*Capitalstar*) von Bombardier, anfangs als 4-Wagen-Züge, doch mittlerweile teils mit einem fünften Wagen ergänzt. Sie können sowohl auf Strecken mit Oberleitung als auch mit Stromschienen eingesetzt werden.

run by Southern. Between Dalston Junction and Surrey Quays, London Overground runs every 3-5 minutes, with trains continuing alternately to one of the four southern termini, while at the northern end, every other train goes to Highbury & Islington. On the Euston – Watford Junction line, which is partly shared with the Bakerloo Line, there is a train every 20 minutes, and between Gospel Oak and Barking, diesel units run every 15 minutes.

The London Overground network saw a significant expansion on 31 May 2015, when the Lea Valley Lines from Liverpool Street to Enfield Town and Cheshunt via Seven Sisters (each terminus served every 30 minutes) as well as to Chingford (every 15 minutes) were taken over by TfL. The link between Romford and Upminster was also integrated. The total length of the London Overground network has thus reached 165 km. By the end of the decade, the Gospel Oak – Barking line will have been electrified and possibly extended to Barking Riverside.

The London Overground network is served by modern EMUs of class 378 (Capitalstar) manufactured by Bombardier. Initially 4-car trains, many have been extended with a fifth car. They can be used on routes with either overhead or third-rail power supply.

Chingford (Lea Valley Lines)

Dalston Junction (East London Line)

Blackfriars (Thameslink)

NATIONAL RAIL

Neben dem S-Bahn-Netz ‚London Overground' besitzt Greater London ein weitreichendes Vorortbahnnetz, vor allem südlich der Themse, wohin andererseits die U-Bahn kaum vordringt. Bis auf Thameslink und die Southern-Verbindung über Kensington Olympia gehen alle Vorortbahnen von den traditionellen Kopfbahnhöfen ab und werden entsprechend in einzelnen ‚Franchises' ausgeschrieben, die verschiedenen Betreiber wechseln von Zeit zu Zeit. Während sich nördlich der Themse dadurch meist klare strahlenförmige Linienbündel ergeben, ist südlich des Flusses nur der Strang von Waterloo Richtung Südwesten deutlich von den übrigen Linien zu unterscheiden, da die Linienführungen der Southern, Southeastern und Thameslink im Süden und Südosten Londons verflochten sind, als innerstädtische Endpunkte fungieren Victoria, Charing Cross, London Bridge und Cannon Street. Die tatsächlichen Linienführungen und Halte einzelner Züge sind für Außenstehende aufgrund fehlender Liniennummern und vereinfachter Darstellung auf Netzplänen kaum nachzuvollziehen. An sämtlichen Vorortbahnhöfen innerhalb von Greater London hält mindestens zweimal pro Stunde ein Zug. Während im Netz nördlich der Themse Elektrifizierung mit Oberleitung vorherrscht, sind die Strecken im Süden alle mit Stromschiene ausgerüstet. Im Bereich von Greater London sind alle ‚National Rail'-Züge in den TfL-Tarif integriert. Lediglich beim Heathrow Express, der von der Flughafengesellschaft direkt betrieben wird, gelten ausschließlich eigene Fahrpreise.

Als bislang einzige Strecke im Stil des Pariser RER wurde 1988 **Thameslink** eingeführt, auch wenn der dafür

In addition to the S-Bahn-style London Overground network, Greater London is also served by an extensive suburban railway network, particularly south of the River Thames, an area the London Underground has barely penetrated. Except for Thameslink and the Southern route via Kensington Olympia, the suburban trains all depart from London's traditional terminal stations. The services are therefore grouped in individual franchises, with the various private operators changing from time to time. While north of the River Thames this has led to mostly clear bundles of lines, the only clearly distinguishable service south of the river is that from Waterloo towards the southwest. The routes included in the Southern, Southeastern and Thameslink franchises in South and Southeast London are interlaced, sharing termini at Victoria, Charing Cross, London Bridge and Cannon Street. The actual routes and stopping patterns are difficult to understand for outsiders due to the lack of line numbers and the simplified representation of the system on network maps. At all suburban stations within Greater London there are at least two trains an hour. While electrification with overhead lines prevails north of the River Thames, the southern lines are all equipped with a third-rail power supply. Within Greater London, all National Rail services are integrated into the TfL fare system, with just Heathrow Express, owned by Heathrow Airport, having its exclusive fares.

*So far, the only route to have been established in the style of the Paris RER is **Thameslink**, which was introduced in 1988, although the Snow Hill Tunnel it runs*

Charing Cross (Southeastern)

genutzte Snow Hill Tunnel durch die Innenstadt bereits 1866 gebaut worden war. Dieser war lange Zeit nur von Güterzügen befahren worden und lag seit 1971 still. 1990 wurde die Station City Thameslink auf einer verschobenen Trasse eröffnet. Thameslink-Züge schalten am Bahnhof Farringdon von Oberleitungs- auf Stromschienenbetrieb um.

Trotz des großen Erfolgs dieser ersten Durchmesserlinie dauerte es mehrere Jahrzehnte, bis endlich das lang diskutierte Projekt **Crossrail** in Angriff genommen wurde. Nachdem die Bauarbeiten dieser unterirdischen Ost-West-Verbindung seit 2009 laufen, ist eine Aufnahme des Betriebs 2018/19 vorgesehen. Zwischen Stratford und Paddington wurden tief liegende Röhrentunnel aufgefahren, daran werden bestehende Vorortbahnstrecken angeschlossen, im Westen über Maidenhead nach Reading und zum Flughafen Heathrow, im Osten nach Shenfield. Gleichzeitig entsteht ein größtenteils unterirdischer Abzweig von Whitechapel über Canary Wharf und Woolwich bis Abbey Wood. Auf dem zentralen Abschnitt, der für 24 Züge pro Stunde ausgelegt ist, wird Crossrail die Central Line erheblich entlasten. Wie London Overground untersteht Crossrail direkt *Transport for London* (TfL). Die Betriebskonzession gewann *MTR Corporation (Crossrail) Ltd.* TfL bestellte im Februar 2014 bei Bombardier 65 Aventra-Züge mit 200 m Länge (Baureihe 345), deren Einsatz Mitte 2017 zwischen Liverpool Street und Shenfield starten soll. Als **TfL Rail** begann der Crossrail-Vorlaufbetrieb auf dieser Strecke bereits am 31. Mai 2015.
[www.crossrail.co.uk]

through had already been built back in 1866. This tunnel connection had long been used only by freight trains and had lain abandoned since 1971. In 1990, City Thameslink station was opened on a diverted alignment. At Farringdon, Thameslink trains switch between overhead and third rail power collection.

Despite the great success of this first cross-city line, it took several decades for the long-debated ***Crossrail*** *project to receive the final go-ahead. With the construction of the underground east-west route launched in 2009, the start of operations is scheduled for 2018/19. Deep tube tunnels are being constructed between Stratford and Paddington, to which existing railway lines will be connected: in the west to Heathrow Airport and via Maidenhead to Reading, and in the east to Shenfield. At the same time, a mostly underground branch is being built from Whitechapel via Canary Wharf and Woolwich to Abbey Wood. On the central portion, which is designed for 24 trains per hour, Crossrail will significantly relieve the Central Line. Like London Overground, Crossrail is directly controlled by Transport for London (TfL). The operating concession has been awarded to MTR Corporation (Crossrail) Ltd. In February 2014, TfL ordered 65 Aventra trains with a length of 200 m (class 345) from Bombardier, which are set to start operating between Liverpool Street and Shenfield in mid-2017. Branded* ***TfL Rail****, a pre-Crossrail service was introduced on this route on 31 May 2015, with trains running every 10 minutes.*
[www.crossrail.co.uk]

Ilford (TfL Rail)

Heathrow T5 (Heathrow Express)

Liverpool Street (TfL Rail)

Farringdon (Thameslink)

Highbury & Islington (Great Northern)

London Bridge (Southern)

Clapham Junction (South West Trains)

King's Cross

Kentish Town (Thameslink)

St. Pancras International (Thameslink)

Bombardier #3022 @ Cemetery Road > Droylsden

MANCHESTER

Die City of Manchester ist mit knapp einer halben Million Einwohner auf 115 km^2 nur ein kleiner Teil der Metropolregion Greater Manchester, zu der auch Salford, Trafford, Tameside, Stockport, Bury, Oldham, Rochdale, Bolton und das etwas abseits gelegene Wigan gehören. Westlich davon schließt direkt Merseyside, der Ballungsraum um Liverpool, an.

Der öffentliche Nahverkehr in der Region Greater Manchester wird von *Transport for Greater Manchester* (TfGM) geplant und koordiniert. Neben dem in den letzten Jahren stark gewachsenen Stadtbahnnetz (Metrolink) wird das Gebiet von zahlreichen, teils nicht elektrifizierten Regionalbahnstrecken durchzogen.

Für Greater Manchester werden unzählige unterschiedliche Tageskarten angeboten, z.B. nur Metrolink, nur Bus, oder Bus+Zug, Bus+Zug+Tram usw. Für Besucher am bequemsten scheint demnach ein *System One DaySaver* für alle drei Verkehrsmittel für 8,60 £ zu sein, will man über die Grenzen hinweg auch nach Warrington oder in den Peak District, dann lohnt sich ein *Wayfarer* für 12,00 £. Wer nur Metrolink nutzen will, kann das einen Tag lang ab 9:30 Uhr mit einer *Adult Day Travelcard* für 5,00 £. Einzelfahrten nur mit Metrolink kosten zwischen 1,20 £ und 4,70 £.

With roughly half a million inhabitants in an area of 115 km^2, the City of Manchester is just a small part of the metropolitan area known as Greater Manchester, which also includes Salford, Trafford, Tameside, Stockport, Bury, Oldham, Rochdale, Bolton and, at some distance, Wigan. To the west, it borders with Merseyside, the conurbation around Liverpool.

Public transport in Greater Manchester is coordinated and planned by 'Transport for Greater Manchester' (TfGM). Besides the light rail system Metrolink, which has seen some significant expansion in recent years, the region is criss-crossed by numerous local railway routes, some of which are non-electrified.

A large selection of day tickets is available for Greater Manchester. These include exclusive tickets for Metrolink or buses, as well as combined tickets for tram+bus, tram+train+bus, etc. For visitors, the easiest ticket to use is probably the 'System One DaySaver', valid for all three types of transport and priced at £8.60, and for those who want to travel further afield, e.g. to Warrington or the Peak District, a Wayfarer for £12.00 is available. A Metrolink-only Adult Day Travelcard valid from 09:30 is sold for £5.00, while single fares for Metrolink range from £1.20 to £4.70.

Bombardier #3031 @ Piccadilly

Die Stadtbahn von Manchester, die so genannte **Metrolink**, ist Eigentum von TfGM (Transport for Greater Manchester) und wird derzeit von *RATP Dev* betrieben. Metrolink war 1992 die erste moderne Stadtbahn Großbritanniens. Es handelt sich dabei um die einzige Hochflurstadtbahn des Landes, die auch im Straßenraum verkehrt. Das Netz wurde in den letzten Jahren erheblich erweitert und erschließt nun bis auf Bolton und Wigan alle Kommunen der Region Greater Manchester. Außerdem wurde innerhalb weniger Jahre der gesamte Fahrzeugpark erneuert, was mit einem kompletten Restyling vom früheren Türkis zum heutigen Gelb einherging.

In den frühen 1970er Jahren entstand das sog. ‚Picc-Vic'-Projekt für eine unterirdische Verbindungsbahn zwischen den beiden Hauptbahnhöfen Piccadilly und Victoria. Ähnlich wie in Liverpool sollten U-Bahnhöfe an den beiden Hauptbahnhöfen sowie an der Whitworth/Princess Street, dem St. Peter's Square und am Royal Exchange mitten im Geschäftsviertel entstehen. 1977 wurde das Projekt wegen Geldmangels aufgegeben.

Das heutige Netz umfasst mittlerweile sieben farblich unterschiedene Linien (Buchstabenkennzeichnungen A-G wurden erstmals im August 2015 eingeführt). Jede Linie verkehrt in der Regel alle 12 Minuten, nach Bury oder Altrincham fährt demnach alle 6 Minuten eine Bahn. Der kurze Ast zur MediaCityUK wird meist in einer Stich-

MANCHESTER
(Greater Manchester)

515 000 | 2 700 000

(1901-1949) 1992

1435 mm

93 km

7

12'

Metrolink
www.metrolink.co.uk

Transport for Greater Manchester
www.tfgm.com
www.systemonetravelcards.co.uk

*The Manchester light rail system is known as **Metrolink**. It is owned by TfGM (Transport for Greater Manchester) and currently operated by RATP Dev. When it opened in 1992, Metrolink was Britain's first new-generation tramway system, and it is still the only system that uses high-floor vehicles on street-running sections. The system has rapidly expanded in recent years, and now serves all of Greater Manchester except Bolton and Wigan. At the same time, the entire rolling stock has been replaced, accompanied by a complete restyling of the system from its former turquoise to the current yellow colour scheme.*

In the early 1970s, an underground scheme referred to as 'Picc-Vic' was proposed to link the city's major railway stations, Piccadilly and Victoria. The project was similar to the Liverpool city centre loop and included underground stations at Whitworth/Princess Street, St. Peter's Square, and at Royal Exchange for the central shopping area, as well as under the respective railway terminals. In 1977, however, the project was abandoned due to a lack of funding.

Today's system comprises seven colour-coded lines (line letters A-G were introduced in August 2015), each operating a basic 12-minute headway. The Altrincham and Bury routes are thus served every 6 minutes. The MediaCityUK spur is mostly served by the Eccles Line. Due to capacity constraints on the existing city centre

MANCHESTER

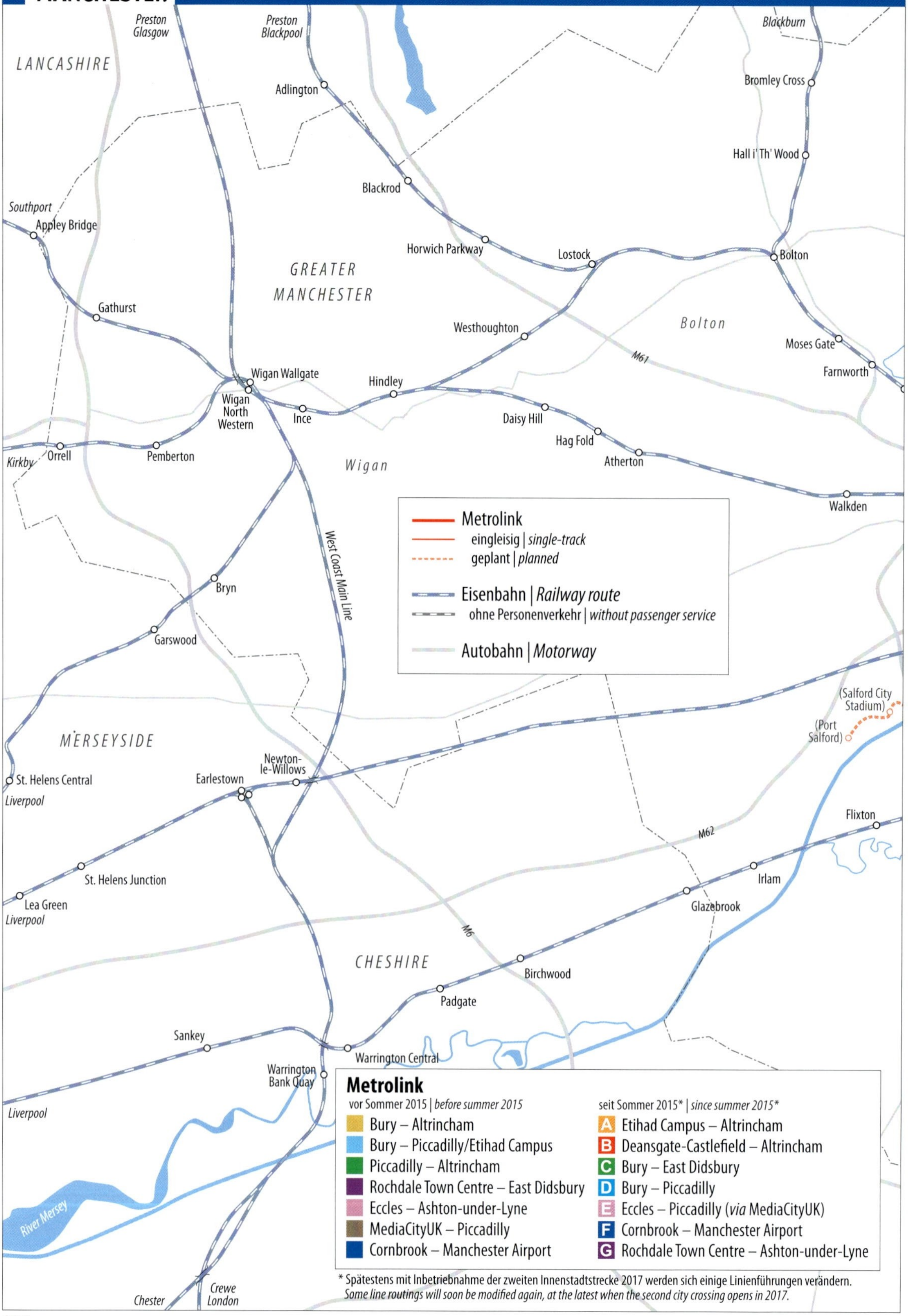

* Spätestens mit Inbetriebnahme der zweiten Innenstadtstrecke 2017 werden sich einige Linienführungen verändern.
Some line routings will soon be modified again, at the latest when the second city crossing opens in 2017.

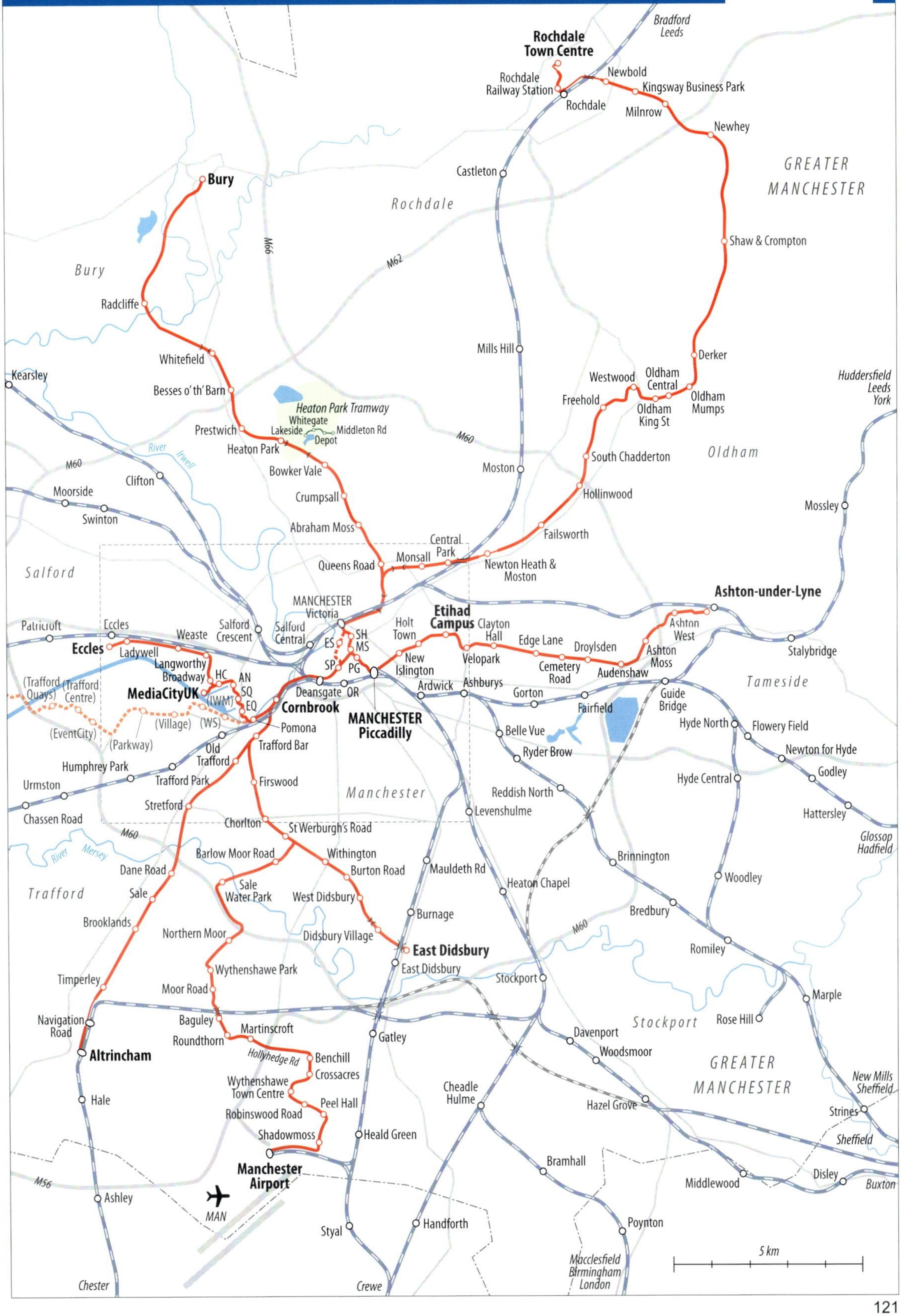
Rochdale Town Centre
Rochdale Railway Station
Rochdale
Newbold
Kingsway Business Park
Milnrow
Newhey
Shaw & Crompton
Derker
Oldham Mumps
Oldham Central
Oldham King St
Westwood
Freehold
South Chadderton
Hollinwood
Failsworth
Newton Heath & Moston
Central Park
Monsall
Queens Road
Abraham Moss
Crumpsall
Bowker Vale
Heaton Park
Prestwich
Besses o' th' Barn
Whitefield
Radcliffe
Bury
Heaton Park Tramway
Whitegate
Lakeside
Depot
Middleton Rd
MANCHESTER Victoria
Salford Central
Salford Crescent
SH
MS
ES
SP
PG
Deansgate
OR
Cornbrook
MANCHESTER Piccadilly
Pomona
Trafford Bar
Old Trafford
Stretford
Dane Road
Sale
Brooklands
Timperley
Navigation Road
Altrincham
Hale
Ashley
Firswood
Chorlton
St Werburgh's Road
Barlow Moor Road
Sale Water Park
Northern Moor
Wythenshawe Park
Moor Road
Baguley
Roundthorn
Martinscroft
Hollyhedge Rd
Benchill
Crossacres
Wythenshawe Town Centre
Peel Hall
Robinswood Road
Shadowmoss
Manchester Airport
MAN
Withington
Burton Road
West Didsbury
Didsbury Village
East Didsbury
Holt Town
New Islington
Etihad Campus
Clayton Hall
Velopark
Edge Lane
Cemetery Road
Droylsden
Audenshaw
Ashton Moss
Ashton West
Ashton-under-Lyne
Eccles
Ladywell
Weaste
Langworthy
Broadway
HC
AN
SQ
EQ
MediaCityUK
(IWM)
(WS)
(Village)
(Parkway)
(EventCity)
(Trafford Quays)
(Trafford Centre)
Patricroft
Kearsley
Clifton
Moorside
Swinton
Humphrey Park
Urmston
Chassen Road
Trafford Park
Castleton
Mills Hill
Moston
Mossley
Stalybridge
Guide Bridge
Hyde North
Flowery Field
Newton for Hyde
Godley
Hattersley
Hyde Central
Woodley
Romiley
Bredbury
Brinnington
Marple
Rose Hill
Strines
New Mills
Sheffield
Disley
Buxton
Middlewood
Hazel Grove
Woodsmoor
Davenport
Stockport
Heaton Chapel
Reddish North
Levenshulme
Ryder Brow
Belle Vue
Gorton
Fairfield
Ardwick
Ashburys
Mauldeth Rd
Burnage
East Didsbury
Gatley
Heald Green
Cheadle Hulme
Bramhall
Poynton
Handforth
Styal
Macclesfield
Birmingham
London
Crewe
Chester
Bradford
Leeds
Huddersfield
Leeds
York
Glossop
Hadfield
GREATER MANCHESTER
Rochdale
Bury
Oldham
Salford
Manchester
Tameside
Trafford
Stockport
River Irwell
River Mersey
M60
M62
M66
M56
5 km

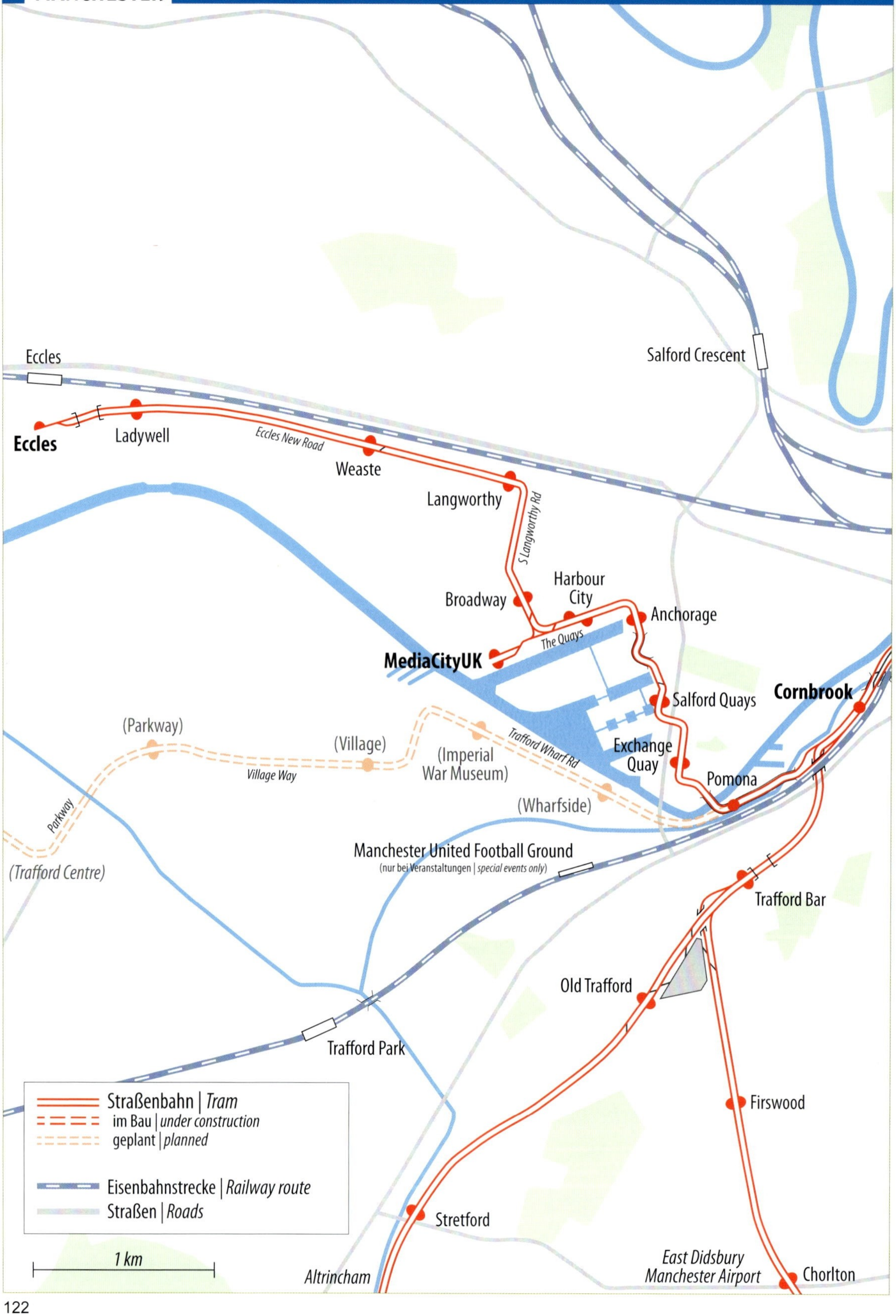

Eccles
Salford Crescent
Eccles
Ladywell
Eccles New Road
Weaste
Langworthy
S Langworthy Rd
Harbour City
Broadway
Anchorage
The Quays
MediaCityUK
Salford Quays
Cornbrook
(Parkway)
(Village)
(Imperial War Museum)
Trafford Wharf Rd
Exchange Quay
Village Way
Pomona
Parkway
(Wharfside)
Manchester United Football Ground
(nur bei Veranstaltungen | special events only)
(Trafford Centre)
Trafford Bar
Old Trafford
Trafford Park
Firswood
Straßenbahn | Tram
im Bau | under construction
geplant | planned
Eisenbahnstrecke | Railway route
Straßen | Roads
Stretford
1 km
East Didsbury
Manchester Airport
Altrincham
Chorlton

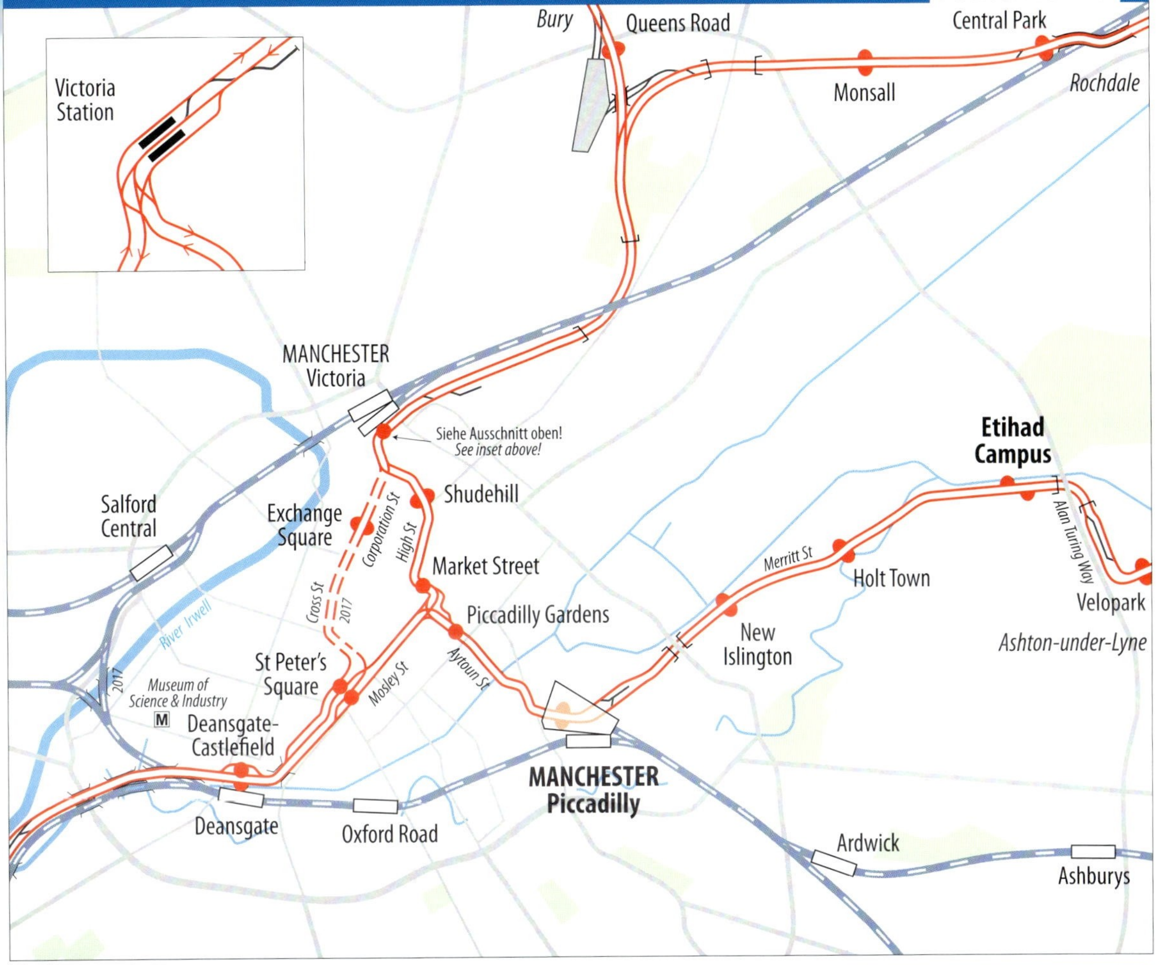

Bombardier #3032 @ Piccadilly > New Islington

Bombardier #3075 @ Ashton-under-Lyne

fahrt von den Zügen nach Eccles angeschlossen. Wegen Überlastung der Innenstadtstrecke enden die Züge vom Flughafen bis zur Inbetriebnahme der zweiten Innenstadtquerung ca. 2017 in Cornbrook.

Für die 1992 eröffnete Nord-Süd-Strecke wurden zwei ehemalige British-Rail-Strecken direkt übernommen und durch eine Innenstadtstrecke miteinander verbunden, so dass es sich um eine Art ‚Tram-Train' handelt, jedoch ohne Mischbetrieb mit anderen Bahnen.

Die **Bury Line**, gebaut 1879, wurde 1916 mit 1200 V Gleichstrom über Stromschiene elektrifiziert. Da dieses System nicht mehr zeitgemäß war, schien ein Umbau zu einer Stadtbahn die beste Möglichkeit, diese Strecke weiterhin zu nutzen. Die 1849 eröffnete **Altrincham Line** war 1931 mit 1500 V Gleichstrom elektrifiziert worden, 1971 wurde die Spannung jedoch auf 25 kV Wechselstrom umgestellt. Für den Stadtbahnbetrieb musste die Spannung dieser Strecke auf 750 V Gleichstrom geändert werden, während die Bury-Linie vollständig mit Oberleitung ausgerüstet werden musste. Alle Stationen beider Linien wurden behindertengerecht ausgebaut, entweder mit Rampen oder Aufzügen.

Wegen der bereits bestehenden Hochbahnsteige an der Bury- und der Altrincham-Linie entschied man sich bei der Metrolink für Hochflurfahrzeuge. Am Bahnhof Victoria wurde die Bury-Linie durch eine Öffnung in der südlichen Bahnhofsmauer mit dem straßenbündigen Abschnitt verbunden. Die Altrincham-Linie erreicht am Ausstellungszentrum, das in der ehemaligen *Central Station* untergebracht ist, über eine Rampe die Straßenebene. Der Metrolink-Bahnhof Piccadilly befindet sich zwischen den Bögen unter dem Fernbahnhof.

1999/2000 folgte die **Eccles Line**. Sie zweigt von der Altrincham-Linie am Bahnhof Cornbrook ab und führt über

route, trains from the airport currently terminate at Cornbrook, and will do so until the second city centre crossing becomes available in 2017.

For the initial Metrolink north-south route opened in 1992, two former British Rail lines were directly taken over and linked via a city centre route, thus creating a kind of 'tram-train', though without any mixed traffic with other trains.

MANCHESTER Metrolink

93 km, 92 Haltestellen | *stops*

06-04-1992: Bury – Victoria (15.9 km)
27-04-1992: Victoria – Deansgate-Castlefield (3.1 km)
15-06-1992: Deansgate-Castlefield – Altrincham (10.4 km)
20-07-1992: Market St/St Peter's Square – Piccadilly (0.7 km)
06-12-1999: Cornbrook – Broadway (3.0 km)
21-07-2000: Broadway – Eccles (3.5 km)
31-03-2003: + Shudehill
02-09-2005: + Cornbrook
20-09-2010: Harbour City – MediaCityUK (0.3 km)
18-04-2011: + Abraham Moss
07-07-2011: Trafford Bar – St Werburgh's Road (2.7 km)
13-06-2012: Victoria – Oldham Mumps (10.7 km)
16-12-2012: Oldham Mumps – Shaw & Crompton (4.1 km)
11-02-2013: Piccadilly – Droylsden (5.9 km)
28-02-2013: Shaw & Crompton – Rochdale Railway Stn (7.4 km)
23-05-2013: St Werburgh's Road – East Didsbury (4.4 km)
09-10-2013: Droylsden – Ashton-under-Lyne (3.4 km)
16-12-2013: + Queens Road*
27-01-2014: Freehold – Oldham Central – Derker (2.5 km)**
31-03-2014: Rochdale Rly Stn – Rochdale Town Centre (0.9 km)
03-11-2014: St Werburgh's Road – Manchester Airport (14.5 km)
2017: St. Peter's Sq. – Victoria via Exchange Sq. (1.0 km)

* statt | *replacing* Woodlands Road
** statt früherer Direktverbindung | *replacing former direct route*

Bombardier #3082 @ Salford Quays

den Manchester Ship Canal und dann durch das Sanierungsgebiet Salford Quays im ehemaligen Hafen. Cornbrook, ursprünglich nur eine Umsteigestation, bekam erst 2005 einen Ausgang zur Straße. Der westliche Abschnitt nach Eccles verläuft hauptsächlich im Straßenraum, teils straßenbündig, teils abmarkiert.

Nach zehn Jahren Pause begann 2011 der ‚Big Bang': In einem bislang in England nicht denkbaren Ausbauprogramm konnte sich das Netz innerhalb weniger Jahre fast verdreifachen. Für die **South Manchester Line** nach East Didsbury (7,1 km), die von der Altrincham-Linie kreuzungsfrei ausfädelt, konnte durchgehend ein seit 1967 stillgelegter Eisenbahnkorridor genutzt werden. Eine Weiterführung bis Stockport wäre möglich. Die davon abgehende **Airport Line** (14,5 km) über Wythenshawe wurde hingegen neu trassiert, diese Strecke weist demnach alles von unabhängigem Gleiskörper über das Mersey-Tal bis hin zu straßenbündigen Abschnitten in Wythenshawe auf. Die Fahrt vom Flughafen ins Stadtzentrum dauert mit der Tram allerdings etwa 50 Minuten mit Umsteigen in Cornbrook, mit einer der häufig verkehrenden Regionalbahnen nur 15 Minuten.

Am Hauptbahnhof Piccadilly startet die **East Manchester Line**, die auf ihrem Weg durch den Osten der Stadt zwei Unterführungen zur Querung von Hauptstraßen bekam. Manche Bahnen enden nun statt am Bahnhof Piccadilly am derzeit von einer arabischen Fluggesellschaft gesponserten Stadion des FC Manchester City. Die anschließende Strecke führt meist straßenbündig entlang der Manchester Road durch den Stadtteil Droylsden der Kommune Tameside. Erst ab Audenshaw bis zur Endstelle in Ashton-under-Lyne steht ein eigener Bahnkörper zur Verfügung.

Die **Oldham and Rochdale Line** ähnelt hingegen wieder den ersten Abschnitten nach Bury und Altrincham. Anders als in den frühen Phasen wurde die von Network

*The **Bury Line**, opened in 1879, had already been electrified at 1200 V DC via a third rail by as early as 1916. As this system had since become obsolete, conversion to light rail was considered the best option for this route. The **Altrincham Line**, opened in 1849, was electrified in 1931 using overhead wires and 1500 V DC, and converted to 25 kV AC in 1971. For light rail operation, the tension on this line had to be switched to 750 V DC, whereas on the Bury line, totally new overhead line equipment had to be installed. All the stations along both lines were made accessible for the mobility-impaired by means of ramps or lifts.*

The choice of high-floor vehicles was based on the existence of high platforms at every station along the two railway lines. At Victoria, the Bury Line was linked to the city centre section via an opening cut into the station's southern wall. The Altrincham Line was connected via a ramp next to the Exhibition Centre, which is housed in the former Central Station. At Piccadilly, the Metrolink station was built in the 'undercroft' of the railway station, between the arches supporting the mainline tracks.

*The next route to open was the **Eccles Line** in 1999/2000. This route diverges from the Altrincham Line at Cornbrook, runs on a viaduct across the Manchester Ship Canal, and then at grade through the redeveloped areas of Salford Quays. Cornbrook, initially just an isolated transfer station, only became accessible from street level in 2005. The western section to Eccles runs mostly on-street, partly marked-off and partly mixed with road traffic.*

*Following a ten-year break, Metrolink's 'big bang' started in 2011: an expansion program previously unthinkable in England almost tripled the system in size within just a few years. The **South Manchester Line** to East*

Bombardier #3014 + 3059 @ Victoria

Rail übernommene Eisenbahnstrecke jedoch völlig von Grund auf erneuert, inklusive Gleisbau, weshalb die ehemalige Oldham Loop Line bereits im Oktober 2009 stillgelegt worden war. Zwischen Juni 2012 und Januar 2014, als die teils straßenbündige Strecke durch Oldham in Betrieb genommen werden konnte, nutzte Metrolink zwischen Freehold und Derker die alte Eisenbahntrasse über den ehemaligen Bahnhof Oldham Mumps (200 m südlich der heutigen Metrolink-Haltestelle). In Rochdale wurde eine eingleisige Brücke über die Bahnanlagen der Strecke nach Leeds errichtet, danach folgt eine Rampe zum Bahnhofsvorplatz und eine teils straßenbündige Strecke mit einem kurzen eingleisigen Abschnitt bis ins Stadtzentrum von Rochdale, wo die Linie am Busbahnhof endet.

Ab 2017 wird die **zweite Innenstadtstrecke** den Bahnhof Victoria mit dem zentralen St. Peter's Square verbinden. Dazu wurde 2014 die Haltestelle im Bahnhof Victoria dreigleisig ausgebaut, am St. Peter's Square entsteht eine viergleisige Anlage mit zwei Mittelbahnsteigen. Stadteinwärts wurde auch die Haltestelle Deansgate-Castlefield zweigleisig erweitert.

Mittelfristig soll eine Neubaustrecke zum Einkaufszentrum Trafford Centre und später eventuell weiter bis Port Salford gebaut werden. Die sog. **Trafford Park Line** wird ab etwa 2020 auf der Hochbahnstrecke westlich von

Didsbury (7.1 km), which diverts from the Altrincham Line in a grade-separated junction, takes advantage of a railway corridor disused since 1967. A further extension to Stockport would also be possible. The branch known as the ***Airport Line*** *(14.5 km) via Wythenshawe, however, was built on a completely new route, and therefore features anything from an independent right-of-way across the Mersey Valley to on-street sections in Wythenshawe. A ride from the airport to the city centre by tram takes approximately 50 minutes and requires a change of trams at Cornbrook, while frequent regional trains cover the same distance in only 15 minutes.*

The ***East Manchester Line*** *starts at Piccadilly, the city's main railway station. On its way through the eastern parts of the city, it boasts two underpasses beneath major roads. Instead of Piccadilly, some trams now terminate at the FC Manchester City stadium, currently sponsored by an Arab airline. The following route runs mostly on-street along Manchester Road through the district of Droylsden in Tameside. A dedicated right-of-way is only available from Audenshaw to the terminus in Ashton-under-Lyne.*

The ***Oldham and Rochdale Line*** *resembles the older Metrolink routes to Bury and Altrincham. Unlike those, however, the railway line purchased from Network Rail*

Metrolink > Fahrzeuge | *Rolling Stock* (750 V DC)

Nummer *Number*	Anzahl *Quantity*	Hersteller *Manufacturer*	Typ *Class*	Länge *Length*	Breite *Width*	Ausgeliefert *Delivered*
3001-3120	100 > 120	Bombardier	M5000 (Flexity Swift)	28.4 m	2.65 m	2009-2017

Bombardier #3062 @ Benchill > Martinscroft

Pomona von der Eccles-Linie abzweigen und als moderne Stadtbahn auf breiten Straßen durch ein Entwicklungs- und Gewerbegebiet verkehren. Von der Haltestelle Wharfside kann man das Stadion von Manchester United erreichen.

Sollte sich das Pilotprojekt in Sheffield als erfolgreich herausstellen, ist auch für Greater Manchester die Einführung eines Tram-Train auf mehreren Strecken, vor allem im Osten der Region, vorstellbar.

Die ursprünglichen 32 Metrolink-Fahrzeuge (Nr. 1001-1026, 2001-2006) von der italienischen Firma FIREMA (heute Ansaldobreda) wurden nach knapp 20 Jahren Einsatz allesamt zwischen 2012 und 2014 ausgemustert und durch neue Fahrzeuge von Bombardier ersetzt. Die als M5000 bezeichneten Wagen basieren auf den in Köln und Bonn eingesetzten K5000-Hochflurwagen und gehören

was completely upgraded, including a new trackbed, which is why the former Oldham Loop Line was decommissioned in October 2009. Between June 2012 and January 2014, when the partly on-street route through Oldham town centre came into service, Metrolink used the old railway route between Freehold and Derker via the former railway station Oldham Mumps (200 m south of the present Metrolink stop). In Rochdale, a single-track bridge was built over the railway to Leeds, followed by a ramp that takes the trams to the station square. From there, they run partly in mixed traffic and with a short single-track section down into the Rochdale town centre, where the line ends at the bus station.

From 2017, a ***second city centre route*** *will connect Victoria railway station with the central stop at St.*

Ansaldo #2006 @ Broadway > Langworthy (2005)

Ansaldo #1008 @ Altrincham (2005)

Central Park

zur Produktfamilie Flexity Swift. Die ursprüngliche Bestellung von nur acht Fahrzeugen wurde schrittweise auf 120 erweitert, die bis 2017 ausgeliefert werden. Sie verkehren meist als Solowagen, in der Hauptverkehrszeit jedoch auch in Doppeltraktion.

Bombardier #3002 @ Piccadilly

Peter's Square. For this purpose, the stop at Victoria station was expanded to three tracks in 2014, while at St. Peter's Square, a four-track station with two island platforms is being built. Inbound trams now also benefit from an expanded two-track platform at Deansgate-Castlefield.

In the medium term, a new line will be built to the Trafford Centre shopping mall, and perhaps later on to Port Salford. In about 2020, the so-called ***Trafford Park Line*** *will diverge from the Eccles Line on the elevated structure just west of Pomona station, and operate as a modern light railway along wide roads through a redevelopment area and industrial zone. The Manchester United stadium will be accessible from the tram stop at Wharfside.*

If the pilot project in Sheffield proves successful, Greater Manchester may also see the implementation of tram-trains on several lines, especially in the eastern part of the region.

The original 32 Metrolink vehicles (nos. 1001-1026 and 2001-2006), manufactured by FIREMA (now Ansaldobreda) of Italy, were all withdrawn between 2012 and 2014 after just 20 years of service. They were replaced with new M5000 vehicles from Bombardier, which are based on the K5000 in service in Cologne and Bonn and are part of the Flexity Swift family. The initial order placed in 2007 was for just eight cars, but this was increased in various stages to the current 120 cars to be delivered by 2017. They mostly operate as single units, but can also be seen as two-car sets during peak hours.

Bombardier Flexity Swift

Bombardier #3069 + 3064 @ MediaCityUK

Trafford Bar

Bombardier #3029 @ Trafford Bar

Bombardier #3087 @ Shudehill

Pacer #142044 @ Manchester Piccadilly

Vorortverkehr

Auf dem dichten Eisenbahnnetz rund um Manchester herrscht reger Regionalverkehr mit Zügen meist im Halbstundentakt, wobei es keinen exklusiven S-Bahn-Verkehr für Greater Manchester gibt, sondern die meisten Regionalzüge Teil eines größeren, von *Northern Rail* betriebenen Netzes sind. Viele Züge werden daher in benachbarte Regionen, z.B. nach Leeds, Liverpool oder Blackpool durchgebunden. An wichtigen Bahnhöfen halten auch die Züge von *TransPennine Express* oder anderen Bahngesellschaften, die Verbindungen zu weiter entfernten Zielen herstellen. Zwischen Manchester Airport und Piccadilly fährt alle paar Minuten eine Bahn und benötigt dafür rund 15-18 Minuten (Metrolink ca. 50 Min.), auch Rochdale und Victoria sind mehrmals stündlich in 16-20 Minuten miteinander direkt verbunden, während Metrolink über Oldham 45 Minuten benötigt.

Lange waren in der Region um Manchester nur die Hauptstrecken nach Süden sowie die Vorortbahn nach Glossop/Hadfield (bis 1984 mit 1500 V DC) elektrifiziert, bis im Mai 2015 *Northern Electrics* den Betrieb zwischen Manchester und Liverpool über Eccles startete. Bis 2017 will Network Rail die Elektrifizierung des Bahnnetzes im Nordwesten Englands auf die Strecken Manchester – Leeds über Stalybridge sowie Manchester – Blackpool über Bolton ausweiten. Der Lokalverkehr ist auf vielen Strecken noch von Schienenbussen der BR 142 (Pacer) geprägt, auf längeren Strecken werden modernisierte Dieseltriebwagen der BR 150 (Sprinter) oder neue der BR 185 (Desiro UK) eingesetzt.

Suburban Rail

The tightly-knit network around Manchester boasts a busy local rail service, with most trains running half-hourly. There is no exclusive S-Bahn-style service for Greater Manchester, but most local trains are part of a larger network operated by Northern Rail. Many services therefore continue into the neighbouring regions, for example to Leeds, Liverpool and Blackpool. Some important railway stations are also served by trains belonging to TransPennine Express or other railway operators, which offer connections to more distant destinations. Between Manchester Airport and Piccadilly, trains run every few minutes, covering the journey in approximately 15-18 minutes (Metrolink takes some 50 minutes). Rochdale and Victoria are directly connected several times an hour in 16-20 minutes, while Metrolink via Oldham takes 45 minutes.

In the Manchester area, until recently only the main routes towards the south as well as the suburban line to Glossop/Hadfield (until 1984 with 1500 V DC) had been electrified, but in May 2015, Northern Electrics trains started running between Manchester and Liverpool via Eccles. By 2017, Network Rail will have expanded the electrification of the railway network in the northwest of England to the Manchester – Leeds route via Stalybridge and the Manchester – Blackpool route via Bolton. Local traffic is still dominated by railbuses of class 142 (Pacer), whereas longer routes are served by refurbished DMUs of class 150 (Sprinter) or new class 185 trains (Desiro UK).

Rochdale

Northern Electric @ Manchester Victoria

Manchester Piccadilly – Durchgangsgleise | *through tracks*

Manchester Deansgate

Siemens Desiro #185116 @ Manchester Piccadilly

Haymarket – erster modernisierter U-Bahnhof | *first modernised underground station*

NEWCASTLE UPON TYNE

Mit unter 300.000 Einwohnern wäre Newcastle keine Stadt für eine Metro, doch ist sie Mittelpunkt des Großraums Tyne and Wear im Nordosten Englands, der die Kommunen Newcastle, Gateshead, North Tyneside, South Tyneside und Sunderland umfasst, wo mehr als 1 Mio. Menschen leben.

Obwohl die **Tyne and Wear Metro** oft als „Light Rail" bzw. Stadtbahn bezeichnet wird, hat sie nicht viel mit anderen Stadtbahnen gemeinsam, da dieser Begriff heute meist für moderne Straßenbahnen, wenn auch größtenteils auf eigenem Gleiskörper, verwendet wird. Die *Tyne and Wear Metro* kann man zwischen S-Bahn und richtiger Metro einreihen. Sie verläuft durchgehend auf eigenem Gleiskörper und bis auf wenige Bahnübergänge auf den äußeren Abschnitten ist sie völlig getrennt vom Straßenverkehr. Die Metro gehört zur *Passenger Transport Executive for Tyne and Wear*, die unter der Marke „Nexus" auftritt, und wird derzeit von *DB Regio Tyne & Wear Ltd* betrieben. Für die Verkehrs- und Infrastrukturplanung ist nun die „North East Combined Authority" zuständig, die neben den Kommunen in der Region Tyne and Wear auch das County Durham und Northumberland einschließt.

Für Einzelfahrten mit der Metro gilt ein 3-Zonen-Tarif, der Fahrpreis beträgt entsprechend £1,80/2,70/3,40. Eine *DaySaver*-Tageskarte kostet entsprechend £2,70/3,70/4,60, sie gilt auch in *Northern Rail*-Zügen zwischen Newcastle und Sunderland sowie auf der Fähre zwischen North Shields und South Shields. Will man auch Busse nutzen, bietet sich ein *Day Rover*-Ticket für £7,00 an.

With less than 300,000 inhabitants, Newcastle would not normally be considered eligible for a metro system. The city is, however, the heart of the conurbation known as Tyne and Wear, which includes the metropolitan boroughs of Newcastle, Gateshead, North Tyneside, South Tyneside and Sunderland, and is home to over a million people.

*Although often referred to as 'light rail', the **Tyne and Wear Metro** does not have much in common with other light rail systems, as this term is nowadays mostly used for modern tramway systems. The Tyne and Wear Metro system could be described as a hybrid between a suburban railway and a proper metro. It runs entirely on its own right-of-way, totally segregated from road traffic, but with a few level crossings on the outer branches. The Metro is owned by Nexus, the 'Passenger Transport Executive for Tyne and Wear', and is currently operated by 'DB Regio Tyne & Wear Ltd'. Transport and infrastructure planning is now in the hands of the North East Combined Authority, which besides the Tyne and Wear region, includes County Durham and Northumberland.*

Fares for single journeys on the Metro are payable according to the number of zones (max. 3 zones) travelled through, costing £1.80/2.70/3.40, respectively. Accordingly, a DaySaver ticket is sold for £2.70/3.70/4.60, and is also valid on Northern Rail trains between Newcastle and Sunderland as well as on the ferry between North Shields and South Shields. For those who wish to use buses too, a Day Rover ticket for £7.00 is on offer.

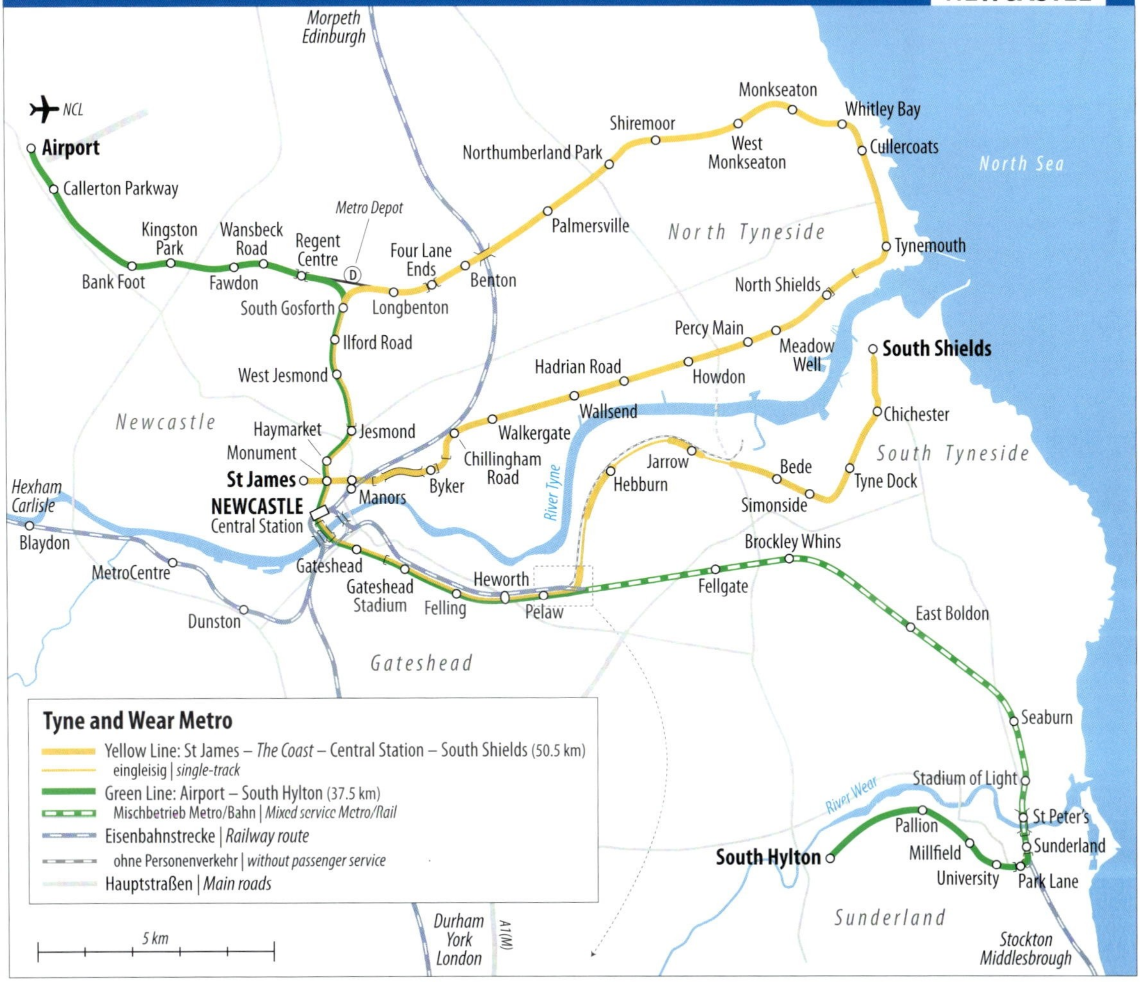

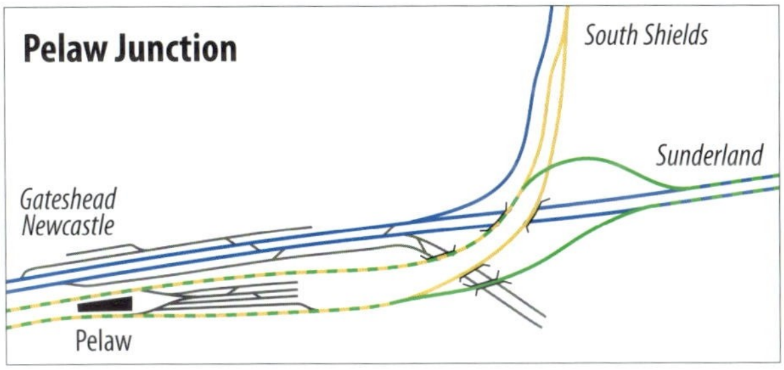

NEWCASTLE UPON TYNE (Tyne and Wear)

280 000 | 1 100 000

1980

1435 mm | 77.5 km | 2 | 12'

Nexus
www.nexus.org.uk

Network One Tickets
www.networkonetickets.co.uk

North East Combined Authority
www.northeastca.gov.uk

TYNE AND WEAR METRO

77.5 km (6.5 km unterirdisch | *underground*), 60 Bahnhöfe | *stations*

Metro-Betrieb | *Metro service:*

11-08-1980: Haymarket – Tynemouth
10-05-1981: South Gosforth – Bank Foot
15-11-1981: Haymarket – Heworth
14-11-1982: St. James – Manors – Tynemouth
24-03-1984: Heworth – South Shields
15-09-1985: + Kingston Park
16-09-1985: + Pelaw
19-03-1986: + Palmersville
17-11-1991: Bank Foot – Airport
31-03-2002: Pelaw – South Hylton
28-04-2002: + Park Lane
11-12-2005: + Northumberland Park
17-03-2008: + Simonside

Whitley Bay

Das Metro-Netz besteht aus zwei farblich gekennzeichneten Linien. Eine Fahrt auf der Green Line vom Airport bis South Hylton in Sunderland dauert 67 Minuten. Die Yellow Line wird aus dem Küstenring durch North Tyneside und dem Ast nach South Shields durch South Tyneside gebildet, die Züge dieser Linien passieren dabei zweimal den U-Bahnhof Monument im Zentrum von Newcastle. Eine Fahrt auf dem Küstenring dauert 54 Minuten, auf der ganzen Linie 82 Minuten. Auf beiden Linien herrscht ein 12-Minuten-Takt, auf dem gemeinsamen Abschnitt zwischen South Gosforth und Pelaw verkehrt demnach tagsüber alle sechs Minuten eine Bahn. Die Metro ist von ca. 5:30 bis Mitternacht in Betrieb.

Die Idee für die *Tyne and Wear Metro* entstand in den späten 1960er Jahren, als sich die einst stark benutzten Vorortbahnen in einem sehr desolaten Zustand befanden und etwas getan werden musste. Nachdem mehrere Strecken stillgelegt worden waren, sollten die übrigen, nämlich der Küstenring und der Ast nach South Shields, umgebaut und in den Zentren von Newcastle sowie Gateshead durch unterirdische Strecken miteinander verbunden werden.

Der Küstenring war ursprünglich zwischen 1839 und 1882 in Betrieb genommen worden, der nördliche Ast endete bis 1909 in Newcastle an der New Bridge Street, bis ein kurzes Verbindungsstück zum Bahnhof Manors gebaut wurde, so dass die Züge im 1850 eröffneten Hauptbahnhof (Central) abfahren und enden konnten. 1879 wurde der Küstenring zwischen Manors und Percy Main durch eine Strecke am Fluss entlang ergänzt. Diese Nebenstrecke, die vor allem den Arbeitern der dortigen Schiffswerften

The Metro system comprises two colour-coded lines. A full journey on the Green Line between Airport and South Hylton in Sunderland takes 67 minutes. The Yellow Line is made up of the North Tyneside loop and the South Shields branch through South Tyneside, with trains running twice through Monument station, which lies in the centre of Newcastle. A trip around the loop takes 54 minutes, and the entire journey to South Shields, 82 minutes. With each line operating every 12 minutes during normal daytime service, there is a train every 6 minutes on the shared section between South Gosforth and Pelaw. The Metro is in service from about 05:30 until midnight.

The Tyne and Wear Metro was conceived in the late 1960s when the once busy suburban railway lines had reached a desolate state and some kind of action was needed. While several branches were closed, the remaining routes, i.e. the coast loop and the South Shields line, were upgraded and linked by underground routes through the Newcastle and Gateshead city centres.

The coast loop was originally built between 1839 and 1882, although the northern leg terminated in Newcastle at New Bridge Street until 1909, when a short link to Manors station opened, enabling trains to depart and arrive at Central Station (opened in 1850). In 1879, the loop was complemented by the Riverside Branch, which served the neighbourhoods and shipyards along the River Tyne between Manors and Percy Main until 1973. These routes were electrified with a third rail at 600 V DC in as early as 1904. In 1967, the ageing EMUs were replaced with diesel trains.

Queen Elizabeth II Bridge (Newcastle Central Station <> Gateshead)

diente, wurde 1973 stillgelegt. Der Küstenring und die Nebenstrecke wurden bereits 1904 mit 600 V Gleichstrom über seitliche Stromschiene elektrifiziert. 1967 wurden die in die Jahre gekommenen elektrischen Triebwagen durch Dieselzüge ersetzt.

Der heutige Ast zum Flughafen folgt der 1905 nach Ponteland eröffneten Bahnstrecke. Diese eingleisige Linie wurde jedoch nur bis 1929 für den Personenverkehr genutzt. Aufgrund mehrerer einfach gestalteter Haltestellen direkt an Bahnübergängen (zweimal mit versetzten Bahnsteigen) gleicht dieser Ast am ehesten einer deutschen Stadtbahn vom Typ Frankfurt am Main.

Auf der Südseite des Flusses Tyne wurden die Strecken, die heute von der Metro benutzt werden, zwischen 1835 und 1872 eröffnet. Die Linie nach South Shields wurde 1938 elektrifiziert, doch 1963 ersetzten Dieseltriebwagen die elektrischen Züge. Zwischen dem Abzweig östlich von Pelaw und Jarrow gibt es auf diesem Ast drei eingleisige Abschnitte, da das danebenliegende Gleis weiterhin von Güterzügen befahren wird.

Der Bau der Metro wurde 1973 beschlossen, die Arbeiten dauerten 11 Jahre. Das Projekt umfasste die Elektrifizierung mit 1500 V Gleichstrom über Oberleitung, den Umbau oder eine Verschiebung einiger Stationen und ca. 10 km neue Strecken (davon 6,4 km im Tunnel, der Rest auf Geländeebene bzw. als Hochbahn). Zu den neuen Strecken gehörten die 350 m lange Queen-Elizabeth-II-Brücke über den Fluss Tyne und der 820 m lange Byker-Viadukt über das Ouseburn-Tal zwischen Byker und Manors. Die eingleisigen Tunnel durch Newcastle und Gateshead

The present Airport branch follows an alignment opened to Ponteland in 1905. This single-track line, however, only carried passengers until 1929. With several rather simple stops located adjacent to level crossings (two having staggered platforms), this branch most resembles a typical German 'Stadtbahn' of the Frankfurt type.

The routes now used by the Metro on the south side of the River Tyne were opened between 1835 and 1872. The line to South Shields was electrified in 1938, but the electric trains were replaced by diesel units in 1963. Between the junction at Pelaw and Jarrow, this branch features three single-track sections as the second track is still used by freight trains.

Approved in 1973, the Metro scheme took 11 years to be completed. The project included electrification at 1500 V DC using overhead line equipment, the upgrading or relocation of existing stations, and the construction of approximately 10 km of new routes. Some 6.4 km of these lies in tunnels, the rest being elevated or at grade, including the 350 m Queen Elizabeth II Bridge across the River Tyne and the 820 m Byker Viaduct across the Ouseburn Valley between Byker and Manors. Using mining techniques, the tunnels through Newcastle and Gateshead were excavated as single-track tubes with a diameter of 4.75 m. The former route between Jesmond and Manors was connected to the east-west tunnel and now functions as a non-revenue track link between the two routes.

The initial network having been completed in 1984, the northwestern branch was extended from Bank Foot to

Byker

wurden bergmännisch mit einem Durchmesser von jeweils 4,75 m gebaut. Die ehemalige Strecke zwischen Jesmond und Manors wurde an den Ost-West-Tunnel angeschlossen und dient heute als Betriebsstrecke.

Nachdem das Grundnetz 1984 fertiggestellt worden war, wurde der nordwestliche Ast 1991 entlang der früheren Strecke nach Ponteland von Bank Foot zum Flughafen verlängert.

Für die Ende der 1990er Jahre errichtete Verlängerung nach Sunderland wurde die bestehende Eisenbahnstrecke nicht übernommen, sondern für einen Mischbetrieb angepasst. Die drei bestehenden Bahnhöfe auf dieser Strecke, Brockley Whins, East Boldon und Seaburn, wurden umgebaut und drei neue Bahnhöfe errichtet. In Sunderland konnte die Trasse der 1984 geschlossenen Bahn nach Durham zum Bau der neuen Strecke genutzt werden. Mit Inbetriebnahme der 18,5 km langen Strecke von Pelaw bis South Hylton war das heutige Netz 2002 vollständig. Zwischen Sunderland und Newcastle wird das Angebot der Metro mit Zügen alle 12 Minuten durch stündliche Regionalzüge von Northern Rail ergänzt, die nur in Heworth halten. Northern betreibt auch den übrigen Regionalverkehr im Nordosten, ein dichter Verkehr herrscht jedoch nur zwischen Hauptbahnhof und MetroCentre (4 Züge pro Stunde).

the airport in 1991, still following the former railway to Ponteland.

For the Sunderland extension, the existing railway line was not taken over, but instead the route was upgraded to allow mixed service. The three stations along the route, Brockley Whins, East Boldon and Seaburn, were rebuilt, and three new stations were added. Within Sunderland, the existing railway formation of the former Sunderland to Durham freight line, abandoned in 1984, was used to build a new route. Finally, the opening of the 18.5 km route from Pelaw to South Hylton in 2002 completed the present network. Between Sunderland and Newcastle, the metro service, with trains every 12 minutes, is complemented by hourly regional Northern Rail trains which only stop at Heworth. Although Northern also operates other regional services in the Northeast, a dense local service is only provided between Central Station and MetroCentre (four trains per hour).

For the opening of the Metro, a total of 88 2-section vehicles (4003-4090) with a Jacobs bogie in the middle were delivered, two prototypes (4001+4002) having previously undergone a lengthy period of testing. The vehicles are usually operated in pairs, and both trains and stations are all fully accessible. Due to a lack of funds necessary for new rolling stock, most of the existing cars, already 35 years old, were refurbished between 2010 and 2015, and now boast a black and yellow livery.

Tyne and Wear Metro > Fahrzeuge | *Rolling Stock* (750 V DC)

Nummer *Number*	Anzahl *Quantity*	Hersteller *Manufacturer*	Typ *Class*	Länge *Length*	Breite *Width*	Ausgeliefert *Delivered*
4001-4090	90	Metro-Cammell	Metrocar (BR Class 994)	27.4 m	2.65 m	1975, 1978-1981

St. Peter's

Central Station

Sunderland

Manors

Nachdem zwei Fahrzeug-Prototypen (4001+4002) über einen längeren Zeitraum getestet worden waren, wurden für den Metro-Betrieb weitere 88 zweiteilige Einheiten (4003-4090) mit einem Jacobs-Drehgestell in der Mitte geliefert. Normalerweise verkehren die Fahrzeuge in Doppeltraktion. Alle Züge und Bahnhöfe sind barrierefrei zugänglich. Da Finanzmittel für eine Neubeschaffung fehlen, wurden fast alle Fahrzeuge zwischen 2010 und 2015 ertüchtigt, dabei bekamen die inzwischen 35 Jahre alten Wagen einen neuen Anstrich in Schwarz/Gelb.

Central Station

Modernisierter Innenraum | *refurbished interior*

Airport

Bombardier #205 + Alstom #225 @ Toton Lane

NOTTINGHAM

Etwa 200 km nördlich von London gelegen, ist Nottingham neben Derby und Leicester eine der großen Städte in der Region East Midlands und Zentrum des Großraums Greater Nottingham.

Für Greater Nottingham werden Tageskarten für Tram, Bus und Bahn (*Kangaroo Day Ticket*) für 4,50 £ angeboten, eine Tageskarte nur für die Tram kostet 4,00 £, Einzelfahrten 2,20 £. Ermäßigungen gibt es bei der Tram mit einer aufladbaren MANGO-Smartcard, die für 3,00 £ erhältlich ist.

Während das Tramnetz in Sheffield seit Inbetriebnahme gar nicht und das in Birmingham nur sehr bescheiden erweitert wurde, gelang es im beschaulichen Nottingham 11 Jahre nach Eröffnung der ersten Strecke im August 2015, die Netzlänge mehr als zu verdoppeln. Der Eisenbahnvorortverkehr spielt eine geringe Rolle, so fahren auf der Nordstrecke parallel zur Tram zwar halbstündlich Züge von East Midlands Trains nach Hucknall und weiter, sie halten jedoch nur stündlich in Bulwell, auch in Attenborough wird nur stündlich gehalten, in Beeston immerhin dreimal stündlich.

NOTTINGHAM
(Nottinghamshire)

- 305 000 / 750 000
- el. (1900-1936) 2004
- 1435 mm
- 31 km
- 2
- 10'
- Nottingham Express Transit (NET) *www.thetram.net*
- Kangaroo *www.kangaroo.co.uk*

Located some 200 km north of London, Nottingham is one of the larger cities in the East Midlands region, along with Derby and Leicester, and the centre of Greater Nottingham.

For Greater Nottingham, 'Kangaroo Day Tickets' are available for tram, bus and train for £4.50, a day ticket just for the tram costs £4.00, and a single ticket £2.20. Discounts for the tram are granted when one uses a rechargeable MANGO SmartCard, sold for £3.00.

While the tram network in Sheffield has not been extended at all since its opening, and the one in Birmingham only very modestly, Nottingham's tram system more than doubled in size in August 2015, 11 years after the original line had been brought into service. Suburban rail traffic plays a minor role in the region; the northern route, which runs parallel to the tramway, has a half-hourly service operated by East Midlands Trains to Hucknall and beyond, but the trains only stop once an hour at Bulwell, and while Attenborough is also just served once an hour, three trains per hour call at Beeston.

NOTTINGHAM Express Transit (NET)

31 km - 48 Haltestellen | *stops*

09-03-2004: Nottingham Station – Hucknall / Phoenix Park (13.5 km)
25-08-2015: Nottingham Station – Clifton South / Toton Lane (17.5 km)

Alstom #237 @ Bulwell

Die Straßenbahn von Nottingham wird offiziell als **Nottingham Express Transit** (NET) bezeichnet. Die Tram wird von *Keolis* betrieben, einem Mitglied im Konsortium *Tramlink Nottingham*, das mit dem Ausbau und Betrieb beauftragt wurde. Das Netz besteht aus zwei Linien, die sich einen rund 7 km langen Abschnitt durch die Innenstadt, wo somit tagsüber mindestens alle 5 Minuten eine Bahn fährt, teilen.

Die erste, 13,5 km lange Strecke wurde im März 2004 eröffnet. Etwa 10 km dieser Strecke verlaufen auf eigenem Gleiskörper, größtenteils parallel zur *Robin Hood Line*, einer lange ungenutzten Eisenbahnstrecke, die erst 1993-1998 stufenweise zwischen Nottingham und Worksop wieder in Betrieb genommen wurde. Der innerstädtische Abschnitt zwischen dem Betriebshof an der Wilkinson Street und dem Bahnhof ist im Gegensatz dazu eine klassische Straßenbahn, straßenbündig mit nur zum Teil abmarkierter Trasse. Die Bahnsteige sind hier meist in die Bürgersteige integriert.

Auch die beiden 2015 eröffneten Südäste weisen längere straßenbündige Abschnitte auf. Das wichtigste Bauwerk für beide Neubaustrecken ist die über den Bahnhof eingeschobene Stahlbrücke. Für die 7,5 km lange Clifton-Linie stand südlich des Flusses Trent eine alte Eisenbahntrasse der *Great Central Railway* mitsamt Unterführung unter der Umgehungsstraße A52 zur Verfügung. Anschließend führt diese Linie übers freie Feld, dann straßenbündig entlang des Southchurch Drive durch Clifton und schließlich auf der Farnborough Road zur Endstelle am Rand des bebauten Gebiets, wo eine Park-and-Ride-Anlage errichtet wurde.

Die rund 10 km lange Beeston-Linie erschließt erst das Gewerbegebiet ng^2 und überquert dann die Bahnstrecke

The Nottingham tram system is officially called ***'Nottingham Express Transit'*** *(NET). It is now run by Keolis, a member of the 'Tramlink Nottingham' consortium, which was set up to develop and operate the system. The current network consists of two unnumbered lines which share an approximately 7 km section through the city centre, resulting in a tram every 5 minutes during daytime off-peak hours.*

The first 13.5 km route opened in March 2004, with about 10 km running on a segregated right-of-way, mainly parallel to the Robin Hood Line, a long out-of-use railway line reopened in stages between 1993 and 1998 from Nottingham to Worksop. In contrast, the central section between the depot at Wilkinson Street and the railway station resembles a classic tramway, with on-street running though on a partly marked-off lane. The platforms are mostly integrated into the pavement.

The two southern branches, which opened in 2015, also feature lengthy on-street sections. The most important structure built for both branches is a steel bridge inserted over the railway station. For the 7.5 km long Clifton line, on the south bank of the River Trent an old railway corridor of the Great Central Railway was available, including an underpass under the ring road A52. After that, the trams run across an open field, then on-street through Clifton along Southchurch Drive and then Farnborough Road before reaching the terminus at the edge of the built-up area, where a park-and-ride facility was established.

The roughly 10 km Beeston line first serves the industrial and business area 'ng^2' before crossing the railway line to London on a purpose-built bridge. While the following section is embedded in the roadway, a

Bombardier #215 @ Southchurch Drive North

Richtung London auf einer eigenen Brücke. Während die anschließende Strecke ebenfalls straßenbündig verläuft, wurde durch das Areal des Queens Medical Centre eine 650 m lange Hochbahnstrecke errichtet, welche auch die Umgehungsstraße A52 überspannt. Entlang des University Boulevard steht dann ein eigener Gleiskörper in Parallellage zur Verfügung, während die Gleise durch Beeston wiederum im Straßenasphalt verlegt wurden. Am Central College verlässt die Tram allerdings den Straßenraum und fährt auf einem Grünstreifen durch ruhige Wohnsiedlungen bis zur Endstelle Toton Lane, wo an der Zufahrtsstraße zur Autobahn M1 eine Park-and-Ride-Anlage eingerichtet wurde. Eine Verlängerung zum geplanten Hochgeschwindigkeitsbahnhof ist eine Option für die späten 2020er Jahre, allerdings ist dessen Lage noch nicht endgültig entschieden.

Die für die ursprüngliche Strecke angeschafften Incentro-Wagen aus dem nahen Derby tragen Namen einer mit Nottingham in Beziehung stehenden Persönlichkeit, z.B. Lord Byron (205), D.H. Lawrence (202) und natürlich Robin Hood (211). Alle Wagen wurden 2013-2015 modernisiert und bekamen einen neuen Anstrich, bei dem das Silber dominiert, während allerdings das dunkle Grün-Türkis anteilig erhalten blieb. Ein ähnliches Farbschema erhielten auch die neuen Citadis-Wagen. Bei ihnen wird die Namensgebung fortgesetzt, z.B. Alan Sillitoe (219).

650 m elevated structure was built through the area of the Queens Medical Centre and also spanning the A52 ring road. On University Boulevard, a dedicated trackbed runs parallel along the southern side of the road, whereas through Beeston, the tracks are again embedded in the roadway. At Central College, however, the trams leave the public roads and run on a green strip through quiet residential areas to the terminus at Toton Lane, where a park-and-ride facility has been set up next to the access road for the M1 motorway. An extension to the planned high-speed rail station is an option for the late 2020s, although its location has not yet been decided.

The original Incentro vehicles, built by Bombardier in nearby Derby, all carry the name of a Nottingham-related personality, among them Lord Byron (#205), D.H. Lawrence (#202) and, of course, Robin Hood (#211). The trams were all refurbished between 2013 and 2015, and now boast a new livery, dominated by silver, though maintaining the share of dark teal they had before. The new Citadis trams were delivered in a similar livery, and the naming convention has been continued, e.g. with Alan Sillitoe (#219).

NET Tram > Fahrzeuge | *Rolling Stock* (750 V DC)

Nummer *Number*	Anzahl *Quantity*	Hersteller *Manufacturer*	Typ *Class*	Länge *Length*	Breite *Width*	Ausgeliefert *Delivered*
201-215	15	Bombardier	Incentro AT6/5	32 m	2.40 m	2002-2003
216-237	22	Alstom	Citadis 302	32 m	2.40 m	2013-2014

Alstom Citadis @ Old Market Square

Alstom Citadis + Bombardier Incentro @ Nottingham Station

Alstom Citadis @ Wilford Lane > Wilford Village

Bombardier #203 @ Moorbridge (2005)

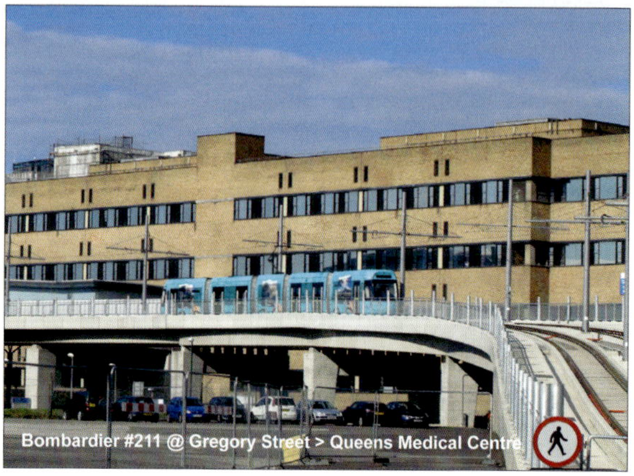
Bombardier #211 @ Gregory Street > Queens Medical Centre

Bombardier #214 @ Lace Market

Alstom Citadis

Queens Medical Centre > University of Nottingham

Bombardier #213 @ Nottingham Trent University > High School

Duewag #107 @ University of Sheffield

SHEFFIELD

Sheffield liegt am südlichen Rand der historischen Grafschaft Yorkshire und gehört heute zusammen mit u.a. Doncaster, Rotherham und Barnsley zum Großraum South Yorkshire (ca. 1,4 Mill. Einw.). Ähnlich wie Stuttgart erstreckt sich die Stadt über mehrere Hügel, wobei das Stadtzentrum in einem Talkessel liegt.

Sheffield verfügt über ein Straßenbahnnetz mit drei farblich gekennzeichneten Linien, die wie ein Teil des städtischen Busnetzes von *Stagecoach* betrieben werden. Eigentümer der Infrastruktur ist *South Yorkshire Passenger Transport Executive* (SYPTE). Die Blue Line (Malin Bridge – Halfway) und die Yellow Line (Middlewood – Meadowhall) verkehren tagsüber alle 10 Minuten, die Purple Line (Cathedral – Herdings Park) nur alle 30 Minuten. Von 9:00 bis 14:00 Uhr fahren die Bahnen der Purple Line auf der Yellow Line weiter nach Meadowhall. Abends und sonntags verkehren alle Linien im 20-Minuten-Takt.

Das Ticketangebot ist sehr reichhaltig, eine einfache Fahrt nur mit der Tram kostet je nach Entfernung 1,50 £ bzw. 2,20 £, Fahrscheine sind beim

SHEFFIELD (South Yorkshire)

552 000 | 700 000

(1899-1960) 1994

1435 mm

29 km

3

Blue & Yellow: 10'; Purple: 30'

Stagecoach Supertram
www.supertram.com

Travel South Yorkshire
www.travelsouthyorkshire.com
www.sytravelmaster.com

South Yorkshire Passenger Transport Executive (SYPTE)
www.sypte.co.uk

Sheffield lies at the southernmost tip of historical Yorkshire and is now part of the metropolitan county of South Yorkshire (incl. Doncaster, Rotherham and Barnsley; 1.4 million inh.). The city is known for its hilly cityscape, with the city centre in the valley and the residential areas spread out over seven hills.

Sheffield boasts a tram network made up of three colour-coded lines, which, like some urban buses, are operated by Stagecoach. The infrastructure is owned by the South Yorkshire Passenger Transport Executive (SYPTE). The Blue Line (Malin Bridge – Halfway) and the Yellow Line (Middlewood – Meadowhall) run every 10 minutes during daytime service, and the Purple Line (Cathedral – Herdings Park) every 30 minutes. Between 09:00 and 14:30, Purple Line trams continue to Meadowhall displaying a yellow route sign. In the evenings and on Sundays, all three lines operate a 20-minute headway.

Sheffield's range of tickets is rather diverse, with a single trip on the tram costing £1.50 or £2.20, depending on the distance travelled.

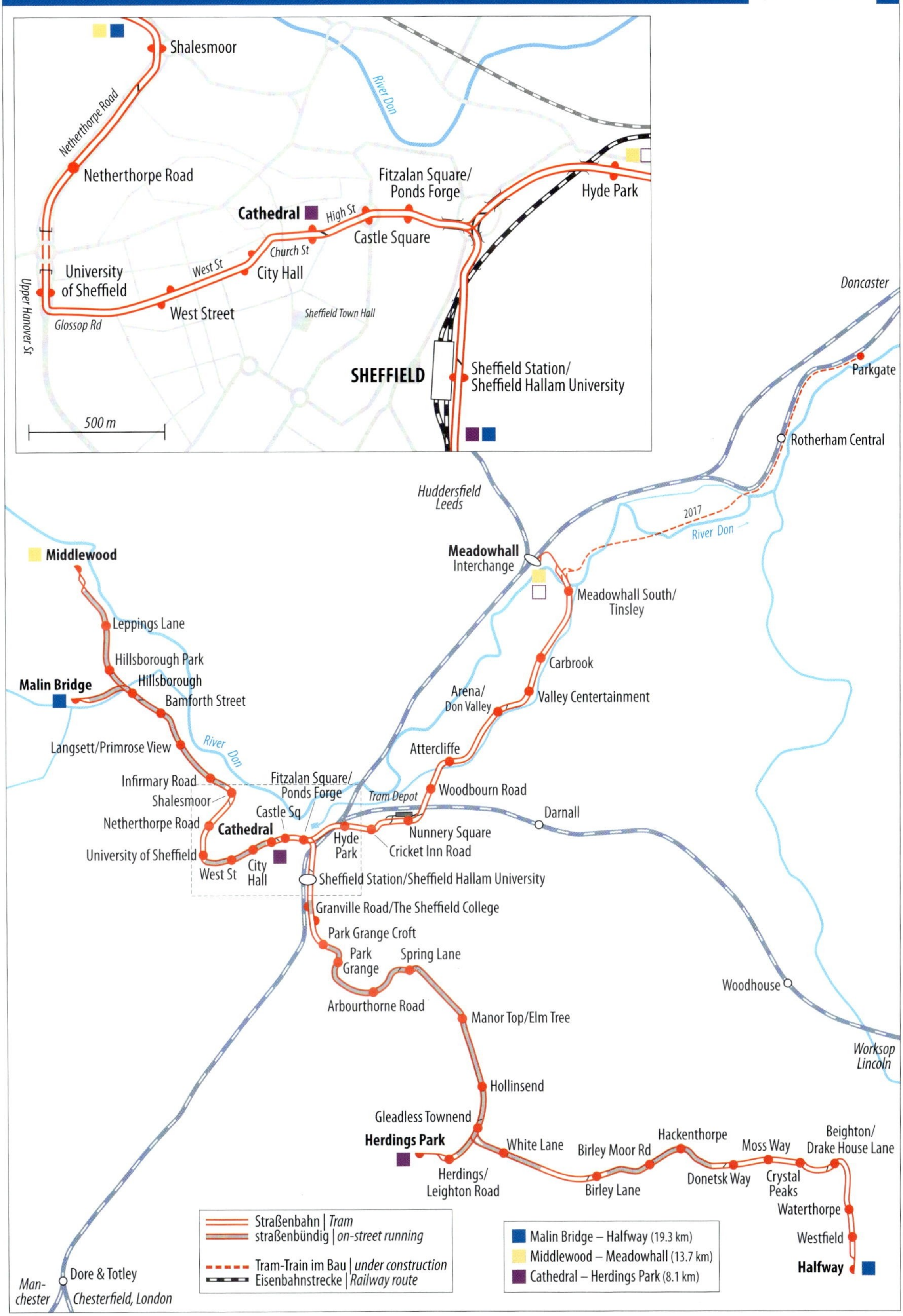
Shalesmoor
Netherthorpe Road
Netherthorpe Road
River Don
Fitzalan Square/
Ponds Forge
Hyde Park
Cathedral
High St
Castle Square
Church St
West St
City Hall
University
of Sheffield
West Street
Glossop Rd
Upper Hanover St
Sheffield Town Hall
SHEFFIELD
Sheffield Station/
Sheffield Hallam University
500 m
Doncaster
Parkgate
Rotherham Central
Huddersfield
Leeds
2017
River Don
Meadowhall
Interchange
Meadowhall South/
Tinsley
Middlewood
Leppings Lane
Hillsborough Park
Malin Bridge
Hillsborough
Bamforth Street
Carbrook
Arena/
Don Valley
Valley Centertainment
Langsett/Primrose View
River Don
Attercliffe
Infirmary Road
Fitzalan Square/
Ponds Forge
Tram Depot
Woodbourn Road
Shalesmoor
Castle Sq
Darnall
Netherthorpe Road
Cathedral
Hyde
Park
Nunnery Square
Cricket Inn Road
University of Sheffield
West St
City
Hall
Sheffield Station/Sheffield Hallam University
Granville Road/The Sheffield College
Park Grange Croft
Park
Grange
Spring Lane
Woodhouse
Arbourthorne Road
Manor Top/Elm Tree
Worksop
Lincoln
Hollinsend
Gleadless Townend
Herdings Park
White Lane
Birley Moor Rd
Hackenthorpe
Moss Way
Beighton/
Drake House Lane
Herdings/
Leighton Road
Birley Lane
Donetsk Way
Crystal
Peaks
Waterthorpe
Westfield
Halfway
Straßenbahn | Tram
straßenbündig | on-street running
Tram-Train im Bau | under construction
Eisenbahnstrecke | Railway route
Malin Bridge – Halfway (19.3 km)
Middlewood – Meadowhall (13.7 km)
Cathedral – Herdings Park (8.1 km)
Dore & Totley
Man-
chester
Chesterfield, London

Duewag #121 @ Leppings Lane > Middlewood

Schaffner in der Tram erhältlich. Ein *Dayrider* für Tram und Stagecoach-Busse für ganz Sheffield ist für 3,90 £ erhältlich, mit einem *Travelmaster Gold* kann man den gesamten Nahverkehr in South Yorkshire inkl. aller Busse und Züge nutzen (7,50 £).

Abgesehen von Blackpool fuhr die letzte städtische Straßenbahn Englands der ersten Generation in Sheffield im Jahr 1960. 1994, also zwei Jahre nach Inbetriebnahme der hochflurigen Stadtbahn in Manchester, war die ***Supertram*** die erste Niederflurstraßenbahn Großbritanniens. Anders als in Manchester wurden für die Supertram keine Eisenbahnstrecken direkt übernommen, weshalb die Entscheidung zugunsten der Niederflurtechnik auf der Hand lag. Das heutige Netz ist eine Mischung aus konventioneller straßenbündiger Straßenbahn und etwa zur Hälfte auf eigenem Gleiskörper verlaufender Stadtbahn. Nur der 7 km lange Ast nach Meadowhall verläuft meist parallel zu einer Gütereisenbahn und ist somit vollkommen vom Straßenverkehr getrennt, aber auch hier gibt es einige Bahnübergänge. Die wichtigsten Bauwerke im Netz sind eine Unterführung unter dem Kreisel am University Square westlich der Innenstadt, drei Viadukte am Gleisdreieck über dem Kreisel am Park Square östlich der Innenstadt sowie ein rund 300 m langer Viadukt zwischen Granville Road und der erst 2001 eingefügten Haltestelle Park Grange Croft. Auf den Abschnitten abseits von Straßen wurden Vignol-Schienen verlegt.

Die Supertram wird mit 25 von Siemens-Duewag in Düsseldorf gebauten Fahrzeugen betrieben. Die dreiteiligen Straßenbahnen sind nur in den Endabschnitten im Türbereich niederflurig (42 cm), der Rest ist über zwei Stufen

Tickets can be bought from the conductor on the trams. A 'Dayrider' pass for the tram and Stagecoach buses in Sheffield is sold for £3.90, while a 'Travelmaster Gold' offers unlimited travel in the entire South Yorkshire region, including all buses and local trains (£7.50).

*Other than Blackpool, England's last first-generation urban tramway closed in Sheffield in 1960. The Sheffield **Supertram** was the first low-floor system in Britain when it opened in 1994, only two years after the high-floor Manchester Metrolink system. As the Sheffield tram does not use any former British Rail passenger lines, however, the choice of low-floor technology was obvious. The system is a mix of conventional street-running tramway and segregated light rail. The share of reserved track is about 50%, with only the 7 km Meadowhall branch, which runs mostly alongside a freight railway, being totally segregated from road traffic, although with several level crossings. The most significant structures built for the system are an underpass to avoid the roundabout at*

SHEFFIELD Supertram

29 km - 48 Haltestellen | *stops*

21-03-1994: Fitzalan Square – Meadowhall
22-08-1994: Fitzalan Square – Spring Lane
05-12-1994: Spring Lane – Gleadless Townend
18-02-1995: Fitzalan Square – Cathedral
27-02-1995: Cathedral – Shalesmoor
27-03-1995: Gleadless Townend – Halfway
03-04-1995: Gleadless Townend – Herdings Park
23-10-1995: Shalesmoor – Middlewood / Malin Bridge
01-12-2001: + Park Grange Croft
2017: Meadowhall South/Tinsley – Rotherham Parkgate (Tram-Train)

Duewag #104 @ Sheffield Station > Fitzalan Square (2005)

erreichbar. Die Stromzufuhr mit 750 V Gleichstrom erfolgt über Oberleitung.

Die Haltestellen sind 26,5 m lang und ermöglichen einen stufenlosen Einstieg bei einer Höhe von 37,5 cm über Schienenoberkante. Die Bahnsteigränder sind mit Blindenmarkierungen versehen. Alle Haltestellen sind gleich ausgestattet und verfügen über einen Unterstand, mittlerweile auch über Fahrzielanzeiger. Die ursprünglich aufgestellten Fahrscheinautomaten wurden bereits 1996 wieder entfernt, heute werden die Fahrscheine von Schaffnern in der Bahn verkauft bzw. kontrolliert.

Das gesamte heutige Netz wurde zwar stufenweise, jedoch innerhalb von nur eineinhalb Jahren (1994/95) eröffnet. Es ist seit 20 Jahren weitgehend unverändert geblieben, lediglich der Anstrich der Fahrzeuge wurde dem jeweiligen *Corporate Image* angepasst, zuletzt 2006. 1997 wurde die *South Yorkshire Supertram Ltd* von der *Stagecoach Holdings PLC* erworben, die derzeit das Netz unter der Bezeichnung Stagecoach Supertram betreibt. Nach anfänglichen Schwierigkeiten wegen des unkoordinierten parallelen Busverkehrs ist die Supertram mittlerweile zu einem beliebten Transportmittel geworden. Eine gute Ampelvorrangschaltung ermöglicht einen reibungslosen Betrieb trotz des hohen Anteils an straßenbündigen Strecken.

University Square on the western side of the city centre, three bridges at the track triangle above the roundabout at Park Square on the eastern side of the city centre, as well as an approximately 300 m long viaduct between Granville Road and a stop called Park Grange Croft, which was only added in 2001. All the off-road sections feature railway-type Vignol tracks.

The Sheffield tram system is operated with a fleet of 25 vehicles, all built by Siemens-Duewag in Düsseldorf. The end sections of these 3-section trams are partially low-floor in the door area (42 cm), whereas the rest is higher and accessible via steps. Power is supplied via an overhead wire at 750 V DC.

The tram stops are 26.5 m long and provide level access into the vehicles from 37.5 cm high platforms. The platform edges are fitted with tactile markings for the blind. The stops all have a standard design with shelters, and have recently been equipped with next-tram indicators. The original ticket machines were withdrawn in as early as 1996, and tickets are now inspected and sold on the tram by conductors.

The entire system as we know it today was opened in stages, but within a period of only 18 months (1994/95). Apart from changes in the trams' livery, with the last repainting done in 2006, there have not been any signifi-

Sheffield Supertram > Fahrzeuge | *Rolling Stock* (750 V DC)

Nummer *Number*	Anzahl *Quantity*	Hersteller *Manufacturer*	Typ *Class*	Länge *Length*	Breite *Width*	Ausgeliefert *Delivered*
101-125	25	Duewag	Supertram	34.8 m	2.65 m	1993-1994
399201-399207	7	Vossloh España	Citylink (BR Class 399)	37.2 m	2.65 m	*2015-2017*

Duewag #115 @ Middlewood

Anfangs waren mehrere Netzerweiterungen geplant, jedoch wurde davon nichts verwirklicht. Im Mai 2012 wurde Sheffield schließlich nach mehrjährigen Diskussionen vom britischen Verkehrsministerium dazu auserkoren, einen ***Tram-Train***, also eine Regio-Stadtbahn nach dem Karlsruher Modell, als zweijährigen Pilotversuch umzusetzen. Ab ca. 2017 werden die Citylink-Fahrzeuge vom Stadtzentrum auf den Gleisen der Yellow Line bis Meadowhall South/Tinsley fahren, von dort über eine neu errichtete 150 m lange Spange eine bestehende Gütereisenbahn erreichen und dann vor Rotherham Central auf die auch von Personenzügen befahrene Strecke treffen. Die Tram-Trains werden etwa 2 km weiter nördlich am Einkaufszentrum Parkgate enden. Dafür müssen rund 5,5 km mit 750 V Gleichstrom elektrifiziert werden. Auch wenn das gesamte Eisenbahnnetz rund um Sheffield bislang nicht elektrifiziert wurde, sind die neuen Fahrzeuge bereits sowohl für das Tramnetz als auch für das Network Rail-Netz mit 25 kV 50 Hz Wechselstrom ausgerüstet.

Langfristig soll der Knoten Meadowhall umgebaut werden, denn unweit der heutigen Endstation der Yellow Line soll frühestens Anfang der 2030er Jahre der Bahnhof an der Hochgeschwindigkeitsstrecke von London bzw. Birmingham nach Leeds bzw. York errichtet werden.

cant modifications in the last 20 years. In 1997, South Yorkshire Supertram Ltd was acquired by Stagecoach Holdings PLC, which now operates the system as Stagecoach Supertram. After some initial difficulties due to parallel bus routes following the deregulation of the bus service, the Supertram has now become a very popular means of transport. Having priority at traffic lights guarantees a fast and reliable service despite the high percentage of on-street running.

Initially, there were several projects for network expansion, but none of them have come to fruition. Eventually in May 2012, after several years of discussion, Sheffield was chosen by the Department for Transport (DfT) for the realisation of a two-year ***tram-train*** *pilot project. From approximately 2017, new Citylink vehicles will run from the city centre on Yellow Line tracks to Meadowhall South/Tinsley, where they will diverge onto the 150 m so-called Tinsley Chord to reach an existing freight line. Just before arriving at Rotherham Central, the tram-trains will join the Sheffield – Rotherham – Doncaster passenger line and terminate some 2 km further north at the Parkgate Shopping Centre. Approximately 5.5 km of tracks will be electrified at 750 V DC. Even though the rail network around Sheffield has not been electrified, the new trains are ready for dual-voltage operation on both tram routes and Network Rail tracks (25 kV 50 Hz AC).*

In the long-term future, the Meadowhall hub may be rebuilt in the early 2030s as it has been chosen as the site of the future high-speed rail station on the line to be built from London/Birmingham to Leeds/York.

Duewag Supertram

Duewag #111 @ University of Sheffield > Netherthorpe Road

Duewag #120 @ Sheffield Station
(2015 im Originalanstrich | *in original livery*)

Duewag #122 @ Fitzalan Square/Ponds Forge

Foto Craig Moore

Duewag #104 @ Attercliffe (2005)

Black Country Living Museum – Wolverhampton District #34 (1919)

Straßenbahnmuseen und Nostalgiebahnen

Auf den folgenden Seiten präsentieren wir Ihnen einige Kostproben aus den zahlreichen Straßenbahnmuseen der Britischen Inseln, wobei kein Anspruch auf Vollständigkeit erhoben wird. Der Leser soll lediglich Hinweise bekommen, was es bei einer Reise nach Großbritannien und Irland neben den modernen Straßenbahnen noch zu entdecken gibt. Für weitere Informationen, besonders bezüglich vollständiger Fahrzeuglisten, finden Sie jeweils die Web-Adresse der einzelnen Museen und Betriebe.

Im Vergleich zur Anzahl moderner Betriebe findet man auf den Britischen Inseln eine sehr hohe Anzahl an Nostalgiestraßenbahnen, sei es in Form eines ganzen „Tramway Village" wie in **Crich** (siehe Seite 154) oder eines Straßenbahnbetriebs innerhalb eines Verkehrs- oder

Tram Museums and Heritage Trams

In the following pages, we will present a few interesting exhibits from the numerous tram museums in the British Isles, without claiming to be complete. We just want to give you some indication as to what there is to discover on a trip to Britain and Ireland besides the modern tramways. For more information, in particular regarding complete fleet lists, we have listed the websites of every museum and heritage tramway company.

Compared to the number of modern tram systems found in the British Isles, the number of heritage trams, whether in the form of an entire 'Tramway Village' like that in ***Crich*** *(see page 154), or a short tram ride within a transport or local museum, is rather high. In addition, of course, the heritage service in* ***Blackpool*** *continues to*

Heaton Park – Manchester #765 (1914)

Foto B. Kußmagk

Seaton – #12 (Nachbau | *Replica car*: London 'Feltham' tram 1930s)

Foto Seaton Tramway

Glasgow Riverside Museum – Pferdebahn | *Horse tram* (Glasgow Corporation Tramways)

Heimatmuseums. Dazu kommt selbstverständlich auch der neben der modernen Tram weiterhin angebotene Nostalgiebetrieb in **Blackpool** (siehe S. 16) sowie der Saisonbetrieb auf der **Isle of Man** (siehe S. 156) und in **Llandudno** (siehe S. 158). Für die übrigen Museen und Nostalgiebahnen hier ein Überblick von Nord nach Süd:

2011 zog das Verkehrsmuseum von **Glasgow** in einen modernen Bau direkt am Fluss Clyde, das *Riverside Museum*, wo man mehrere Ausstellungsstücke zum Thema Straßenbahn, aber auch zur *Subway* von Glasgow findet. Der Eintritt ist frei.

Im *Museum of Scottish Industrial Life* im ehemaligen Stahlwerk **Summerlee** in Coatbridge, rund 15 km östlich von Glasgow, steht eine etwa 400 m lange Tramstrecke zur Verfügung, auf der drei betriebsbereite Fahrzeuge verkehren, zwei aus der Region und eins aus Düsseldorf.

*exist in parallel with the modern tramway (see page 16). We have dedicated special pages to the seasonal operation on the **Isle of Man** (see page 156) and in **Llandudno** (see page 158). For other museums and heritage tramways, we have prepared an overview from north to south:*

*In 2011, **Glasgow**'s Transport Museum moved to a modern building right by the River Clyde, the 'Riverside Museum', where you will find a number of exhibits about trams, but also about the Glasgow Subway. Admission is free.*

*The 'Museum of Scottish Industrial Life' at **Summerlee**, the former steelworks in Coatbridge, some 15 km east of Glasgow, has an approximately 400 m long tram route used by three operational vehicles, two from the region and one from Düsseldorf.*

Websites
Glasgow: www.glasgowlife.org.uk/museums/riverside
Summerlee: www.visitlanarkshire.com
Beamish: www.beamish.org.uk
Heaton Park: www.heatonparktramway.co.uk
Birkenhead: www.mtps.co.uk
Dudley: www.bclm.com
London: www.ltmuseum.co.uk
Lowestoft: www.eatm.org.uk
Brighton: www.volkselectricrailway.co.uk
Seaton: www.tram.co.uk
Howth: www.nationaltransportmuseum.org

Glasgow Riverside Museum – Glasgow Corporation Tramways #1392

Beamish – Gateshead and District Tramways #10 (1925)

Foto Bernhard Kußmagk, 1997

Einzelne Wagen sind im Museum des *North Eastern Electrical Traction Trust* in **Sunderland** sowie im *Streetlife Museum of Transport* in **Hull** zu sehen. Die interessanteste Sammlung im Nordosten Englands ist allerdings im Freilichtmuseum in **Beamish** im County Durham, rund 10 km südlich von Newcastle, zu sehen. Diese umfasst 14 Fahrzeuge, von denen meist 4 bis 6 auf einer 2,4 km langen Rundstrecke unterwegs sind. Wie in Crich ist die Eintrittskarte (18,50 £) ein Jahr lang gültig.

Im **Heaton Park** im Norden von Manchester (siehe Karte S. 121) verkehren an Sommerwochenenden drei Fahrzeuge auf einem originalen 750 m langen Abschnitt der Manchester Tramway.

800 m misst die Strecke der *Wirral Heritage Tramway* in **Birkenhead**, von Liverpool einfach mit Merseyrail erreichbar (siehe Karte S. 49). Die Straßenbahn ist Teil des *Wirral Transport Museum* und verkehrt an Wochenenden, in den Schulferien teils auch wochentags.

*While a few tramcars can be seen in the 'Museum of the North Eastern Electrical Traction Trust' in **Sunderland** as well as in the 'Streetlife Museum of Transport' in **Hull**, the most interesting collection in the northeast of England can be seen in the open-air museum in **Beamish** in County Durham, approximately 10 km south of Newcastle. This includes 14 vehicles, of which usually 4 to 6 run on a 2.4 km circular route. As in Crich, the entrance ticket (£18.50) is valid for a year.*

*In **Heaton Park** in the north of Manchester (see map on page 121), three vehicles operate on an original 750 m long section of the Manchester Tramway on summer weekends.*

*The track of the 'Wirral Heritage Tramway' in **Birkenhead** measures 800 m. The line can easily be reached from Liverpool on Merseyrail (see map on page 49). The tramway is part of the 'Wirral Transport Museum' and runs on weekends (during school holidays on some weekdays, too).*

Beamish – Porto #196 (1935)

Foto B. Kußmagk, 1997

London Transport Museum – #102 (West Ham Corporation Tramways, 1910)

Birkenhead – Wallasey Corporation Tramways #78 (1920)
Foto Brendan Fox

Eine kurze Tramstrecke existiert auch im *Black Country Living Museum* in **Dudley**, rund 13 km westlich von Birmingham. Lediglich zwei Straßenbahnfahrzeuge sind im *London Transport Museum* in **Covent Garden** zu sehen. Das *East Anglia Transport Museum* in **Lowestoft** verfügt über fünf betriebsbereite Wagen, die in den Sommermonaten auf einer 400 m langen Strecke unterwegs sind.

Nicht unerwähnt bleiben darf die *Volk's Electric Railway* in **Brighton**. Seit 1883 in Betrieb, gehört sie zu den ältesten elektrischen Bahnen der Welt. Die Stromzufuhr erfolgt über eine Stromschiene (110 V Gleichstrom).

Bei der *Seaton Tramway* in **Seaton**, an der Südküste von Devon, verkehren von März bis Oktober im Halbstundentakt sogar bis zu 14 verschiedene Fahrzeuge auf einer 4,8 km langen ehemaligen Eisenbahnstrecke.

Das *National Transport Museum of Ireland* in **Howth**, nordöstlich von Dublin, beherbergt fünf irische Tram-Fahrzeuge.

A short tram route is also available at the 'Black Country Living Museum' in ***Dudley****, some 13 km west of Birmingham. Only two tramcars can be seen in the 'London Transport Museum' at* ***Covent Garden****. The 'East Anglia Transport Museum' in Lowestoft has five operational cars that during the summer months run on a 400 m long track.*

Also worthy of mention is the 'Volk's Electric Railway' in ***Brighton****. Opened in 1883, it is one of the oldest electric railways in the world. Power is supplied via a third rail (110 V DC).*

The 'Seaton Tramway' in ***Seaton****, on the south coast of Devon, operates up to 14 different vehicles every half an hour on a 4.8 km former railway line from March to October.*

The 'National Transport Museum of Ireland' in ***Howth****, in the northeastern outskirts of Dublin, is home to five Irish tram vehicles.*

Volk's Electric Railway
Foto David Ettefer

Birkenhead – Birkenhead Corporation Tramways #20 (1900)
Foto Brendan Fox

Crich

London #331 (Metropolitan Electric Tramways, 1930)

Das „**Crich Tramway Village**“ mit dem „National Tramway Museum“ befindet sich am Rand des kleinen Dorfs Crich, rund 25 km nordwestlich von Nottingham und 35 km südlich von Sheffield im ländlichen Derbyshire.

Die Sammlung des Museums umfasst über 50 verschiedene Fahrzeuge, viele aus Nordengland, aber auch aus anderen Landesteilen und Schottland sowie aus dem Ausland, darunter z. B. ein Reko-Wagen aus Berlin und ein Tatra-Wagen aus Halle. Auch Prag, Johannesburg, Den Haag, New York und Porto steuerten Fahrzeuge bei. Auf einer 1,3 km langen Strecke sind stets mehrere Fahrzeuge abwechselnd unterwegs. Den Abschnitt im Museumsdorf säumen mehrere historische Originalbauten aus der Region. Der Eintrittspreis von 14,00 £ ermöglicht eine mehrfache Rückkehr innerhalb eines Jahres.

*The '**Crich Tramway Village**' with the 'National Tramway Museum' is located just outside the small village of Crich, in rural Derbyshire, some 25 km northwest of Nottingham and 35 km south of Sheffield.*

The museum's collection includes more than 50 different vehicles. Many of them are from northern England, but there are also trams from other parts of the country and Scotland as well as from abroad, for example from Germany, a Reko car from Berlin and a Tatra car from Halle. But Prague, Johannesburg, The Hague, New York and Porto have also contributed some vehicles. The 1.3 km tram route is continuously served by various alternating cars. The section through the heritage village is flanked by several original buildings transferred from the region. The entrance fee of £14.00 allows multiple visits within a year.

Website: www.tramway.co.uk

Blackpool Boat Car #236 (1934) + Chesterfield #7 (1904)

Ausstellungshalle | *Exhibition hall*

Sheffield #74 (1900)

Sheffield #510 (1950) + Leeds #180 (1931)

Leicester #76 (1904) + Glasgow #1115 (1929)

Berlin #223006 (1969)

Blackpool #167 (1928)

Douglas Bay Horse Tramway – Derby Castle – *Trammer* 'Robert' zieht Wagen 21, links dahinter der Wagenschuppen, rechts der Bahnhof der *Manx Electric*
– trammer 'Robert' pulling car #21, in the background on the left, the car barn, and the Manx Electric station on the right

Mit knapp 85.000 Einwohnern und einer Fläche von 572 km^2 ist die Isle of Man ein kleines Paradies für Bahnfreunde. Entlang der Strandpromenade der Hauptstadt Douglas findet man die letzte aus der Ursprungszeit überlebende Pferdestraßenbahn Großbritanniens. Seit 1876 verbindet die „**Douglas Bay Horse Tramway**" auf ihrer 2,6 km langen Strecke den Fährhafen mit der Endstation der „Manx Electric Railway" in Derby Castle. Die Spurweite der nur in der Sommersaison verkehrenden Bahn (20-Minuten-Takt) beträgt 914 mm. Es stehen rund 20 verschiedene Wagen zur Verfügung, je nach Wetter werden offene oder geschlossene eingesetzt. Eine Einzelfahrt kostet 3,00 £. Es gibt Pläne, die Gleise aus dem Straßenraum herauszunehmen und auf die Strandpromenade zu verlegen.

*With a population of some 85,000 inhabitants and an area of 572 km^2, the Isle of Man is a little paradise for railway enthusiasts. Along the seaside promenade of the capital Douglas, the '**Douglas Bay Horse Tramway**', the last original line of its kind in Britain, has linked the ferry terminal to the terminus of the 'Manx Electric Railway' at Derby Castle on a 2.6 km route since 1876. With a track gauge of 914 mm, the horse trams operate every 20 minutes, but just in the summer season. Some 20 different cars are available for service, with open or enclosed carriages being used depending on the weather. A single ticket costs £3.00. There are plans to remove the tracks from the roadway and relocate them to the esplanade.*

Website: www.douglashorsetramway.net

'Rocky' + #43 @ Derby Castle

Wagen 18 vor dem Gaiety Theatre | *Car #18 passing Gaiety Theatre*

Manx Electric Railway – Derby Castle – Triebwagen 20 steht mit Beiwagen 46 fast bereit zur Abfahrt Richtung Ramsey; rechts die Pferdebahnstation
– motor car #20 with trailer #40 almost ready to depart for Ramsey, with the horse tram stop to the right

Die durchgehend zweigleisig errichtete „**Manx Electric Railway**" (Spurweite 914 mm; 550 V Gleichstrom) aus dem Jahr 1893 fährt in den Sommermonaten von Derby Castle über Laxey bis ins 27,4 km nördlich von Douglas gelegene Ramsey. In Laxey kann man zur 1895 eröffneten „**Snaefell Mountain Railway**" umsteigen. Die 8 km lange zweigleisige Bergbahn hat 1067 mm Spurweite und Rechtsverkehr, für die Stromzufuhr mit 550 V Gleichstrom nutzt sie einen Bügelstromabnehmer. Zwischen den Schienen liegt abschnittsweise eine Bremsschiene nach dem System Fell.

Neben diesen Bahnen kann man mit einer Tageskarte für 16 £ auch die Dampfeisenbahn von Douglas nach Port Erin sowie alle Buslinien auf der Insel nutzen, Einzelkarten sowie günstigere Mehrtageskarten sind auch erhältlich.

*Opened in 1893, the '**Manx Electric Railway**' (track gauge 914 mm; 550 V DC) was built double-track throughout. During the summer months, it runs from Derby Castle via Laxey to Ramsey, a town 27.4 km north of Douglas. In Laxey, interchange is provided to the '**Snaefell Mountain Railway**', which opened in 1895. The 8 km double-track mountain railway has 1067 mm gauge and right-hand running. It uses a bow collector for the 550 V DC power supply. Mounted between the rails on some sections, there is an additional Fell system rail for braking.*

In addition to these railways, a day ticket for £16 is also valid on the steam train from Douglas to Port Erin as well as on all the bus services on the island; single tickets and cheaper multi-day tickets are also available.

Website: www.manxelectricrailway.co.uk

Laxey – Snaefell Mountain Railway (links | *left*) **& Manx Electric Railway** (rechts | *right*)

Snaefell Mountain Railway – Tw. 1 auf dem Berggipfel | *car #1 on summit*

Great Orme Tramway – Wagen 4 auf dem unteren Abschnitt mit Blick über die Llandudno Bay | *Car #4 on the lower section with a view of Llandudno Bay*

Vom nordwalisischen Seebad Llandudno fährt seit über 100 Jahren eine Bahn auf den Hausberg Great Orme, daher der Name „**Great Orme Tramway**“. Sie erreichte 1902 die Zwischenstation und ein Jahr später den Berggipfel. Allerdings handelt es sich dabei nicht um eine Tram, sondern um zwei unabhängig voneinander betriebene Standseilbahnen, wobei das Seil der unteren Bahn (797 m) ähnlich den Kabelbahnen von San Francisco im Untergrund läuft, da die Bahn auf diesem Abschnitt teils im Straßenraum wie eine Straßenbahn verkehrt. Auf dem oberen Abschnitt (756 m) liegt das Seil hingegen frei. An der Station Halfway muss umgestiegen werden. Die Spurweite beträgt 1067 mm. Die Great Orme Tramway fährt von Ende März bis Oktober, eine Hin- und Rückfahrt kostet 6,50 £.

*In North Wales, the **'Great Orme Tramway'** has carried visitors from the seaside resort of Llandudno to the summit of its namesake for over 100 years. It reached the intermediate station in 1902, and the top of the mountain a year later. However, this is not a classic tramway, but in fact two independently operated funiculars, with the cable on the lower 797 m section hidden in an underground conduit, similar to the cable cars in San Francisco, as the trams on this section travel partly on the street like a proper tramway. On the upper section (756 m), however, the cable is visible between the tracks. Passengers have to change trains at Halfway station. The track gauge is 1067 mm. The Great Orme Tramway runs from late March until October, with a return ticket costing £6.50.*

Website: www.greatormetramway.co.uk

Wagen 6 auf dem oberen Abschnitt | *Car #6 on the upper section*

Wagen 5 auf dem unteren Abschnitt | *Car #5 on the lower section*

TRAM ATLAS - EUROPA

NEU
NEW

METRO & TRAM ATLAS SPANIEN | SPAIN

09/2015 - ISBN 978 3 936573 46 6
19.50 EUR

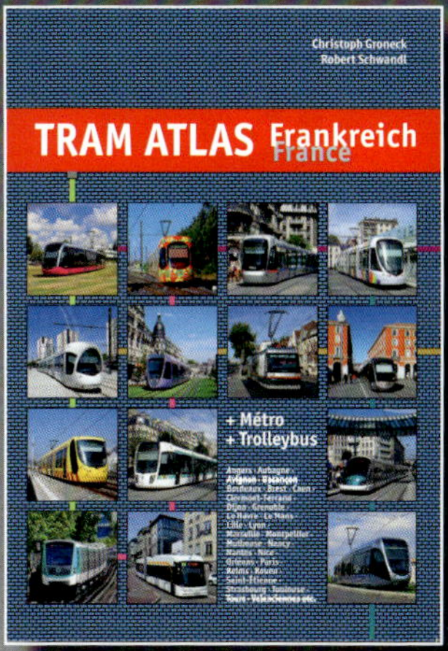

TRAM ATLAS FRANKREICH | FRANCE

+ Métro & Trolleybus

03/2014 - ISBN 978 3 936573 42 8
19.50 EUR

TRAM ATLAS NORDEUROPA NORTHERN EUROPE

Skandinavien & Baltikum
Scandinavia & Baltic States

10/2013 - ISBN 978 3 936573 41 1
19.50 EUR

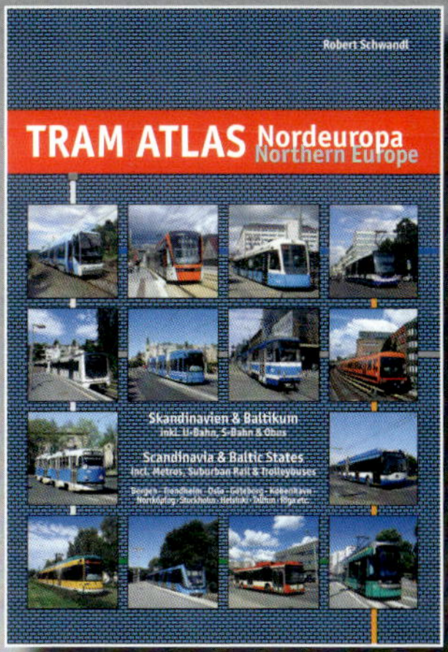

Was kommt dann? What's next?

TRAM ATLAS MITTELEUROPA | CENTRAL EUROPE

Tschechien, Slowakei & Ungarn
Czech Republic, Slovakia & Hungary

~10/2016 - ISBN 978 3 936573 48 0

TRAM ATLAS POLEN | POLAND

~2017 - ISBN 978 3 936573 50 3

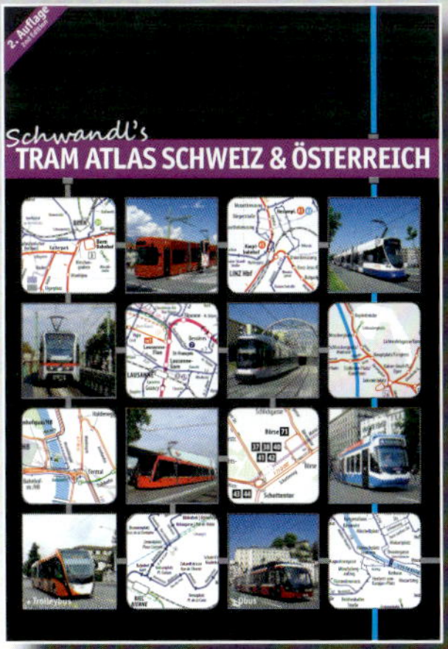

Schwandl's

TRAM ATLAS SCHWEIZ & ÖSTERREICH

2. Auflage Juni 2014
Second edition June 2014
ISBN 978 3 936573 44 2
14.50 EUR

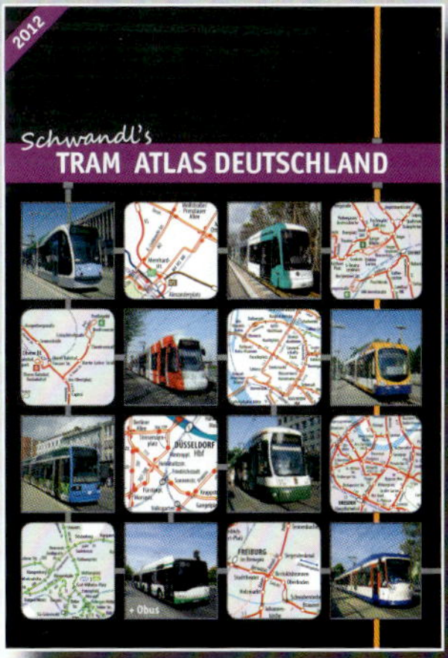

Schwandl's

TRAM ATLAS DEUTSCHLAND

Derzeit vergriffen > 4. Auflage geplant Herbst 2016
Currently out-of-print > 4th edition planned autumn 2016
ISBN 978 3 936573 49 7

Robert Schwandl Verlag

Außerdem erhältlich | Also available:

Metros & Trams in Japan - 1

ISBN 978 3 936573 47 3

... und mehr ... and more ...

Robert Schwandl Verlag, Hektorstraße 3, 10711 Berlin
Tel. +49 (0) 30 - 3759 1284, Fax +49 (0) 30 - 3759 1285
books@robert-schwandl.de - www.robert-schwandl.de